The brag sheet, which is not to be confused with a student resume fo letters of recommendation. However, it is similar to a student resume in that it high... leadership abilities, and employment throughout your secondary education. Brag sheets allow you to assist your educator(s) in writing letters of recommendation on your behalf. This form provides them with more information about who you are outside of school and your interests. You may not need a brag sheet right now, but it would be a good idea to practice filling out this form and sharing it with your parents, counselor, or teacher to request a letter of recommendation!

NAME: _____

BRAG SHEET
College Planning

What colleges are you going to apply to?

_____

What is your anticipated college major?

_____

HS Activities: Please list your HS activities, including clubs, teams, etc., and write the grade in which you participated.	**Grade**

Community Service: Please list your volunteer work and/or church activities.

Awards: Please list any awards (academic and non-academic)

List 3 adjectives to describe yourself:

How excited are you about your future?

Rating

BRAG
SHEET
Life Skill

GPA and class rank (if available)

_____

Students generally have little control over their recommendation letters other than who they choose to write them for and the relationships that necessitate them.

The purpose of a brag sheet is to benefit you while making the writing process as easy for your recommender as possible. As the title suggests, it's one of the best opportunities to brag about yourself. While the primary purpose of a brag sheet is to help guide a teacher recommendation letter, it can also be used for a variety of other purposes.

When you go to an interview for a college that you applied to, bring your brag sheet with you and hand it to the interviewer. It will provide them with a quick overview of your hobbies, academic performance, and future goals. Not only will it highlight the best aspects of you, but it may also lead to more in-depth conversations because they won't have to waste time asking about basic information that you were able to cover in your brag sheet.

Additionally, you can use it when applying to schools and writing essays. It can be difficult and overwhelming to come up with a topic for your essays.

Describe an event or activity that has had an impact on your life.

_____

_____

_____

_____

_____

_____

_____

What are you most proud of and why.

_____

_____

_____

_____

_____

_____

_____

List the positive influences in your life (family, friends, sports, teacher. etc.)

_____

_____

_____

_____

_____

_____

_____

_____

_____

_____

Math Algebraic Equation

Score: _____

Date: _____

Algebraic equations are made up of two algebraic expressions that are equal on either side of an equal sign. Constants, variables, and exponents are included, and they are also considered polynomial equations when the exponents are positive whole numbers.

1. An algebraic equation is the same thing as _____ being set equal to one another.
   a. three expressions
   b. 1 algebraic 2 expressions
   c. two algebraic expressions

2. The word equation is related to the word 'equal' meaning that there is___.
   a. an equal sign between the two expressions
   b. an equal sign between the x and y.
   c. an equal sign after y and x.

3. Polynomials are algebraic expressions that are created by ___,
   a. dividing by a variable
   b. combining negative exponents
   c. combining numbers and variables

4. A linear equation is one that usually only has two variables ____.
   a. 'x' and 'y'
   b. 'y' and 'z'
   c. 'x' and 'l'

5. Linear equations will only have ___line when graphed.
   a. two
   b. one
   c. three

6. A quadratic equation is an _____ equation of the second degree.
   a. coefficient
   b. polynomial
   c. quadratic equations

7. Linear equations sometimes can have ___ variables.
   a. zero
   b. only one
   c. one, two or three

8. When solving algebraic equations, the goal is to find out what number the ___ is representing.
   a. variable
   b. expression inside first
   c. figures

9. What type of equation is -2x + 7 = 4?
   a. proportional to
   b. linear equation
   c. integers

10. What type of equation is 7x^2 + 5x + 3 = 0?
    a. cubic equation
    b. positive number
    c. quadratic equation

* History Reading Comprehension: Storming of the Bastille

Score: _____

Date: _____

oppression	fortress	prison	prisoners	fortress
military	1000	weapons	battle	French
assassinated	ruled	commoners	Fearful	craftsmen

Tip: After you've answered the easy ones, go back and work the harder ones.

On July 14, 1789, the Bastille was stormed in Paris, France. The _____ Revolution began with a violent attack on the government by the people of France.

During the Hundred Years' War, the Bastille was a _____ built in the late 1300s to protect Paris. By the late 1700s, King Louis XVI had primarily used the Bastille as a state _____.

The majority of the revolutionaries who stormed the Bastille were Paris-based _____ and store owners. They belonged to the Third Estate, a French social class. Approximately _____ men carried out the attack.

The Third Estate had recently made the king's demands, including a more significant say in government for the _____. They were concerned that he was preparing the French army to launch an attack. To arm themselves, they first took over the Hotel des Invalides in Paris to obtain muskets. However, they lacked gun powder. The Bastille was rumored to be full of political _____ and symbolized the king's _____ to many. It also had gunpowder stores, which the revolutionaries required for their _____.

The revolutionaries approached the Bastille on the morning of July 14. They demanded that the Bastille's _____ commander, Governor de Launay, hand over the prison and the gunpowder. He flatly refused. The crowd became agitated as the negotiations dragged on. They were able to gain access to the courtyard in the early afternoon. They began to try to break into the main _____ once they were inside the courtyard. _____ soldiers in the Bastille opened fire on the crowd. The _____ had begun. When some of the soldiers joined the crowd's side, the fight took a turn for the worse. De Launay quickly realized the situation was hopeless. He handed over the fort to the revolutionaries, who took control.

During the fighting, approximately 100 revolutionaries were killed. The crowd _____ Governor de Launay and three of his officers after they surrendered.

The storming of the Bastille triggered a chain of events that culminated in King Louis XVI's deposition and the French Revolution. The revolutionaries' success inspired commoners throughout France to rise up and fight against the nobles who had _____ them for so long.

July 14, the date of the storming of the Bastille, is now celebrated as French National Day. In the same way that the Fourth of July is celebrated in the United States. It is known as "The National Celebration" or "The Fourteenth of July" in France.

Write in your own words, what happened in the storming of the Bastille.

* Geography Multiple Choice
Quiz: Mountain Range

Select the best answer for each question.

1. The _____ run for 1,500 miles along the east coast of the US from northern Alabama to Maine.
   a. Sierra Nevada
   b. Rocky Mountains
   c. Appalachian Mountains

2. Which is of the following is famous for its tall peaks and stretches 1,491 miles through much of central Asia?
   a. Himalayas
   b. Andres
   c. Urals

3. The _____ are the world's longest mountain range, stretching approximately 4,300 miles.
   a. Alps
   b. Rockies
   c. Andes

4. Fault-block mountains were formed along a fault in the Earth's crust. Which of the following is a fault-block mountain?
   a. Appalachian
   b. Sierra Nevada
   c. Rockies

5. What is the process by which the world's tallest mountain ranges are formed?
   a. seafloor spreading
   b. continental drift
   c. plate tectonics

6. The theory of continental drift was proposed by which German meteorologist?
   a. Charles Thomson Rees Wilson
   b. Alfred Wegener
   c. John Dalton

7. Which of the following mountain ranges is the highest and most extensive in Europe?
   a. The Appalachian
   b. The Alps
   c. The Andes

8. What is the highest point of the Rockies that is 14,440 feet above sea level?
   a. Mount Elbert
   b. Mount Chamberlin
   c. Mount Whitney

9. The _____ is a mountain range in northeast New York.
   a. Alaska Range
   b. Adirondacks
   c. Brooks Range

10. Which famous city was built atop a mountain of the Andes Mountain range?
    a. Machu Picchu
    b. Tikal
    c. Tenochtitlan

11. What is the highest mountain range in North America?
    a. Brooks Range
    b. Cascade Range
    c. Alaska Range

12. The _____ is the largest mountain range between the Appalachians and the Rockies.
    a. Ozarks
    b. Urals
    c. Adirondacks

Grammar: Contractions Multiple Choice

A *contraction* is a way of making two words into one. Circle the correct answer.

1. aren't
   a. are not
   b. not are
   c. arenot

2. can't
   a. cants
   b. cannot
   c. cant

3. couldn't
   a. couldnt
   b. couldnts
   c. could not

4. didn't
   a. didn'ts
   b. did nots
   c. did not

5. don't
   a.
   b. do not

6. hadn't
   a. had not
   b. had nots
   c. hadn'ts

7. hasn't
   a. has nots
   b. has not
   c. hasnot

8. haven't
   a. have nots
   b. haven'ts
   c. have not

9. I'm
   a. I am
   b. I'ms
   c. I'am

10. I've
   a. I have
   b. I'ves
   c. I'have

11. isn't
   a. isn'ts
   b. is not
   c. is'not

12. let's
   a. lets
   b. let'us
   c. let us

13. mightn't
   a. mightnt
   b. might not
   c. might'not

14. mustn't
   a. mustnt
   b. must'not
   c. must not

* History Reading Comprehension: The Great Depression

During the 1930s, the United States experienced a severe economic downturn known as the Great Depression. It started in the United States, Wall Street to be exact, but quickly spread throughout the rest of the world. Many people were out of work, hungry, and homeless during this period. People in the city would wait for hours at soup kitchens to get a bite to eat. Farmers struggled in the Midwest, where a severe drought turned the soil into dust, resulting in massive dust storms.

America's "Great Depression" began with a dramatic stock market crash on "Black Thursday," October 24, 1929, when panicked investors who had lost faith in the American economy quickly sold 16 million shares of stock. However, historians and economists attribute the Great Depression to a variety of factors, including drought, overproduction of goods, bank failures, stock speculation, and consumer debt.

When the Great Depression began, Herbert Hoover was President of the United States. Many people held Hoover responsible for the Great Depression. The shantytowns where homeless people lived were even dubbed "Hoovervilles" after him. Franklin D. Roosevelt was elected president in 1933. He promised the American people a "New Deal."

The New Deal was a set of laws, programs, and government agencies enacted to aid the country in its recovery from the Great Depression. Regulations were imposed on the stock market, banks, and businesses as a result of these laws. They assisted in putting people to work and attempted to house and feed the poor. Many of these laws, such as the Social Security Act, are still in effect today.

The Great Depression came to an end with the outbreak of World War II. The wartime economy re-employed many people and filled factories to capacity.

The Great Depression left an indelible imprint on the United States. The New Deal laws expanded the government's role in people's daily lives significantly. In addition, public works improved the country's infrastructure by constructing roads, schools, bridges, parks, and airports.

Between 1929 and 1933, the stock market lost nearly 90% of its value.
During the Great Depression, approximately 11,000 banks failed, leaving many people without savings.

1. The Great Depression began with the _____.
   a. World War II
   b. economy drought
   c. stock market crash

2. Who was President when the Great Depression began?
   a. Herbert Hoover
   b. George W Bush
   c. Franklin D. Roosevelt

3. The New Deal was a set of _____.
   a. laws, programs, and government agencies
   b. city and state funding
   c. stock market bailout

4. The Great Depression came to an end with the outbreak of ____.
   a. new laws
   b. investors funding
   c. World War II

* The Metric System

Tip: After you've answered the easy ones, go back and work on the harder ones.

gram	metric	liter	Meter	Gram
centimeter	liter	weight	Celsius	Liter
meter	10	milliliters	kilogram	Celsius

Scientists all over the world use the _____ system. There's a very good reason for this-it's so everyone is doing the measuring the same way, all over the world. Most other countries already use the metric system for measuring everything.

Another good reason to use metric is that you don't have so much to remember-no 12 inches in a foot or 5,280 feet in a mile. It's all decimal! The larger or smaller units go up or down by _____, 100, or 1,000.

_____ is for length. A _____ is a little longer than a yard. For long distances, there is the kilometer (a thousand meters). For small things, there is the _____ (100 centimeters in a meter).

_____ is for volume. A _____ is a little larger than a quart. There are a thousand _____ in a _____.

_____ is for _____. A _____ is a little more than the weight of a paper clip. For heavier things, there is the _____ (a thousand grams).

Temperatures are in degrees Celsius (also called centigrade). Water freezes at 0 degrees _____ and boils at 100 degrees _____. That's easy!

Cursive Writing Practice

Score: _____ **Date:** _____

Why did the teacher wear

sunglasses? (Because her

students were bright!) Why

was the teacher cross-eyed?

(She couldn't control her

pupils!) How do bees get to

school? (By school buzz!)

What did the paper say to

the pencil? (Write on!) How

do you get straight As? (Use

Cursive Writing Practice

a ruler!) What building has

the most stories? (The

library!) What do you get

when you throw a million

books into the ocean? (A

title wave!) What is snake's

favorite subject? (Hiss-tory!)

Why did the teacher write on

the window? (To make the

lesson very clear!)

* Geography Multiple Choice
Quiz: Islands

Score: _____

Date: _____

Select the best answer for each question.

1. An island is a body of land smaller than a continent that is surrounded _____ by water.
   a. entirely
   b. on three sides
   c. on two sides

2. A group of related islands, such as the Philippines, is called _____ .
   a. a continent
   b. an island
   c. an archipelago

3. _____ form when volcanoes erupt on the ocean floor.
   a. Artificial Island
   b. Continental islands
   c. Oceanic islands

4. Which of the following islands are classified as oceanic islands?
   a. Padre Island and Cape Hatteras
   b. Greenland and Madagascar
   c. Iceland and Hawaiian

5. Which of the following is the world's largest non-continental island?
   a. Madagascar
   b. Greenland
   c. Great Britain

6. Located off the southeast coast of Africa, _____ is the world's fourth largest island.
   a. Seychelles
   b. Madagascar
   c. Mauritius

7. _____are sections of the continental shelf that have become isolated due to sea-level rise.
   a. Oceanic islands
   b. Continental islands
   c. Barrier islands

8. Home to the famous volcano Mount Fuji, ____ is Japan's largest island.
   a. Hokkaido
   b. Honshu
   c. Kyushu

9. What is the largest island in the Mediterranean Sea?
   a. Sardinia
   b. Sicily
   c. Cyprus

10. Napoleon Bonaparte, Emperor of France was born on which island in France?
    a. Port-Cros
    b. Levant Island
    c. Corcica

11. _____ is the world's ninth largest island, the largest island in the British Isles, and the world's third most populous island.
    a. Great Britain
    b. Isle of Man
    c. Ireland

12. The largest and southernmost island in the Mariana Islands chain, located in the North Pacific Ocean is _____.
    a. Guam
    b. Saipan
    c. Tinian

* Geography Multiple Choice
Quiz: Antarctic

Score: _____

Date: _____

Select the best answer for each question.

1. _____ is the fifth-largest continent in terms of total area.
   a. Antarctic
   b. Artic
   c. Antarctica

2. _____ is composed of older, igneous and metamorphic rocks.
   a. Lesser Antarctica
   b. Greater Antarctica
   c. Antarctica

3. Antarctica is:
   a. Nearly all exposed land with some glaciers
   b. About half ice and half exposed land
   c. Mainly ice, with a few areas of exposed land

4. Antarctica has the world's largest?
   a. Mountains
   b. Ice
   c. Desert

5. In 1983, the coldest temperature ever recorded in Antarctica is?
   a. -108.5°F
   b. -118.0°F
   c. -128.6°F

6. The Antarctic region has an important role in _____.
   a. global climate processes
   b. Earth's heat balance
   c. Earth's atmosphere

7. The _____ is one of the driest _____ in the world.
   a. Antarctic desert and deserts
   b. Antarctic continent and deserts
   c. Antarctic archipelago and continent

8. One of the apex, or top, predators in Antarctica is the?
   a. penguin
   b. sperm whales
   c. leopard seal

9. _____ study climate patterns, including the "ozone hole" that hovers over the Antarctic.
   a. Climatologists
   b. Meteorologists
   c. Geographers

10. _____ is the largest single piece of ice on Earth.
    a. Antarctic Ice Sheet
    b. Glacial Ice
    c. Ross Ice Shelf

11. _____, is part of the "Ring of Fire," a tectonically active area around the Pacific Ocean.
    a. Antarctica
    b. Greater Antarctica
    c. Lesser Antarctica

12. _____ in the Antarctic is hard to measure as it always falls as snow.
    a. Evaporation
    b. Condensation
    c. Precipitation

* Geography Multiple Choice
Quiz: Deserts

Score: _____

Date: _____

Select the best answer for each question.

1. Which is the only continent with no large deserts?
   a. Europe
   b. North America
   c. Australia

2. Which desert in Asia stretches across parts of China and Mongolia?
   a. Great Victoria desert
   b. Sahara desert
   c. Gobi desert

3. What percentage of the world's land surface is a desert?
   a. 15
   b. 25
   c. 20

4. The _____ is the world's largest hot desert.
   a. Sahara
   b. Sonoran
   c. Kalahari

5. Which of the following is one of the most oil-rich places in the world?
   a. Mohave desert
   b. Arabian desert
   c. Kalahari desert

6. An oasis is a place in the desert with _____.
   a. a collection of desert edible plants
   b. a supply of fresh water
   c. a horde of desert animals

7. A subtropical desert is _____.
   a. a desert that exists near the leeward slopes of some mountain ranges
   b. sometimes called inland deserts
   c. caused by the circulation patterns of air masses

8. The _____ is a large desert located in Mexico and parts of the Southwestern United States.
   a. Great Victoria desert
   b. Sonoran desert
   c. Gobi desert

9. The amount of _____ in a desert often greatly exceeds the annual rainfall.
   a. condensation
   b. precipitation
   c. evaporation

10. _____ deserts exist near the leeward slopes of some mountain ranges.
    a. rain shadow
    b. costal
    c. interior

11. A home to Death Valley, the hottest and lowest spot in the US is the _____.
    a. Sonoran desert
    b. Mohave desert
    c. Kalahari desert

12. The Atacama Desert on the Pacific shores of Chile, is a _____, where some areas of it are often covered by fog.
    a. subtropical desert
    b. coastal desert
    c. interior desert

* Geography Multiple Choice Quiz: Glaciers

Score: _____

Date: _____

Select the best answer for each question.

1. A glacier is a huge mass of _____ that moves slowly over _____.
   a. snow and clouds
   b. hail and water
   c. ice and land

2. Glaciers that cover more than 50,000 square kilometers are called?
   a. Alpine
   b. Ice caps
   c. Ice sheets

3. _____ form on mountainsides and move downward through valleys.
   a. Alpine glaciers
   b. Ice caps
   c. Ice sheets

4. A complex of _____ glaciers burying much of a mountain range is called an _____.
   a. valley and ice sheet
   b. hill and ice cap
   c. mountain and ice field

5. Glaciers also exist high in _____ such as the _____ and the _____.
   a. mountain ranges, Himalayas and Andes
   b. Plateaus, Arctic and Antarctica
   c. Hills, Australia and South Africa

6. Melting _____ contribute to rising sea levels.
   a. ice caps
   b. ice field
   c. ice sheets

7. Glaciers carry great amounts of _____, _____, and _____.
   a. snow, water and rock
   b. ice, rock and clay
   c. soil, rock and clay

8. A _____ is one that ends in a body of water like a lake or an ocean.
   a. hanging glaciers
   b. cirque glaciers
   c. calving glacier

9. A _____ glacier is one that is formed in an area where the temperature is always below the freezing point.
   a. temperate
   b. polar
   c. piedmont

10. Most glaciers are located near the _____ or _____.
    a. Greenland or Iceland
    b. Arctic or Antarctic
    c. North or South Poles

11. _____ refers to all processes that contribute mass to a glacier.
    a. Transformation
    b. Ablation
    c. Accumulation

12. _____ is a simple consequence of the weight and creep properties of ice.
    a. Glacier flow
    b. Ablation
    c. Accumulation

* Simple Math Refresher

1. Perform the following operation: 12 + 1 + 8 =
   a. 21
   b. 20
   c. 18

2. Solve 1,056 divided by 22.
   a. 92
   b. 48
   c. 36

3. Division is the math operation that tells you to _____ and is represented by the symbols _____.
   a. separate or combine two numbers together; - and /
   b. separate something into parts; ÷ and /
   c. combine three numbers together; - and /

4. Brad saved $605 for his yearly vacations. He has 11 days of vacation and wants to spend the same amount of money each day, how much will he spend each day?
   a. $95
   b. $55
   c. $104

5. Convert 3/7 to a percent.
   a. 38.1%
   b. 5.9%
   c. 42.9%

6. Change 0.142 to a fraction.
   a. 1/7
   b. 2/4
   c. 1/8

7. Change 2/5 to a decimal.
   a. 0.4
   b. 0.9
   c. 0.5

8. Write 4 8/9 as an improper fraction.
   a. 32/5
   b. 40/8
   c. 44/9

9. A(n) _____ is an improper fraction written with a whole number and a proper fraction.
   a. decimal
   b. proper fraction
   c. mixed number

10. Write 50% as a fraction.
   a. 1/2
   b. 0/5
   c. 5/0

11. Change 79.5% to a decimal.
   a. 0.795
   b. .79.5%
   c. 79.05%

12. Which of the following number has the highest numerical value?
   a. 2.8
   b. 0.28
   c. 4.5%

13. Order the following numbers from smallest to greatest: 0.25, 4.54, 0.015, 1.24

    a. 1.24, 4.54, 0.015, 0.25

    b. 0.015, 0.25, 1.24, 4.54

    c. 4.54, 0.015, 0.25, 1.24

14. What is the 28% of 80?

    a. 28.0

    b. 84%

    c. 22.4

15. Convert 6/7 to a percent.

    a. 7.6%

    b. 6.7%

    c. 86%

16. What is the denominator of 7/9?

    a. 7.9

    b. 7

    c. 9

17. Write 18.7% as a decimal.

    a. 0.187

    b. 1.87

    c. 18.7%

18. Convert 0.00047 to scientific notation.

    a. 4.0×10^{-7}

    b. 4.7×4^{-0}

    c. 4.7×10^{-4}

19. Multiply 4.25×10^{-5} by 4.

    a. 1.7×10^{-4}

    b. 2.7×10^{-4}

    c. 4.5×10^{1}

20. Janes Market sells a pack of 500 napkins for $2.50 and Taylor Grocery sells a pack that has 750 of the same napkins for $3.75. Which pack is the best deal?

    a. Janes Market

    b. Both packs have the same price per napkin

    c. Taylor Grocery

21. Maya earned $4,575 in 3 months. If earned the same amount each month, how much did she earn each month?

    a. $2,575

    b. $925

    c. $1,525

22. The independent variable of an exponential function is the _____.

    a. exponent

    b. logarithm

    c. fraction

23. Solve for X in the following equation $8 + 3^X = 35$

    a. X = 3

    b. X = 8

    c. X = 35

24. Grams. liters and centimeters are all examples of _____ units.

    a. pounds

    b. kilogram

    c. metric

25. One kilogram is equivalent to _____ grams.

    a. 100

    b. 10

    c. 1,000

* Proofreading Shakespeare: Romeo and Juliet

There are **24** mistakes in this passage. 5 capitals missing. 3 unnecessary capitals. 4 unnecessary apostrophes. 3 punctuation marks missing or incorrect. 2 incorrect homophones. 7 incorrectly spelled words.

In 1597, William Shakespeare published "Romeo and Juliet" which would go on to become one of the world's most famous love stories. The plot of Shakespeare's pley takes place in Verona, where the two main characters romeo and Juliet, meet and fall in love Both are descended from two feuding families, the Capulets, and the Montagues. As a result, thay choose to keep their luve hidden and are married by Friar Laurence. Romeo gets into a fight with Juliet"s cousin Tybalt, whom he Kills in a Brawl despite his best efforts. Romeo is expelled from Verona and escapes to Mantua.

When juliet's parents press her to marry, she Seeks the assistance of Friar Laurence once more, who provides her with a sleeping potion designed to simulate her death. In a letter that never reaches Romeo, he explains his plan. Disgusted by the alleged death of his beloved Juliet, Rumeo returns to Verona and commits suicide at Juliet's open coffin. Juliet awakens from her slumber, sees what has happened, and decides to end her liphe. The two feuding families now recognize their complicity and reconcile at their children's graves.

The medieval old town of Verona is ideal for putting oneself in the shoes of Romeo and juliet. Every year, many loving couples and tourists come to walk in the footsteps of romeo and Juliet. A photograph of Juliet's famous balcony, a visit to Romeo's home, or sum queit time spent at Julia's grave. No matter were you look in the city, you wall find loving couple's who stick declarations of love and initials on small slips of paper to the walls or immortalize themselve's on the walls or stones of house's - often illegally.

Although Shakespeare's drama never corresponded to reality, verona has a unique charm, especially for lovers, who imagine they can feel the true story behind the literary work, almost as if Romeo and Juliet had really existed.

* Spelling Words Multiple Choice Quiz

Circle the best definition meaning for each spelling word provided below.

1. emboss
  a. to design with a sunken or recessed pattern
  b. to decorate with a raised pattern or design
  c. to print a material with flat pattern or design

2. perseverance
  a. the act or power of continuing to do something in spite of difficulties
  b. the act of giving up on something because it is difficult
  c. the act of being uninterested, unenthusiastic, or unconcerned

3. chagrin
  a. a feeling of being safe or protected
  b. a feeling of being annoyed by failure or disappointment
  c. a feeling of being sleepy and lethargic

4. mediocre
  a. not very often
  b. not very effective
  c. not very good

5. frugal
  a. careful, unwavering attention or persistent application
  b. careful in spending or using supplies
  c. careful in spending time and effort

6. benefactor
  a. someone who helps another especially by giving money
  b. someone who helps another find a job
  c. someone who helps another buy a house

7. personnel
  a. a group of kids who are members of a sports club
  b. a group of people employed in a business or an organization
  c. a group of elderly citizens that are members of senior social programs

8. journal
  a. a book in which we collect photographs
  b. a book in which you write down your personal experiences and thoughts
  c. a book in which map are compiled and collected

9. amphitheater
  a. a room built to enable an audience to hear and watch performances
  b. an arena with seats rising in curved rows around an open space
  c. a large room for public meetings or performances

10. horticulture
  a. the science and art of cultivating silkworms to produce silk
  b. the science and art of growing fruits, vegetables, flowers, or ornamental plants
  c. the science and art of cultivating plants and livestock

* Word of The Day

Use the dictionary to write the definition
and divide the words for each day
below into syllables.

○ MONDAY WORD: *UNICYCLE*

EXAMPLE:
A unicycle is a vehicle that touches the
ground with only one wheel.

u-ni-cy-cle

TUESDAY **WORD: oviparous**

WEDNESDAY **WORD: absenteeism**

THURSDAY **WORD: disenfranchise**

FRIDAY **WORD: kefir**

SATURDAY / SUNDAY **WORD: opacity**

Write Words In ABC Order

For each word, find one
synonym & one antonym. (if
none: write word + none)

* Health: Check Your Symptoms

Score: _____

Date: _____

Healthy habits aid in the development of happy and healthy children as well as the prevention of future health issues such as diabetes, hypertension, high cholesterol, heart disease, and cancer.

Chronic diseases and long-term illnesses can be avoided by leading a healthy lifestyle. Self-esteem and self-image are aided by feeling good about yourself and taking care of your health.

Maintain a consistent exercise schedule.

No, you don't have to push yourself to go to the gym and do tough workouts, but you should be as active as possible. You can maintain moving by doing simple floor exercises, swimming, or walking. You can also remain moving by doing some domestic chores around the house.

What matters is that you continue to exercise. At least three to five times a week, devote at least twenty to thirty minutes to exercise. Establish a regimen and make sure you get adequate physical activity each day.

Be mindful of your eating habits.

You must continue to eat healthily in order to maintain a healthy lifestyle. Eat more fruits and vegetables and have fewer carbs, salt, and harmful fat in your diet. Don't eat junk food or sweets.

Avoid skipping meals since your body will crave more food once you resume eating. Keep in mind that you should burn more calories than you consume.

1. **I've got a pain in my head.**
   a. Stiff neck
   b. headache

2. **I was out in the sun too long.**
   a. Sunburn
   b. Fever

3. **I've got a small itchy lump or bump.**
   a. Rash
   b. Insect bite

4. **I might be having a heart attack.**
   a. Cramps
   b. Chest pain

5. **I've lost my voice.**
   a. Laryngitis
   b. Sore throat

6. **I need to blow my nose a lot.**
   a. Runny nose
   b. Blood Nose

7. **I have an allergy. I have a**
   a. Rash
   b. Insect bite

8. **My shoe rubbed my heel. I have a**
   a. Rash
   b. Blister

9. **The doctor gave me antibiotics. I have a/an**
   a. Infection
   b. Cold

10. **I think I want to vomit. I am**
    a. Nauseous
    b. Bloated

* Science: Different Blood Types

compatible	transfusion	recipient's	antibodies	survive
donate	bloodstream	eight	negative	antigens

Tip: After you've answered the easy ones, go back and work the harder ones.

What comes to mind when you think of blood? It may be the color red, a hospital, or even a horror film! Blood is something that your body requires to _____, regardless of how you feel about it. Did you realize, though, that not everyone has the same blood type? There are _____ different kinds in total! The letters A, B, and O, as well as positive or _____ signs, distinguish these blood types. O+, O-, A+, A-, B+, B-, AB+, and AB- are the eight blood types.

What Is the Importance of Blood Types?

Don't be concerned if your blood type differs from that of others! There is no such thing as a better or healthier blood type. The sole reason to know your blood type is in case you need to _____ or give blood to someone in an emergency. A blood _____ is a process of transferring blood from one person to another.

Blood transfusions are only effective when the donor's blood is _____ with the _____ blood. Some blood types don't mix well because the body produces antibodies to fight off any unfamiliar _____ that enter the _____. Antibodies act as warriors in your blood, guarding you against alien intruders. Assume you have Type A blood, which contains A antigens solely, and someone with Type B blood wishes to donate blood to you. Your body does not recognize B antigens; thus, _____ are produced to combat them! This has the potential to make you sick. As a result, people with Type A blood should only receive blood from those with Type A blood or Type O blood, as O blood lacks both A and B antigens.

* Reading Comprehension: Social Media Safety

Tip: After you've answered the easy ones, go back and work the harder ones.

Interactions	policies	relationship	post	pop-ups
incidents	identity	connect	Personal	logins
negative	harmful	restrictive	steal	privacy
passwords	viruses	platform	abuse	security

In the last 20 years, socializing has evolved dramatically. _____ between people are referred to as socializing. At one time, socializing meant getting together with family and friends. It now frequently refers to accessing the Internet via social media or websites that allow you to _____ and interact with other people.

One of the first things you can do to protect yourself while online occurs before you even visit a social media website. Ascertain that your computer is outfitted with up-to-date computer _____ software. This software detects and removes _____ that are harmful to your computer. When you use your computer, these viruses can sometimes hack into it and _____ your information, such as _____. Create strong _____ for all of your social media accounts. This is necessary to prevent others from accessing your social media account.

Internet security settings are pre-installed on all computers. These can be as loose or as _____ as you want them to be. To be safe, it is recommended that the Internet security settings be set to medium or higher. This enables your computer to block _____ and warn you when you are about to visit a potentially harmful website.

Two things to keep in mind

- Don't _____ anything you wouldn't want broadcast to the entire world.

- The 'Golden Rule' of life is to treat others as you would like to be treated.

_____ information about one's identity should not be posted or shared on social media. Phone numbers, addresses, social security numbers, and family information are all included. This information can be used to recreate your _____ and should never be made public.

Make use of the _____ settings on the social media website. These can be used to control who can post information to your wall as well as who can see what is posted on it. Let's face it: there are some things you don't mind if your family and close friends know about, but you don't necessarily want your coworkers to find out about them through online posts.

Be positive.
Be cautious about what you post on any social media _____. Posting something _____ about someone hurts their character and opens the door for them, or someone else, to do the same to you. If you are not in a good mood or are upset, think twice. What you post could be _____ to you or someone else. Once you've made a post, it's always there. Even if you delete the post, this remains true!

If you are in a bad social media _____ and are being harassed or bullied, you can report it to the social media company. They all have _____ in place to deal with people who _____ their websites. Make a note of these _____ and report them to the company. You may also save the life of another person.

* Word of The Day

Use the dictionary to write the definition
and divide the words for each day
below into syllables.

MONDAY Word: **adolescent**

○

Write Words In ABC Order

TUESDAY **WORD: strenuous**

WEDNESDAY **WORD: facsimile**

For each word, find one
synonym & one antonym. (if
none: write word + none)

THURSDAY **WORD: subtle**

FRIDAY **WORD: scorned**

SATURDAY / SUNDAY **WORD: robust**

* Word of The Day

Use the dictionary to write the definition
and divide the words for each day
below into syllables.

MONDAY Word: **emigrant**

○

Write Words In ABC Order

_____
_____
_____
_____
_____
_____
_____

TUESDAY **WORD: parallelogram**

WEDNESDAY **WORD: unconscionable**

For each word, find one
synonym & one antonym. (if
none: write word + none)

THURSDAY **WORD: zoophyte**

_____
_____
_____
_____
_____

FRIDAY **WORD: accustomed**

_____
_____
_____
_____

SATURDAY / SUNDAY **WORD: omitted**

_____
_____
_____
_____
_____

* Art: Henri Matisse

Tip: After you've answered the easy ones, go back and work on the harder ones.

influenced	impressionism	bar	France	masterpiece
rules	appendicitis	modern	emotions	bright

Henri Matisse was born in the north of _____. Henri's father was a grain merchant who was strict

with him. He went to law school in Paris and graduated from there. In 1888, he passed the _____

and began working as a law clerk.

Henri was diagnosed with _____ in 1889. During his recovery, his mother bought him some art

supplies to keep him occupied. He became enamored with painting and art. He decided to pursue a career as an

artist, which made his father extremely dissatisfied. His mother encouraged him to break the _____

of art and experiment with new techniques and paint his _____. He studied art for a year at the

Academie Julian in Paris before leaving to train under the artist Gustave Moreau, where he could experiment with

more _____ painting styles. Matisse met painter John Peter Russell in 1897. Russell introduced him

to _____ and van Gogh's work.

In 1897, Matisse completed his first _____. It was known as The Dinner Table. He continued to

paint, _____ by artists such as Vincent van Gogh and Paul Cezanne. He also studied the works of

J.M.W. Turner and adopted some of Seurat's Pointillism style.

Matisse developed a new style in the early 1900s. He began to paint with _____ masses of freely

applied colors. He used colors to express emotion, often using colors that had nothing to do with the subject's

natural colors. Along with fellow artists Maurice de Vlaminck and Andre Derain, Matisse introduced their new style

to the world in 1905. One critic referred to them as "fauves," which translates as "wild beasts." The name stuck,

and their art style became known as Fauvism.

Antonyms
Identify antonyms.

Circle the word that has the opposite meaning of the given word.

Examples:

night is the opposite of day   small is the opposite of big

1. clumsy	funny	graceful	shameful
2. late	tardy	early	tired
3. shiny	dull	bright	flashy
4. yell	talk	loud	whisper
5. poverty	beggar	riches	happiness
6. borrow	lend	steal	return
7. calm	excited	sad	mellow
8. cloudy	rainy	gray	clear
9. pure	tainted	chilly	color
10. similar	alike	clear	different
11. serious	funny	angry	neutral
12. attack	arrive	defend	raise

Homophones
Identify homophones.

Read each sentence carefully. Choose the correct homophone to fill in the blanks.

Homophones are words that sound the same but have different meanings and spellings.

---

1. bored, board
   The boys were _____ so they decided to go outside and
   skate_____ .

2. buy, by
   She went_____the store to_____some snacks for the party.

3. cent, sent
   I_____ the postcard. It cost 49 _____s.

4. blew, blue
   Sarah_____up fifty_____balloons to decorate the party.

5. hair, hare
   The gray and white_____ed _____hopped down the trail.

6. aloud, allowed
   Are you _____to say that secret_____?

7. dessert, desert
   We went to the _____for a hike. On the way home we stopped to
   get _____ .

8. sight, site
   The historical_____ is now in my _____.

* Art: Recycled Art

Recycled art is an unusual but very creative art form in which existing materials are reused and recycled to create works of art. This is in contrast to more traditional art forms in which artists use paint, drawing materials, clay, or other mediums associated with artwork creation. Sometimes the materials used in recycled art are essentially garbage, while other materials are created for a purpose other than art and are being given a new lease on life. Recycled art can be made for several reasons. When people have limited materials to work with, it is often created out of necessity. In other cases, as discussed in this lesson, the materials used in the art are deliberately chosen to challenge viewers' perceptions of what is art, what is trash, and what is beautiful and meaningful. Many recycled art artists use their mediums to convey powerful environmental messages.

There are two types of recycled art: upcycled art and downcycled art. These are two complementary approaches that make use of recycled materials in opposing ways. Upcycled art transforms materials that are typically considered trash into beautiful and meaningful art. This practice is considered more common in the recycled art world because it allows artists to make powerful statements about waste. Upcycled art is created by an artist who creates a portrait out of discarded computer parts that would otherwise end up in a landfill.

Downcycled art is the inverse of upcycled art in that artists deconstruct or destroy objects before transforming them into art. Downcycled art is created by an artist who takes an old armchair and rips the stuffing out of it in an installation piece. While downcycled art exists, it is less common because the goal of recycled art is often to elevate materials that are considered worthless by incorporating them into art.

1. Sometimes the materials used in recycled art are essentially _____.
   a. wood
   b. garbage
   c. luxury items

2. _____ art transforms materials that are typically considered trash into beautiful and meaningful art.
   a. Abstract
   b. Acrylic paint
   c. Upcycled

3. _____ art is the inverse of upcycled art in that artists deconstruct or destroy objects before transforming them into art.
   a. Enamel
   b. Fine art
   c. Downcycled

4. There are two types of recycled art: _____ art and _____ art.
   a. decorative and airbrush
   b. upcycled and downcycled
   c. abstract and recycled

A cash receipt is a printed confirmation of the amount of money received in a transaction involving the transfer of cash or cash equivalents.

Receipt No.   EXAMPLE

Write the date of the cash purchase

Date: _____

Write the cash amount received from the customer

Amount: _____

Write the item(s) purchase

Item: **Blue socks and purple shoes** _____

Write who paid you

From: **Tommy Roberson** _____

Write who the payment is for. Could be a company or individual name

To: **Kiddy Clothes Store** _____

Write the name who received the payment

Write date you received the payment. In most cases, it can be the same day as the purchase date.

Received by: **Janet Miller** _____

Date: _____

Pretend someone has just bought something from you, then fill out the receipt to reflect the transaction.

Receipt No.

Date: _____

Amount: _____

Item: _____

From: _____

To: _____

Received by: _____

Date: _____

Receipt No.

Date: _____

Amount: _____

Item: _____

From: _____

To: _____

Received by: _____

Date: _____

Letter "F" Science Spelling Words

Circle the correct spelling of each word.

	A	B	C	D
1.	Fasett	Facet	Facett	Faset
2.	Farming	Farmyng	Farrmyng	Farrming
3.	Faullt	Fault	Fuallt	Fualt
4.	Fuana	Faona	Foana	Fauna
5.	Faldspar	Felldspar	Feldspar	Falldspar
6.	Fernment	Ferrnment	Ferment	Ferrment
7.	Fermentasion	Ferrmentasion	Fermentation	Ferrmentation
8.	Fission	Fistion	Fision	Fition
9.	Fisore	Fissure	Fiscure	Fisure
10.	Flood Plain	Flod Plian	Floud Plain	Flod Plain
11.	Fluding	Floding	Flooding	Flouding
12.	Fllura	Fllora	Flora	Flura
13.	Flloorish	Fllourish	Floorish	Flourish
14.	Flluwstone	Fllowstone	Fluwstone	Flowstone
15.	Folliage	Folaige	Foliage	Follaige
16.	Fod chian	Food chain	Foud chain	Fod chain
17.	Food relasionships	Fod relationships	Food relationships	Fod relasionships
18.	Fod Web	Food Web	Foud Web	Fud Web
19.	Forradge	Foradge	Forage	Forrage
20.	Furrecast	Forecast	Furecast	Forrecast
21.	Forrensics	Forensics	Furensics	Furrensics
22.	Forrmasions	Formasions	Forrmations	Formations
23.	Fosil fuel	Foussil fuel	Fousil fuel	Fossil fuel
24.	Francis torbine	Frrancis turbine	Frrancis torbine	Francis turbine

Fill in the blanks with a definition for each of the science spelling words:

Fictional vs. Fictitious vs. Fictive

Fictional is invented as part of a work of fiction

SYNONYMS:
Fabricated
Imaginary

Fictitious is created, taken, or assumed for the sake of concealment; not genuine; false

SYNONYMS:
Bogus
Counterfeit

Fictive - fictitious; imaginary. pertaining to the creation of fiction
- is capable of imaginative creation.

SYNONYMS:

Make-believe
Fabricated

1. He dismissed recent rumors about his private life as _____.
   a. fictitious
   b. fictional
   c. fictive

2. I have the impression that this _____ marriage of ours is like a ghost in a play.
   a. fictional
   b. fictitious
   c. fictive

3. The setting is a _____ island in the Chesapeake River.
   a. fictitious
   b. fictional
   c. fictive

4. The writer has _____ talent.
   a. fictitious
   b. fictional
   c. fictive

5. Almost all _____ detectives are unreal.
   a. fictitious
   b. fictional
   c. fictive

6. The names of the shops are entirely _____.
   a. fictive
   b. fictional
   c. fictitious

Extra Credit: Fun Idioms You Might Know

Download the free **Google Translate** app. Select the conversation option via the app. Speak each English word or phrase into your device. You'll *hear* the *translation* spoken aloud in Spanish as well written in Spanish. Write down the Spanish version for each below.

1. As easy as ABC

    a. _____

    b. _____

2. Cross your fingers

    a. _____

    b. _____

3. Call it a day

    a. _____

    b. _____

4. Cool as a cucumber

    a. _____

    b. _____

5. Fell on deaf ears

    a. _____

    b. _____

6. Crack a book

    a. _____

    b. _____

7. Raining cats and dogs

    a. _____

    b. _____

8. Giving the cold shoulder

    a. _____

    b. _____

9. Down to the wire

    a. _____

    b. _____

10. Fill in the blanks

    a. _____

    b. _____

11. Get cold feet

    a. _____

    b. _____

12. Cat got your tongue?

    a. _____

    b. _____

13. Get a kick out of it

    a. _____

    b. _____

14. I'm all ears

    a. _____

    b. _____

15. Busy as a bee

    a. _____

    b. _____

16. A little birdie told me

    a. _____

    b. _____

17. It cost an arm and a leg

    a. _____

    b. _____

18. Cry crocodile tears

    a. _____

    b. _____

19. Put a bug in his ear

    a. _____

    b. _____

20. Wolf in sheep's clothing

    a. _____

    b. _____

21. Have a change of heart

    a. _____

    b. _____

22. Get your act together

    a. _____

    b. _____

23. Play it by ear

    a. _____

    b. _____

24. Hold your horses

    a. _____

    b. _____

25. Let the cat out of the bag

    a. _____

    b. _____

26. Give it a shot

    a. _____

    b. _____

27. See eye to eye

    a. _____

    b. _____

28. Night owl

    a. _____

    b. _____

29. Mixed feelings

    a. _____

    b. _____

30. Have second thoughts

    a. _____

    b. _____

31. Curiosity killed the cat

    a. _____

    b. _____

32. In hot water

    a. _____

    b. _____

33. In the same boat

    a. _____

    b. _____

34. I've got your number

    a. _____

    b. _____

35. Get off your high horse

    a. _____

    b. _____

36. Slipped my mind

    a. _____

    b. _____

37. Miss the boat

    a. _____

    b. _____

38. Mumbo jumbo

    a. _____

    b. _____

39. Out of the blue

    a. _____

    b. _____

40. Speak your mind

    a. _____

    b. _____

41. Pass with flying colors

    a. _____

    b. _____

42. Piece of cake

    a. _____

    b. _____

Introvert vs. Extrovert

Introvert is a person who prefers calm environments, limits social engagement, or embraces a greater than average preference for solitude.

SYNONYMS:
brooder
loner
solitary

Extrovert is an outgoing, gregarious person who thrives in dynamic environments and seeks to maximize social engagement.

SYNONYMS:
character
exhibitionist
show-off
showboat

Fill in the blank with the correct word. [introvert, introverts, extrovert, extroverts]

1. Sue is the _____ in the family; opinionated, talkative and passionate about politics.

2. He was described as an _____, a reserved man who spoke little.

3. _____ are often described as the life of the party.

4. An _____ is often thought of as a quiet, reserved, and thoughtful individual.

5. _____ enjoy being around other people and tend to focus on the outside world.

6. Typically _____ tend to enjoy more time to themselves.

7. Jane is an _____ whose only hobby is reading.

8. I am still not as "outgoing" as an _____ is.

9. I had been a very _____ person, living life to the full.

10. I am an _____, I am a loner.

11. Because Pat is an _____ who enjoys chatting with others, she is the ideal talk show host.

12. She is basically an _____, uncomfortable with loud women and confrontations.

Weather Vocabulary Words
Match Up

Score: _____

Date: _____

The weather is simply the state of the atmosphere at any given time, which includes temperature, precipitation, air pressure, and cloud cover. Winds and storms cause daily changes in the weather. Seasonal changes are caused by the Earth's rotation around the sun.

The sun's rays do not fall evenly on the land and oceans because the Earth is round rather than flat. The sun shines more directly near the equator, bringing more warmth to these areas. On the other hand, the polar regions are at such an angle to the sun that they receive little or no sunlight during the winter, resulting in colder temperatures. These temperature differences cause a frantic movement of air and water in great swirling currents, distributing heat energy from the sun across the planet. When the air in one region is warmer than air in another, it becomes less dense and begins to rise, drawing more air in beneath it. Cooler, denser air sinks elsewhere, pushing air outward to flow along the surface and complete the cycle.

Match to the correct answer.

1	Anemometer		something that happens quickly usually due to heavy rain	A
2	Barometer		tiny water droplets floating in the atmosphere that you can see	B
3	Blizzard		A region with low air pressure and warm, moist air	C
4	Cloud		A region with high air pressure and cool, dry air	D
5	Coriolis effect		line on a weather map that represents a given barometric pressure	E
6	Flash flood		meteorological instrument used to measure the atmospheric pressure	F
7	High-pressure system		It affects weather patterns - affects an object that's moving over something that's rotating	G
8	Hurricane		meteorological instrument used to measure wind speed	H
9	Isobar		snow storm that has winds of 35 miles per hour or more	I
10	Low-pressure system		tropical cyclone that formed in the North Atlantic Ocean	J

A credit application is a lender's first step in acquiring consumer information. Informed decisions and information gathering are easier when they know more about you. A credit application is a request for credit from a lender.

* Life Skills — Credit Application

Name:	Date Birth:	SSN:

Current Address:		Phone:

City:	State:	ZIP:

Own Rent (Please circle)	Monthly payment or rent:	How long?

Previous Address:		

City:	State:	ZIP:

Owned Rented (Please circle)	Monthly payment or rent:	How long?

Employment Information

Current Employer:	How long?

Employer Address:	Phone:

Position:	Hourly Salary (Please circle)	Annual Income:

Previous Employer:

Address:	How long?

Phone:	E-mail:	Fax:

Position:	Hourly Salary (Please circle)	Annual Income:

Name and relationship of a relative not living with you:

Address:

City:	State:	ZIP:	Phone:

Co-Applicant Information, if for a joint account

Name:	Date Birth:	SSN:

Current Address:		Phone:

City:	State:	ZIP:

Own Rent (Please circle)	Monthly payment or rent:	How long?

Previous Address:		

City:	State:	ZIP:

Owned Rented (Please circle)	Monthly payment or rent:	How long?

Employment Information

Current Employer:	How long?

Employer Address:	Phone:

Position:	Hourly Salary (circle)	Annual Income:

Previous Employer:

Address:

Phone:	E-mail:	Fax:

Position:	Hourly Salary (circle)	Annual Income:

Name and relationship of a relative not living with you:

Address:

City:	State:	ZIP:	Phone:

Credit Cards

Name	Account No.	Current Balance	Monthly Payment

Mortgage Company

Account No.:	Address:

Auto Loans

Auto Loans	Account No.	Balance	Monthly Payment

Other Loans, Debts, or Obligations

Description	Account No.	Amount

Other Assets or Sources of Income

	Monthly Value: $
	Monthly Value: $

I/We authorize _____ to verify information provided on this form regarding credit and employment history.

Signature of Applicant	Date

Signature of Co-Applicant, if for joint account	Date

* Jobs and Careers

Tip: After you've answered the easy ones, go back and work on the harder ones.

skill	climbing	monetary	professional	hourly
variety	salaried	experience	graduate	achieve

You might have heard that the education you receive and the information you learn in school will help you get a job when you _____. Or your abilities and skills will benefit you in your future careers. So, what's the truth? How do people decide whether they want a job or a career?

There are several common misconceptions regarding the distinctions between a job and a career. Some people believe that a job is simply an _____ position, whereas a _____ position is a career. Others believe that a career requires a longer educational path that results in exceptional skills and knowledge. The truth is not what most people believe.

A job is a position or set of duties performed for _____ gain, whereas a career is a focused path or journey that a person takes to achieve their professional goals. A career can include a variety of jobs along a career path.

Parents and teachers frequently ask their children what they want to be when they grow up. A career is the answer to that question. A career is a path or _____ journey that a person follows throughout their working life. A career can necessitate extensive education, such as that of a doctor or a lawyer, or it can require extensive _____ training, such as that of an electrician or plumber.

The words "career" and "path" are frequently used interchangeably. A career path is a path that people take to _____ their professional objectives. Many people work for decades on their career paths, which often include a _____ of jobs along the way. With each job, a person gains _____ and skills that will help them get a better job and achieve their career goals.

Another term associated with careers is the concept of people _____ a "career ladder". When people climb the metaphorical career ladder, they progress step by step from one better job to the next. Careers take years to develop and achieve. Sometimes a lot of education is required at the start of a career before a person can start moving up the ladder, whereas other careers require years of experience in the field to get to the top.

A job application's purposes is to gather information that will help shape the selection process, supply recruiters with the information they need to build interview questions, and ensure that you're qualified for the position and grasp the nature of the working relationship.

* Life Skills: Practice Employee Application

Applicant

Name: Date:

Referral: Phone No.

Fax No.   Email:

Address:

Are You...

A U.S. Citizen?	☐ Yes	☐ No
Over 18 years old?	☐ Yes	☐ No
Licensed to drive?	☐ Yes	☐ No

Employment

Position: Department:

Type: ☐ Full-Time   ☐ Part-Time   ☐ Other (Seasonal/Temp):

Start Date: Starting Salary:

Current Employment: May we contact? ☐ Yes   ☐ No

Education History

High School

College

Graduate

Other Training/Classes:

Workshops/Certifications:

Employment History

References

Applicant Signature   Date

* Biology: Famous Biologists Research

Score: _____

Date: _____

Oswald Avery was a biologist who discovered that DNA contains genetic information passed down from generation to generation.

Rachel Carson: This biologist made a breakthrough in the field of environmental biology by discovering the impact of chemicals on the environment and the food we eat.

Marie Curie: This biologist made a discovery related to the elements that we now see on the periodic table, and she was among the first to experiment with radiation and tumor treatment. Today, this experiment is widely used to treat cancers and tumors, demonstrating the significance of this discovery.

Charles Darwin: This biologist studied the concept of species evolution as well as the origins of species.

William Harvey: This biologist discovered that blood leaves the heart and travels around the body before returning to the heart, forming a circuit.

Research each biologist and write 2 amazing facts about them

....

....

....

....

....

....

....

....

....

....

* Biology: ANIMAL KINGDOM

Score: _____

Date: _____

Animals are the most numerous and diverse of the five kingdoms of living things. Over two million animal species have been identified so far. All animals share certain characteristics. Animals, unlike plants, obtain their energy from food. They are all made up of many cells, and many animals move quickly. Most reproduce sexually and have sense organs that allow them to respond rapidly to their environment.

Jellyfish, for example, has a relatively simple structure. They lack a skeleton, have few muscles, and move in an uncoordinated manner? They float along with the ocean currents. Jellyfish are classified as invertebrates because, like 98% of all animals, they lack a backbone.

Animals with backbones, such as these zebras, are known as vertebrates. Vertebrates include mammals, birds, fish, amphibians, and reptiles. Zebras are classified as mammals. Mammalian animals, which include humans, are the most complex in the animal kingdom.

1. What are 5 examples of a vertebrate?

2. What are 5 examples of invertebrates?

3. What exactly is a mammal?

4. Amphibians are a class of what cold-blooded vertebrates?

5. Reptiles use a variety of methods to defend themselves such as...

6. What are the 4 types of arthropods?

7. Oviparous animals lay eggs where?

8. An herbivore is an organism that mostly feeds on what?

9. A carnivore is an organism that mostly eats?

10. An omnivore is an organism that eats?

* Biology: Excretory System

Score: _____

Date: _____

chloride	pressure	bladder	filtering	bloodstream
molecules	concentrate	urine	muscular	detoxifies
kidneys	substances	glomeruli	reabsorbing	converts

Tip: After you've answered the easy ones, go back and work the harder ones.

Toxins are present in all animals' bodies and must be eliminated. The human liver _____ and modifies dangerous _____ so that they can be quickly and easily removed from the body. For example, ammonia is very toxic, so the liver _____ it to urea, which is far less toxic and easily removed from the body.

The _____ are the organs responsible for _____ waste products from the blood and regulating blood composition and pressure. The outer layer of the kidneys contains structures known as _____, which are ball-like structures made up of very porous capillaries. Large amounts of water and small molecules, including urea, are forced out through the pores by the blood _____ in these capillaries, but blood cells and larger _____ that are too large to fit through the pores remain in the _____.

The glomeruli are surrounded by the ends of the renal tubules, which are long, looping tubes in the kidney that collect blood filtrate and _____ it into the urine. The filtrate travels through the tubules, _____ nutrients, water, and sodium _____ from the renal tubules and returning them to the blood. Waste products are concentrated in the tubules and become urine as water and nutrients are reabsorbed. Urine is stored in the _____ after the kidneys have concentrated it. Most people can control when they empty their bladder by controlling a _____ valve at the exit point. When this valve is opened and the bladder muscles contract, _____ enters the urethra, where it travels before exiting the body.

Biology: Reading Comprehension Viruses

When we catch a cold or get the flu, we are dealing with the effects of a viral infection. Viruses, despite sharing some characteristics with living organisms, are neither cellular nor alive. The presence of cells, the ability to reproduce, the ability to use energy, and the ability to respond to the environment are all important characteristics of living organisms. A virus cannot perform any of these functions on its own.

A virus, on the other hand, is a collection of genetic material encased in a protective coat, which is typically made of proteins. Viruses are obligate parasites because they must replicate on the host. To replicate itself, a virus must first attach to and penetrate a host cell, after which it will go through the various stages of viral infection. These stages are essentially the virus lifecycle. A virus can enter the host cell via one of several methods by interacting with the surface of the host cell. The virus can then replicate itself by utilizing the host's energy and metabolism.

Bacteriophages, viruses that infect bacteria, either use the lysogenic cycle, in which the host cell's offspring carry the virus, or the lytic cycle, in which the host cell dies immediately after viral replication. Once viral shedding has occurred, the virus can infect additional hosts. Viral infections can be productive in the sense that they cause active infection in the host, or they can be nonproductive in the sense that they remain dormant within the host. These two types of infection can result in chronic infections, in which the host goes through cycles of illness and remission, as well as latent infections, in which the virus remains dormant for a period of time before causing illness in the host.

1. A virus is encased in a protective coat, which is typically made of _____.
    a. proteins
    b. molecules
    c. cells

2. To replicate itself, a virus must first attach to and penetrate a ____ cell.
    a. healthy
    b. living atom
    c. host

3. Viruses are neither cellular nor __.
    a. alive
    b. moving
    c. a threat

4. The virus can replicate itself by utilizing the host's ____ and ____.
    a. cells and DNA
    b. molecules and cell
    c. energy and metabolism

5. A virus can remain _____ for a period of time before causing illness in a host.
    a. metabolized
    b. dormant
    c. infected

* Spelling Words Word Search

Circle the 20 words listed below. Words appear straight across, back- word straight across, up and down.

```
V   B   U   E   T   A   R   U   S   N   E   M   M   O   C   E
C   F   P   M   D   R   S   U   O   I   C   A   L   L   A   F
K   D   H   M   S   I   E   E   T   N   E   S   B   A   H   D
A   M   Z   P   Y   S   G   L   J   W   E   G   N   M   A   I
Y   M   C   J   L   L   U   A   B   G   R   C   E   V   U   S
U   E   E   P   W   A   A   O   Z   I   O   J   T   X   V   E
E   D   Y   H   X   J   U   I   H   P   T   A   E   N   C   N
N   E   B   G   T   X   P   S   N   P   A   S   J   B   O   F
C   S   V   W   M   A   P   T   I   N   R   C   E   T   L   R
Y   J   H   S   I   D   N   A   R   B   E   O   H   M   L   A
C   O   N   S   U   L   T   A   N   T   L   I   M   O   O   N
L   N   B   E   L   V   E   D   E   R   E   E   B   A   Q   C
I   D   E   S   U   O   I   T   I   T   C   I   F   V   U   H
C   A   R   C   I   N   O   G   E   N   C   Y   M   F   I   I
A   Q   O   S   D   E   L   I   N   E   A   T   E   R   A   S
L   E   L   B   I   S   S   E   C   C   A   N   I   F   L   E
```

consultant	inaccessible	fictitious	brandish	plausible
absenteeism	accelerator	amorphous	anathema	belvedere
biennial	carcinogen	colloquial	comestible	commensurate
delineate	disenfranchise	encyclical	fallacious	gazpacho

Biology Vocabulary Words Crossword

Score: _____

Date: _____

Across

1. organelle in which photosynthesis takes place
4. a substance used to kill microorganisms and cure infections
5. any substance that stimulates an immune response in the body
6. a chamber connected to other chambers or passageways
8. major ecological community with distinct climate and flora
9. substance that initiates or accelerates a chemical reaction
13. an eyelike marking
15. any toxin that affects neural tissues

Down

2. a process in which one substance permeates another
6. any of the forms of a gene that can occupy the same locus
7. a digestive juice secreted by the liver
10. a major division of the vertebrate brain
11. the act of dispersing something
12. the environment as it relates to living organisms
14. that which has mass and occupies space

ATRIUM   BIOME   ANTIGEN
ECOLOGY
CHLOROPLAST   MATTER
ABSORPTION   ANTIBIOTIC
DIFFUSION   ALLELE
EYESPOT   NEUROTOXIN
BILE   CEREBELLUM
CATALYST

* Geometry Reading Comprehension

Score: _____

Date: _____

90-degree	segment	Acute	angles	Obtuse
directions	straight	halves	height	formulas

Tip: After you've answered the easy ones, go back and work the harder ones.

The study of shapes and space is known as geometry. It provides answers to size, area, and volume questions. The earliest known geometry works date back to 2000 BC and are from Egypt. There were _____ for lengths, areas, and volumes, as well as one for pyramids. Thales of Miletus calculated the _____ of pyramids in the 7th century BC, and the Greek mathematician Pythagoras proved the well-known Pythagorean Theorem.

Euclid, another Greek mathematician, introduced Euclidean geometry around 300 BC by demonstrating how to prove theorems using basic definitions and truths. We still use Euclidean geometry to prove theorems today.

Geometric terms include points, lines, and _____. A point is a non-dimensional object with no length or width. A dot is commonly used to represent it. A line is an object that extends in both _____ without end. It is usually depicted with arrowheads to indicate that it continues indefinitely. A line _____ is a section of a line that has two ends. A ray is one-half of a line with a single endpoint. Two rays with the same endpoint form an angle. The angle is called a straight angle if the rays are the two _____ of a single line. A straight angle is analogous to a book open flat on a desk. A right angle is defined as an angle that is opened half that far.

Angles are expressed in degrees. A right angle is defined as a _____ angle. _____ angles are those that are less than a right angle. _____ angles are those that are larger than a right angle but smaller than a _____ angle.

Biology Vocabulary Words Crossword

Score: _____

Date: _____

Across

1. organelle in which photosynthesis takes place
4. a substance used to kill microorganisms and cure infections
5. any substance that stimulates an immune response in the body
6. a chamber connected to other chambers or passageways
8. major ecological community with distinct climate and flora
9. substance that initiates or accelerates a chemical reaction
13. an eyelike marking
15. any toxin that affects neural tissues

Down

2. a process in which one substance permeates another
6. any of the forms of a gene that can occupy the same locus
7. a digestive juice secreted by the liver
10. a major division of the vertebrate brain
11. the act of dispersing something
12. the environment as it relates to living organisms
14. that which has mass and occupies space

ATRIUM   BIOME   ANTIGEN
ECOLOGY
CHLOROPLAST   MATTER
ABSORPTION   ANTIBIOTIC
DIFFUSION   ALLELE
EYESPOT   NEUROTOXIN
BILE   CEREBELLUM
CATALYST

When the index and radicand of two or more radicals are the same, radicals can be combined. Like radicals are radicals that have the same index and radicand. It is often helpful to treat radicals similarly to variables: radicals can be added and subtracted in the same way that like variables can. Before you can add or subtract like terms, you may need to simplify a radical expression.

Adding and Subtracting Radical Expressions

Simplify the Radical E pressions

1) $\sqrt{28} + \sqrt{28} - \sqrt{28}$

2) $-3\sqrt{2} - 5\sqrt{2} + 4\sqrt{2}$

3) $\sqrt{45} - \sqrt{45}$

4) $4\sqrt{3} - 2\sqrt{3} - 7\sqrt{3}$

5) $\sqrt{80} + \sqrt{80} + \sqrt{80}$

6) $\sqrt{2} + 6\sqrt{2} + \sqrt{18}$

7) $-\sqrt{11} + \sqrt{176}$

8) $4\sqrt{11} + 7\sqrt{44}$

9) $-\sqrt{18} + \sqrt{63} + \sqrt{8}$

10) $-5\sqrt{3} - 7\sqrt{3} - 2\sqrt{48}$

Tips:
Determine the slope, m. This can be done by using the slope formula to calculate the slope between two known points on a line.

Determine the y-intercept. This can be achieved by entering the slope and coordinates of a point (x, y) on the line into the slope-intercept formula and solving for b.

Once you have both m and b, simply enter them into the equation at their respective positions.

Score : _____

Date : _____

Find the Slope and Y-intercept

1) $y = -\frac{7}{5}x - 3$ slope = _____

y-intercept = _____

2) $y = \frac{1}{5}x + 5$ slope = _____

y-intercept = _____

3) $y = 3x + 2$ slope = _____

y-intercept = _____

4) $y = \frac{3}{2}x + 3$ slope = _____

y-intercept = _____

5) $y = -x + 2$ slope = _____

y-intercept = _____

6) $y = 2x - 4$ slope = _____

y-intercept = _____

7) $y = -\frac{4}{9}x - 3$ slope = _____

y-intercept = _____

8) $y = -\frac{7}{6}x + 10$ slope = _____

y-intercept = _____

9) $y = \frac{5}{2}x - 4$ slope = _____

y-intercept = _____

10) $y = -x + 3$ slope = _____

y-intercept = _____

When faced with a math expression that contains several operations or parentheses, the order in which you tackle the operations may affect the solution.

Simplify the expressions contained within parentheses (), brackets [], braces, and fractions bars.

- Evaluate all powers.
- All multiplications and divisions must be done from left to right.
- All additions and subtractions must be done from left to right.

Evaluate each expression.   # Order of Operations

1) $(-3)x - (-6) \div (-3) \cdot (-2)x$

2) $3x - (-8)x \cdot 5 - 9x + 3x$

3) $(-11)x + (-8)x \cdot 4 - (-10)x$

4) $60x \div 5 - 5x \cdot 3 + 2x$

5) $3x - 11x \cdot 2 - 7x$

6) $(-11) \cdot (-2)x - (-10)x - (-3)x \cdot (-5)$

7) $66x \div 11 - 6x \cdot 2$

8) $4x \cdot 54x \div 9x - 5x - 9x$

9) $(-2)x - (-4) \div (-2) \cdot (-12)x$

10) $8x + 7x \cdot (-2) - (-3)x + 5x$

11) $(-8)x \cdot (-78)x \div 13x - (-3)x$

12) $(-6) \cdot (-7)x - (-4)x - (-3)x \cdot (-2)$

* History: King Tut Reading Comprehension

Tutankhamun was born around 1341 BC as a prince in Egypt's royal court. Pharaoh Akhenaten was his father. Tut was actually born Tutankhaten, but he changed his name after his father died.

Tut was born to one of his father's lesser wives rather than his father's main wife, the powerful Nefertiti. His presence may have caused some tension in the royal courts, as Nefertiti had only daughters and desperately desired to have her own son to succeed to the throne.

Tut's father died when he was seven years old. Tut married his sister (as was common for Pharaohs in Ancient Egypt) and became Pharaoh a few years later. Because he was so young, he needed help ruling the country. Horemheb, a powerful general, and Ay, Tutankhamun's vizier, were the true rulers.

Tutankhamun died when he was about nineteen years old. Archaeologists have no idea what killed him. Some believe he was assassinated, but the most likely cause of death was a leg wound. Scientists discovered that his mummy's leg was broken and infected before he died. This injury was most likely caused by an accident.

Today, Tut is best known for his tomb in the Valley of the Kings. His tomb was most likely built for someone else and was used to bury the young Pharaoh when he died unexpectedly. This may have aided in keeping his tomb hidden from thieves for thousands of years. As a result, when archeologist Howard Carter discovered the tomb in 1922, it was filled with treasure and artifacts not found in any other Pharaoh's tomb.

Did you know that? Lord Carnarvon, Carter's patron (who was best known as the financial backer of the search for and excavation of Tut), died four months after first entering the tomb. Prompting journalists to popularize a "Curse of the Pharaohs," claiming that hieroglyphs on the tomb walls foretold the death of those who disturbed King Tut.

1. **What was King Tut's real name?**
   a. Tutankhaion
   b. Tutankhaten
   c. Tutankhamun

2. **Tut's father died when he was _____ years old.**
   a. 19 yrs old
   b. Twenty-Two
   c. seven

3. **Tutankhamun died when he was about _____ years old.**
   a. nineteen
   b. 16 years old
   c. 21

4. **Nefertiti was the wife of____.**
   a. Tut
   b. Horemheb
   c. Pharaoh Akhenaten

5. **The tomb of young pharaoh Tut is located in the _____.**
   a. Tuts King Egypt
   b. Maine Valley Sons
   c. Valley of the Kings

* Spelling Words Word Scramble

Tips:
Separate the consonants from the vowels.
Try to find letters that often go together in words like "BR" or "TH".

Look carefully at the jumbled words and unscramble the spelling words below.

1. eenegtl   _ _ n _ _ _ l

2. luieedbg   _ _ g _ _ _ e _

3. tramanel   _ _ _ e _ n _ _

4. ucmuevialt   c u _ _ _ t _ _ _

5. dandeut   _ _ _ n t _ _

6. lnarabmo   a _ _ _ _ m _ _

7. geossua   _ a _ _ o _ _

8. rirantpiopoap   _ p _ _ _ _ r _ _ _ i _ _

9. iamlemd   _ i _ _ m _ _

10. lmaedu   m _ u _ _ _

11. iinnutoti   _ n _ _ _ _ i _ _

12. tiuneaecn   _ _ u _ c _ _ _ _

13. ioeaulgd   _ _ _ _ o _ u _

14. orecirtd   c _ _ _ i _ _ _

15. iietdcfne   d _ _ i _ _ _ _ _

16. lntceleie   _ l _ _ _ _ _ _ e

17. mtoidte   _ m i _ _ _ _

18. inoocslvun   _ _ _ _ u l _ _ _ n

19. ietlxpo   _ x _ l _ _ _

20. roancgi   o _ _ _ n _ _

* Music: Wolfgang Amadeus Mozart

Wolfgang Amadeus Mozart (January 27, 1756 – December 5, 1791; pronounced MOHT-sart) was an Austrian composer, instrumentalist, and music teacher. Johannes Chrysostomus Wolfgangus Theophillus Mozart was his full baptismal name. He was the youngest child of Leopold and Anna Maria Mozart and was born in Salzburg, Austria. The young Mozart displayed exceptional musical talent from an early age. He toured Europe with his parents and older sister "Nannerl," performing for royalty and the aristocratic elite for several years.

Mozart attempted but failed to establish himself as a composer in Paris as a young man. He returned to Salzburg and briefly worked in the Archbishop of Salzburg's court. He was restless, aware of his brilliance, and thought Salzburg was too small for him. He moved to Vienna, where he had some success. He married Constance Weber and had two sons with her.

Mozart composed over 600 musical works, all of which are of the highest quality. The operas, The Marriage of Figaro, Don Giovanni, Cos fan tutte, and The Magic Flute; the symphonies in E-flat major, G minor, and C major ("Jupiter"); concertos for piano, violin, and various wind instruments; and numerous chamber pieces, and the Requiem are among his works. Along with Bach and Beethoven, Mozart is regarded as one of the greatest composers of all time.

There are several stories about Mozart's final illness and death, and it's difficult to know what happened. He was working on The Magic Flute, one of his best works and still a popular opera today. It is written in German rather than Italian, as are the majority of his other operas. It's similar to an English pantomime in some ways. At the same time, he was working on this, he was approached by a stranger and asked to compose a requiem. He was instructed to write this in private. Then he was commissioned to write the Italian opera La Clemenza di Tito, which premiered in Prague in September 1791. The Magic Flute received its first performance at the end of September. The Requiem was then a labor of love for Mozart. He must have realized that he was already gravely ill and that the Requiem (a mass for the dead) was for himself in some ways. He died in Vienna before completing it. Constanze commissioned another composer, Franz Xaver Süssmayr, to complete the work. Mozart was laid to rest in the St. Marx Cemetery.

1. When Mozart returned to Salzburg, he worked in the_____.
   a. Archbishop of Salzburg's court
   b. Salzburg's Music Store
   c. Archbishop High School

2. Mozart was an Austrian _____.
   a. composer, English teacher, singer
   b. science teacher, piano player and composer
   c. composer, instrumentalist, and music teacher

3. Mozart married _____ and had two sons with her.
   a. Constance Weber
   b. Courtney Webber
   c. Countesses Wilson

4. Mozart was laid to rest in the _____.
   a. Mozart family cemetery
   b. Dr. Mary Cemetery
   c. St. Marx Cemetery

* Music Vocabulary Crossword

Music has most likely existed for as long as humans have, which could be over a hundred thousand years! The earliest music is thought to have involved singing and clapping, and then early humans began drumming with sticks or other natural objects. Flutes carved from bones, such as bear and woolly mammoth bones, were among the first known musical instruments. Some of these bone instruments date back to 45,000 years!

Scholars agree that there are no 100% reliable methods for determining the exact chronology of musical instruments across cultures. Comparing and organizing instruments based on their complexity is deceptive because technological advances in musical instruments have sometimes reduced complexity. Early slit drums, for example, required felling and hollowing out large trees; later slit drums were made by opening bamboo stalks, a much simpler task.

Across

1. the distinctive property of a complex sound
2. the speed at which a composition is to be played
3. having or denoting a high range
5. the lowest part of the musical range
7. compatibility in opinion and action

Down

4. an interval during which a recurring sequence occurs
5. hit repeatedly
6. a succession of notes forming a distinctive sequence
8. a strong rod or stick with a specialized utilitarian purpose
10. a brief written record

BASS   BEAT   STAFF
TIMBRE   HARMONY
TREBLE   MELODY   NOTE
RHYTHM   TEMPO

Occupation **Lawyer, university administrator, writer,**

BORN DATE: **January 27, 1954**   Nationality **American**

DEATH DATE: **still alive and well**   Education **Princeton & Harvard University**   Children **2 girls**

Childhood and Family Background Facts

Born as Mary Robinson in Chicago, Illinois.

Dad's name John Robinson III & mom's name Rose Robinson.

One brother named Malcolm Robinson, he's a college basketball coach.

Her great-great-great-grandmother, Cindy Shields, was born into slavery in South Carolina.

Her childhood home was in New York.

Her great-aunt who was a piano teacher, taught her how to play the piano.

Work and Career Facts

- First job was babysitting.
- Mary majored in sociology at Princeton, where she graduated with honors, and went to Harvard Law School.
- She once worked in public service as an assistant to the mayor.
- She was the Vice President of Community and External Affairs at the University of Chicago Medical Center.

Friends, Social Life and Other Interesting Facts

- When she was a teen, she became friends with Kim Jackson.
- Her college bestie Suzanne Alele died from cancer at a young age in 1990.
- Her two favorite children's books: "Goodnight Moon" and "Where the Wild Things Are."
- Celebrity Crush: Denzel & Will Smith

Children, Marriage or Significant Relationships

- She suffered a heartbreaking miscarriage.
- Gave birth to two beautiful daughters Monica and Jennifer.
- She met her husband Tom when she was assigned to be his mentor when he was a summer associate at the law firm she worked at.

Did you enjoy researching this person?

Rating: ☆ ☆ ☆ ☆ ☆

GRADE_____

DATE_____   **RESEARCH: Galileo Galilei**

Occupation _____

BORN DATE:_____   Nationality _____

DEATH DATE:_____   Education _____   #Children _____

Childhood and Family Background Facts

Work and Career Facts

Children, Marriage and or Significant Relationships

Friends, Social Life and Other Interesting Facts

Did you enjoy researching this person?

Give a Rating: ☆ ☆ ☆ ☆ ☆

GRADE_____

DATE_____

RESEARCH: Mark Twain

Occupation _____

BORN DATE:_____   Nationality _____

DEATH DATE:_____   Education _____   #Children _____

Childhood and Family Background Facts

Work and Career Facts

Children, Marriage and or Significant Relationships

Friends, Social Life and Other Interesting Facts

Did you enjoy researching this person?

Give a Rating: ☆ ☆ ☆ ☆ ☆

GRADE_____

DATE_____   **RESEARCH: Marie Curie**

Occupation _____

BORN DATE:_____   Nationality _____

DEATH DATE:_____   Education _____   #Children _____

Childhood and Family Background Facts

Work and Career Facts

Children, Marriage and or Significant Relationships

Friends, Social Life and Other Interesting Facts

Did you enjoy researching this person?

Give a Rating: ☆ ☆ ☆ ☆ ☆

TODAY IS RESEARCH DAY!

GRADE_____

DATE_____

RESEARCH: Princess Diana

Occupation _____

BORN DATE:_____   Nationality _____

DEATH DATE:_____   Education _____   #Children _____

Childhood and Family Background Facts

Work and Career Facts

Children, Marriage and or Significant Relationships

Friends, Social Life and Other Interesting Facts

Did you enjoy researching this person?

Give a Rating: ☆ ☆ ☆ ☆ ☆

GRADE_____

DATE_____   **RESEARCH: Andrew Jackson**

Occupation _____

BORN DATE:_____   Nationality_____

DEATH DATE:_____   Education_____   #Children _____

Childhood and Family Background Facts

Work and Career Facts

Children, Marriage and or Significant Relationships

Friends, Social Life and Other Interesting Facts

Did you enjoy researching this person?

Give a Rating: ☆ ☆ ☆ ☆ ☆

GRADE_____

DATE_____

RESEARCH: John F. Kennedy

Occupation _____

BORN DATE:_____ Nationality_____

DEATH DATE:_____ Education_____ #Children_____

Childhood and Family Background Facts

Work and Career Facts

Children, Marriage and or Significant Relationships

Friends, Social Life and Other Interesting Facts

Did you enjoy researching this person?

Give a Rating: ☆ ☆ ☆ ☆ ☆

GRADE_____

DATE_____

RESEARCH: King Arthur

Occupation _____

BORN DATE:_____   Nationality_____

DEATH DATE:_____   Education_____   #Children _____

Childhood and Family Background Facts

Work and Career Facts

Children, Marriage and or Significant Relationships

Friends, Social Life and Other Interesting Facts

Did you enjoy researching this person?

Give a Rating: ☆ ☆ ☆ ☆ ☆

DATE_____

RESEARCH: Napoleon Bonaparte

Occupation _____

BORN DATE:_____   Nationality _____

DEATH DATE:_____   Education _____   #Children _____

Childhood and Family Background Facts

Work and Career Facts

Children, Marriage and or Significant Relationships

Friends, Social Life and Other Interesting Facts

Did you enjoy researching this person?

Give a Rating: ☆ ☆ ☆ ☆ ☆

GRADE_____

DATE_____

RESEARCH: Mother Teresa

Occupation _____

BORN DATE:_____ Nationality_____

DEATH DATE:_____ Education_____ #Children_____

Childhood and Family Background Facts

Work and Career Facts

Children, Marriage and or Significant Relationships

Friends, Social Life and Other Interesting Facts

Did you enjoy researching this person?

Give a Rating: ☆ ☆ ☆ ☆ ☆

Math Algebraic Equation

Algebraic equations are made up of two algebraic expressions that are equal on either side of an equal sign. Constants, variables, and exponents are included, and they are also considered polynomial equations when the exponents are positive whole numbers.

1. An algebraic equation is the same thing as _____ being set equal to one another.
   a. three expressions
   b. 1 algebraic 2 expressions
   c. two algebraic expressions

2. The word equation is related to the word 'equal' meaning that there is___.
   a. an equal sign between the two expressions
   b. an equal sign between the x and y.
   c. an equal sign after y and x.

3. Polynomials are algebraic expressions that are created by ___,
   a. dividing by a variable
   b. combining negative exponents
   c. combining numbers and variables

4. A linear equation is one that usually only has two variables ____.
   a. 'x' and 'y'
   b. 'y' and 'z'
   c. 'x' and 't'

5. Linear equations will only have ___line when graphed.
   a. two
   b. one
   c. three

6. A quadratic equation is an _____ equation of the second degree.
   a. coefficient
   b. polynomial
   c. quadratic equations

7. Linear equations sometimes can have ___ variables.
   a. zero
   b. only one
   c. one, two or three

8. When solving algebraic equations, the goal is to find out what number the ___ is representing.
   a. variable
   b. expression inside first
   c. figures

9. What type of equation is -2x + 7 = 4?
   a. proportional to
   b. linear equation
   c. integers

10. What type of equation is 7x^2 + 5x + 3 = 0?
    a. cubic equation
    b. positive number
    c. quadratic equation

* **History Reading Comprehension: Storming of the Bastille**

1. The French Revolution began with a violent attack on the government by the people of France.
2. During the Hundred Years' War, the Bastille was a fortress built in the late 1300s to protect Paris.
3. By the late 1700s, King Louis XVI had primarily used the Bastille as a state prison .
4. The majority of the revolutionaries who stormed the Bastille were Paris-based craftsmen and store owners.
5. They belonged to the Third Estate, a French social class. Approximately 1000 men carried out the attack.
6. The Third Estate had recently made the king's demands, including a more significant say in government for the commoners .
7. The Bastille was rumored to be full of political prisoners and symbolized the king's oppression to many.
8. It also had gunpowder stores, which the revolutionaries required for their weapons .
9. They demanded that the Bastille's military commander, Governor de Launay, hand over the prison and the gunpowder.
10. They began to try to break into the main fortress once they were inside the courtyard.
11. **Fearful** soldiers in the Bastille opened fire on the crowd.
12. The battle had begun. When some of the soldiers joined the crowd's side, the fight took a turn for the worse.
13. The crowd assassinated Governor de Launay and three of his officers after they surrendered.
14. The revolutionaries' success inspired commoners throughout France to rise up and fight against the nobles who had ruled them for so long.

* Geography Multiple Choice
Quiz: Mountain Range

Select the best answer for each question.

1. The _____ run for 1,500 miles along the east coast of the US from northern Alabama to Maine.
   - a. Sierra Nevada
   - b. Rocky Mountains
   - c. Appalachian Mountains

2. Which is of the following is famous for its tall peaks and stretches 1,491 miles through much of central Asia?
   - a. Himalayas
   - b. Andes
   - c. Urals

3. The _____ are the world's longest mountain range, stretching approximately 4,300 miles.
   - a. Alps
   - b. Rockies
   - c. Andes

4. Fault-block mountains were formed along a fault in the Earth's crust. Which of the following is a fault-block mountain?
   - a. Appalachian
   - b. Sierra Nevada
   - c. Rockies

5. What is the process by which the world's tallest mountain ranges are formed?
   - a. seafloor spreading
   - b. continental drift
   - c. plate tectonics

6. The theory of continental drift was proposed by which German meteorologist?
   - a. Charles Thomson Rees Wilson
   - b. Alfred Wegener
   - c. John Dalton

7. Which of the following mountain ranges is the highest and most extensive in Europe?
   - a. The Appalachian
   - b. The Alps
   - c. The Andes

8. What is the highest point of the Rockies that is 14,440 feet above sea level?
   - a. Mount Elbert
   - b. Mount Chamberlin
   - c. Mount Whitney

9. The _____ is a mountain range in northeast New York.
   - a. Alaska Range
   - b. Adirondacks
   - c. Brooks Range

10. Which famous city was built atop a mountain of the Andes Mountain range?
    - a. Machu Picchu
    - b. Tikal
    - c. Tenochtitlan

11. What is the highest mountain range in North America?
    - a. Brooks Range
    - b. Cascade Range
    - c. Alaska Range

12. The _____ is the largest mountain range between the Appalachians and the Rockies.
    - a. Ozarks
    - b. Urals
    - c. Adirondacks

Contractions Multiple Choice

A *contraction* is a way of making two words into one. Circle the correct answer.

1. aren't
a. are not
b. not are
c. arenot

2. can't
a. cants
b. cannot
c. cant

3. couldn't
a. couldnt
b. couldnts
c. could not

4. didn't
a. didn'ts
b. did nots
c. did not

5. don't
a.
b. do not

6. hadn't
a. had not
b. had nots
c. hadn'ts

7. hasn't
a. has nots
b. has not
c. hasnot

8. haven't
a. have nots
b. haven'ts
c. have not

9. I'm
a. I am
b. I'ms
c. I'am

10. I've
a. I have
b. I'ves
c. I'have

11. isn't
a. isn'ts
b. is not
c. is'not

12. let's
a. lets
b. let'us
c. let us

13. mightn't
a. mightnt
b. might not
c. might'not

14. mustn't
a. mustnt
b. must'not
c. must not

* History Reading Comprehension: The Great Depression

During the 1930s, the United States experienced a severe economic downturn known as the Great Depression. It started in the United States, Wall Street to be exact, but quickly spread throughout the rest of the world. Many people were out of work, hungry, and homeless during this period. People in the city would wait for hours at soup kitchens to get a bite to eat. Farmers struggled in the Midwest, where a severe drought turned the soil into dust, resulting in massive dust storms.

America's "Great Depression" began with a dramatic stock market crash on "Black Thursday," October 24, 1929, when panicked investors who had lost faith in the American economy quickly sold 16 million shares of stock. However, historians and economists attribute the Great Depression to a variety of factors, including drought, overproduction of goods, bank failures, stock speculation, and consumer debt.

When the Great Depression began, Herbert Hoover was President of the United States. Many people held Hoover responsible for the Great Depression. The shantytowns where homeless people lived were even dubbed "Hoovervilles" after him. Franklin D. Roosevelt was elected president in 1933. He promised the American people a "New Deal."

The New Deal was a set of laws, programs, and government agencies enacted to aid the country in its recovery from the Great Depression. Regulations were imposed on the stock market, banks, and businesses as a result of these laws. They assisted in putting people to work and attempted to house and feed the poor. Many of these laws, such as the Social Security Act, are still in effect today.

The Great Depression came to an end with the outbreak of World War II. The wartime economy re-employed many people and filled factories to capacity.

The Great Depression left an indelible imprint on the United States. The New Deal laws expanded the government's role in people's daily lives significantly. In addition, public works improved the country's infrastructure by constructing roads, schools, bridges, parks, and airports.

Between 1929 and 1933, the stock market lost nearly 90% of its value.
During the Great Depression, approximately 11,000 banks failed, leaving many people without savings.

1. The Great Depression began with the _____.
  a. World War II
  b. economy drought
  c. stock market crash

2. Who was President when the Great Depression began?
  a. Herbert Hoover
  b. George W Bush
  c. Franklin D. Roosevelt

3. The New Deal was a set of _____.
  a. laws, programs, and government agencies
  b. city and state funding
  c. stock market bailout

4. The Great Depression came to an end with the outbreak of ____.
  a. new laws
  b. investors funding
  c. World War II

* The Metric System

Tip: After you've answered the easy ones, go back and work on the harder ones.

gram	metric	liter	Meter	Gram
centimeter	liter	weight	Celsius	Liter
meter	10	milliliters	kilogram	Celsius

Scientists all over the world use the __metric__ system. There's a very good reason for this-it's so everyone is doing the measuring the same way, all over the world. Most other countries already use the metric system for measuring everything.

Another good reason to use metric is that you don't have so much to remember-no 12 inches in a foot or 5,280 feet in a mile. It's all decimal! The larger or smaller units go up or down by __10__, 100, or 1,000.

__Meter__ is for length. A __meter__ is a little longer than a yard. For long distances, there is the kilometer (a thousand meters). For small things, there is the __centimeter__ (100 centimeters in a meter).

__Liter__ is for volume. A __liter__ is a little larger than a quart. There are a thousand __milliliters__ in a __liter__.

__Gram__ is for __weight__. A __gram__ is a little more than the weight of a paper clip. For heavier things, there is the __kilogram__ (a thousand grams).

Temperatures are in degrees Celsius (also called centigrade). Water freezes at 0 degrees __Celsius__ and boils at 100 degrees __Celsius__. That's easy!

* Geography Multiple Choice
Quiz: Islands

Select the best answer for each question.

1. An island is a body of land smaller than a continent that is surrounded _____ by water.
   a. entirely
   b. on three sides
   c. on two sides

2. A group of related islands, such as the Philippines, is called _____ .
   a. a continent
   b. an island
   c. an archipelago

3. _____ form when volcanoes erupt on the ocean floor.
   a. Artificial Island
   b. Continental islands
   c. Oceanic islands

4. Which of the following islands are classified as oceanic islands?
   a. Padre Island and Cape Hatteras
   b. Greenland and Madagascar
   c. Iceland and Hawaiian

5. Which of the following is the world's largest non-continental island?
   a. Madagascar
   b. Greenland
   c. Great Britain

6. Located off the southeast coast of Africa, _____ is the world's fourth largest island.
   a. Seychelles
   b. Madagascar
   c. Mauritius

7. _____are sections of the continental shelf that have become isolated due to sea-level rise.
   a. Oceanic islands
   b. Continental islands
   c. Barrier islands

8. Home to the famous volcano Mount Fuji, ____ is Japan's largest island.
   a. Hokkaido
   b. Honshu
   c. Kyushu

9. What is the largest island in the Mediterranean Sea?
   a. Sardinia
   b. Sicily
   c. Cyprus

10. Napoleon Bonaparte, Emperor of France was born on which island in France?
    a. Port-Cros
    b. Levant Island
    c. Corcica

11. _____ is the world's ninth largest island, the largest island in the British Isles, and the world's third most populous island.
    a. Great Britain
    b. Isle of Man
    c. Ireland

12. The largest and southernmost island in the Mariana Islands chain, located in the North Pacific Ocean is _____.
    a. Guam
    b. Saipan
    c. Tinian

* Geography Multiple Choice
Quiz: Antarctic

Select the best answer for each question.

1. _____ is the fifth-largest continent in terms of total area.

    a. Antarctic

    b. Artic

    c. Antarctica

2. _____ is composed of older, igneous and metamorphic rocks.

    a. Lesser Antarctica

    b. Greater Antarctica

    c. Antarctica

3. Antarctica is:

    a. Nearly all exposed land with some glaciers

    b. About half ice and half exposed land

    c. Mainly ice, with a few areas of exposed land

4. Antarctica has the world's largest?

    a. Mountains

    b. Ice

    c. Desert

5. In 1983, the coldest temperature ever recorded in Antarctica is?

    a. -108.5°F

    b. -118.0°F

    c. -128.6°F

6. The Antarctic region has an important role in _____.

    a. global climate processes

    b. Earth's heat balance

    c. Earth's atmosphere

7. The _____ is one of the driest _____ in the world.

    a. Antarctic desert and deserts

    b. Antarctic continent and deserts

    c. Antarctic archipelago and continent

8. One of the apex, or top, predators in Antarctica is the?

    a. penguin

    b. sperm whales

    c. leopard seal

9. _____ study climate patterns, including the "ozone hole" that hovers over the Antarctic.

    a. Climatologists

    b. Meteorologists

    c. Geographers

10. _____ is the largest single piece of ice on Earth.

    a. Antarctic Ice Sheet

    b. Glacial Ice

    c. Ross Ice Shelf

11. _____, is part of the "Ring of Fire," a tectonically active area around the Pacific Ocean.

    a. Antarctica

    b. Greater Antarctica

    c. Lesser Antarctica

12. _____ in the Antarctic is hard to measure as it always falls as snow.

    a. Evaporation

    b. Condensation

    c. Precipitation

* Geography Multiple Choice
Quiz: Deserts

Select the best answer for each question.

1. **Which is the only continent with no large deserts?**
   a. Europe
   b. North America
   c. Australia

2. **Which desert in Asia stretches across parts of China and Mongolia?**
   a. Great Victoria desert
   b. Sahara desert
   c. Gobi desert

3. **What percentage of the world's land surface is a desert?**
   a. 15
   b. 25
   c. 20

4. **The _____ is the world's largest hot desert.**
   a. Sahara
   b. Sonoran
   c. Kalahari

5. **Which of the following is one of the most oil-rich places in the world?**
   a. Mohave desert
   b. Arabian desert
   c. Kalahari desert

6. **An oasis is a place in the desert with _____.**
   a. a collection of desert edible plants
   b. a supply of fresh water
   c. a horde of desert animals

7. **A subtropical desert is -**
   a. a desert that exists near the leeward slopes of some mountain ranges
   b. sometimes called inland deserts
   c. caused by the circulation patterns of air masses

8. **The _____ is a large desert located in Mexico and parts of the Southwestern United States.**
   a. Great Victoria desert
   b. Sonoran desert
   c. Gobi desert

9. **The amount of _____ in a desert often greatly exceeds the annual rainfall.**
   a. condensation
   b. precipitation
   c. evaporation

10. **_____ deserts exist near the leeward slopes of some mountain ranges.**
    a. rain shadow
    b. costal
    c. interior

11. **A home to Death Valley, the hottest and lowest spot in the US is the _____.**
    a. Sonoran desert
    b. Mohave desert
    c. Kalahari desert

12. **The Atacama Desert, on the Pacific shores of Chile, is a _____, where some areas of it are often covered by fog.**
    a. subtropical desert
    b. coastal desert
    c. interior desert

* Geography Multiple Choice
Quiz: Glaciers

Select the best answer for each question.

1. A glacier is a huge mass of _____ that moves slowly over _____.

   a. snow and clouds

   b. hail and water

   c. ice and land

2. Glaciers that cover more than 50,000 square kilometers are called?

   a. Alpine

   b. Ice caps

   c. Ice sheets

3. _____ form on mountainsides and move downward through valleys.

   a. Alpine glaciers

   b. Ice caps

   c. Ice sheets

4. A complex of _____ glaciers burying much of a mountain range is called an _____.

   a. valley and ice sheet

   b. hill and ice cap

   c. mountain and ice field

5. Glaciers also exist high in _____ such as the _____ and the _____.

   a. mountain ranges, Himalayas and Andes

   b. Plateaus, Arctic and Antarctica

   c. Hills, Australia and South Africa

6. Melting _____ contribute to rising sea levels.

   a. ice caps

   b. ice field

   c. ice sheets

7. Glaciers carry great amounts of _____, _____, and _____.

   a. snow, water and rock

   b. ice, rock and clay

   c. soil, rock and clay

8. A _____ is one that ends in a body of water like a lake or an ocean.

   a. hanging glaciers

   b. cirque glaciers

   c. calving glacier

9. A _____ glacier is one that is formed in an area where the temperature is always below the freezing point.

   a. temperate

   b. polar

   c. piedmont

10. Most glaciers are located near the _____ or _____.

   a. Greenland or Iceland

   b. Arctic or Antarctic

   c. North or South Poles

11. _____ refers to all processes that contribute mass to a glacier.

   a. Transformation

   b. Ablation

   c. Accumulation

12. _____ is a simple consequence of the weight and creep properties of ice.

   a. Glacier flow

   b. Ablation

   c. Accumulation

* **Simple Math Refresher**

1. Perform the following operation: 12 + 1 + 8 =

    a. 21

    b. 20

    c. 18

2. Solve 1,056 divided by 22.

    a. 9.2

    b. 48

    c. 36

3. Division is the math operation that tells you to _____ and is represented by the symbols _____.

    a. separate or combine two numbers together; - and /

    b. separate something into parts; ÷ and /

    c. combine three numbers together; - and /

4. Brad saved $605 for his yearly vacations. He has 11 days of vacation and wants to spend the same amount of money each day, how much will he spend each day?

    a. $95

    b. $55

    c. $104

5. Convert 3/7 to a percent.

    a. 33.1%

    b. 5.9%

    c. 42.9%

6. Change 0.142 to a fraction.

    a. 1/7

    b. 2/4

    c. 1/8

7. Change 2/5 to a decimal.

    a. 0.4

    b. 0.9

    c. 0.5

8. Write 4 8/9 as an improper fraction.

    a. 32/5

    b. 40/8

    c. 44/9

9. A(n) _____ is an improper fraction written with a whole number and a proper fraction.

    a. decimal

    b. proper fraction

    c. mixed number

10. Write 50% as a fraction.

    a. 1/2

    b. 0/5

    c. 5/0

11. Change 79.5% to a decimal.

    a. 0.795

    b. 79.5%

    c. 79.05%

12. Which of the following number has the highest numerical value?

    a. 2.8

    b. 0.28

    c. 4.5%

13. Order the following numbers from smallest to greatest: 0.25, 4.54, 0.015, 1.24

    a. 1.24, 4.54, 0.015, 0.25

    b. 0.015, 0.25, 1.24, 4.54

    c. 4.54, 0.015, 0.25, 1.24

14. What is the 28% of 80?

    a. 28.0

    b. 84%

    c. 22.4

15. Convert 6/7 to a percent.

    a. 7.6%

    b. 6.7%

    c. 86%

16. What is the denominator of 7/9?

    a. 7.9

    b. 7

    c. 9

17. Write 18.7% as a decimal.

    a. 0.187

    b. 1.87

    c. 18.7%

18. Convert 0.00047 to scientific notation.

    a. 4.0×10^{-7}

    b. 4.7×4^{-0}

    c. 4.7×10^{-4}

19. Multiply 4.25×10^{-5} by 4.

    a. 1.7×10^{-4}

    b. 2.7×10^{-4}

    c. 4.5×10^{1}

20. Janes Market sells a pack of 500 napkins for $2.50 and Taylor Grocery sells a pack that has 750 of the same napkins for $3.75. Which pack is the best deal?

    a. Janes Market

    b. Both packs have the same price per napkin

    c. Taylor Grocery

21. Maya earned $4,575 in 3 months. If earned the same amount each month, how much did she earn each month?

    a. $2,575

    b. $925

    c. $1,525

22. The independent variable of an exponential function is the _____.

    a. exponent

    b. logarithm

    c. fraction

23. Solve for X in the following equation $8 + 3^{X} = 35$

    a. X = 3

    b. X = 8

    c. X = 35

24. Grams. liters and centimeters are all examples of _____ units.

    a. pounds

    b. kilogram

    c. metric

25. One kilogram is equivalent to _____ grams.

    a. 100

    b. 10

    c. 1,000

* Proofreading Shakespeare: Romeo and Juliet

> There are **24** mistakes in this passage. 5 capitals missing. 3 unnecessary capitals. 4 unnecessary apostrophes. 3 punctuation marks missing or incorrect. 2 incorrect homophones. 7 incorrectly spelled words.

In 1597, William Shakespeare published "Romeo and ~~Juliet"~~ Juliet," which would go on to become one of the world's most famous love stories. The plot of Shakespeare's ~~pley~~ play takes place in Verona, where the two main ~~characters~~ characters, ~~romeo~~ Romeo and Juliet, meet and fall in ~~love~~ love. Both are descended from two feuding families, the Capulets, and the Montagues. As a result, ~~thay~~ they choose to keep their ~~luve~~ love hidden and are married by Friar Laurence. Romeo gets into a fight with ~~Juliet"s~~ Juliet's cousin Tybalt, whom he ~~Kills~~ kills in a ~~Brawl~~ brawl despite his best efforts. Romeo is expelled from Verona and escapes to Mantua.

When ~~juliet's~~ Juliet's parents press her to marry, she ~~Seeks~~ seeks the assistance of Friar Laurence once more, who provides her with a sleeping potion designed to simulate her death. In a letter that never reaches Romeo, he explains his plan. Disgusted by the alleged death of his beloved Juliet, ~~Rumeo~~ Romeo returns to Verona and commits suicide at Juliet's open coffin. Juliet awakens from her slumber, sees what has happened, and decides to end her ~~liphe.~~ life. The two feuding families now recognize their complicity and reconcile at their children's graves.

The medieval old town of Verona is ideal for putting oneself in the shoes of Romeo and ~~juliet.~~ Juliet. Every year, many loving couples and tourists come to walk in the footsteps of ~~romeo~~ Romeo and Juliet. A photograph of Juliet's famous balcony, a visit to Romeo's home, or ~~sum~~ some ~~queit~~ quiet time spent at Julia's grave. No matter ~~were~~ where you look in the city, you ~~wall~~ will find loving ~~couple's~~ couples who stick declarations of love and initials on small slips of paper to the walls or immortalize ~~themselve's~~ themselves on the walls or stones of ~~house's~~ houses - often illegally.

Although Shakespeare's drama never corresponded to reality, ~~verona~~ Verona has a unique charm, especially for lovers, who imagine they can feel the true story behind the literary work, almost as if Romeo and Juliet had really existed.

* Spelling Words Quiz

Circle the best definition meaning for each spelling word provided below.

1. emboss

   a. to design with a sunken or recessed pattern

   b. to decorate with a raised pattern or design

   c. to print a material with flat pattern or design

2. perseverance

   a. the act or power of continuing to do something in spite of difficulties

   b. the act of giving up on something because it is difficult

   c. the act of being uninterested, unenthusiastic, or unconcerned

3. chagrin

   a. a feeling of being safe or protected

   b. a feeling of being annoyed by failure or disappointment

   c. a feeling of being sleepy and lethargic

4. mediocre

   a. not very often

   b. not very effective

   c. not very good

5. frugal

   a. careful, unwavering attention or persistent application

   b. careful in spending or using supplies

   c. careful in spending time and effort

6. benefactor

   a. someone who helps another especially by giving money

   b. someone who helps another find a job

   c. someone who helps another buy a house

7. personnel

   a. a group of kids who are members of a sports club

   b. a group of people employed in a business or an organization

   c. a group of elderly citizens that are members of senior social programs

8. journal

   a. a book in which we collect photographs

   b. a book in which you write down your personal experiences and thoughts

   c. a book in which map are compiled and collected

9. amphitheater

   a. a room built to enable an audience to hear and watch performances

   b. an arena with seats rising in curved rows around an open space

   c. a large room for public meetings or performances

10. horticulture

   a. the science and art of cultivating silkworms to produce silk

   b. the science and art of growing fruits, vegetables, flowers, or ornamental plants

   c. the science and art of cultivating plants and livestock

* Health: Check Your Symptoms

1. **I've got a pain in my head.**
   - a. Stiff neck
   - b. headache

2. **I was out in the sun too long.**
   - a. Sunburn
   - b. Fever

3. **I've got a small itchy lump or bump.**
   - a. Rash
   - b. Insect bite

4. **I might be having a heart attack.**
   - a. Cramps
   - b. Chest pain

5. **I've lost my voice.**
   - a. Laryngitis
   - b. Sore throat

6. **I need to blow my nose a lot.**
   - a. Runny nose
   - b. Blood Nose

7. **I have an allergy. I have a**
   - a. Rash
   - b. Insect bite

8. **My shoe rubbed my heel. I have a**
   - a. Rash
   - b. Blister

9. **The doctor gave me antibiotics. I have a/an**
   - a. Infection
   - b. Cold

10. **I think I want to vomit. I am**
    - a. Nauseous
    - b. Bloated

11. **My arm is not broken. It is**
    - a. Scratched
    - b. Sprained

12. **My arm touched the hot stove. It is**
    - a. Burned
    - b. Bleeding

13. **I have an upset stomach. I might**
    - a. Cough
    - b. Vomit

14. **The doctor put plaster on my arm. It is**
    - a. Sprained
    - b. Broken

15. **If you cut your finger it will**
    - a. Burn
    - b. Bleed

16. **I hit my hip on a desk. It will**
    - a. Burn
    - b. Bruise

17. **When you have hay-fever you will**
    - a. Sneeze
    - b. Wheeze

18. **A sharp knife will**
    - a. Scratch
    - b. Cut

* Science: Different Blood Types

| compatible | transfusion | recipient's | antibodies | survive |
| donate | bloodstream | eight | negative | antigens |

What comes to mind when you think of blood? It may be the color red, a hospital, or even a horror film! Blood is something that your body requires to survive , regardless of how you feel about it. Did you realize, though, that not everyone has the same blood type? There are eight different kinds in total! The letters A, B, and O, as well as positive or negative signs, distinguish these blood types. O+, O-, A+, A-, B+, B-, AB+, and AB- are the eight blood types.

What Is the Importance of Blood Types?

Don't be concerned if your blood type differs from that of others! There is no such thing as a better or healthier blood type. The sole reason to know your blood type is in case you need to donate or give blood to someone in an emergency. A blood transfusion is a process of transferring blood from one person to another.

Blood transfusions are only effective when the donor's blood is compatible with the recipient's blood. Some blood types don't mix well because the body produces antibodies to fight off any unfamiliar antigens that enter the bloodstream . Antibodies act as warriors in your blood, guarding you against alien intruders. Assume you have Type A blood, which contains A antigens solely, and someone with Type B blood wishes to donate blood to you. Your body does not recognize B antigens; thus, antibodies are produced to combat them! This has the potential to make you sick. As a result, people with Type A blood should only receive blood from those with Type A blood or Type O blood, as O blood lacks both A and B antigens.

* Reading Comprehension:
Social Media Safety

1. In the last 20 years, socializing has evolved dramatically. Interactions between people are referred to as socializing.
2. It now frequently refers to accessing the Internet via social media or websites that allow you to connect and interact with other people.
3. Ascertain that your computer is outfitted with up-to-date computer security software.
4. This software detects and removes viruses that are harmful to your computer.
5. When you use your computer, these viruses can sometimes hack into it and steal your information, such as logins .
6. Create strong passwords for all of your social media accounts.
7. These can be as loose or as restrictive as you want them to be.
8. This enables your computer to block pop-ups and warn you when you are about to visit a potentially harmful website.
9. - Don't post anything you wouldn't want broadcast to the entire world.
10. Personal information about one's identity should not be posted or shared on social media.
11. This information can be used to recreate your identity and should never be made public.
12. Make use of the privacy settings on the social media website.
13. Be cautious about what you post on any social media platform .
14. Posting something negative about someone hurts their character and opens the door for them, or someone else, to do the same to you.
15. If you are not in a good mood or are upset, think twice.
16. What you post could be harmful to you or someone else.
17. If you are in a bad social media relationship and are being harassed or bullied, you can report it to the social media company.
18. They all have policies in place to deal with people who abuse their websites.
19. Make a note of these incidents and report them to the company. You may also save the life of another person.

* **Art: Henri Matisse**

1. Henri Matisse was born in the north of _France_ . Henri's father was a grain merchant who was strict with him. He went to law school in Paris and graduated from there.

2. In 1888, he passed the _bar_ and began working as a law clerk.

3. Henri was diagnosed with _appendicitis_ in 1889.

4. His mother encouraged him to break the _rules_ of art and experiment with new techniques and paint his _emotions_ .

5. He studied art for a year at the Academie Julian in Paris before leaving to train under the artist Gustave Moreau, where he could experiment with more _modern_ painting styles.

6. Russell introduced him to _impressionism_ and van Gogh's work.

7. In 1897, Matisse completed his first _masterpiece_ . It was known as The Dinner Table.

8. He continued to paint, _influenced_ by artists such as Vincent van Gogh and Paul Cezanne.

9. Matisse developed a new style in the early 1900s. He began to paint with _bright_ masses of freely applied colors.

Antonyms
Identify antonyms.

Circle the word that has the opposite meaning of the given word.

Examples:

night is the opposite of day   small is the opposite of big

1. clumsy	funny	(graceful)	shameful
2. late	tardy	(early)	tired
3. shiny	(dull)	bright	flashy
4. yell	talk	loud	(whisper)
5. poverty	beggar	(riches)	happiness
6. borrow	lend	steal	(return)
7. calm	(excited)	sad	mellow
8. cloudy	rainy	gray	(clear)
9. pure	(tainted)	chilly	color
10. similar	alike	clear	(different)
11. serious	(funny)	angry	neutral
12. attack	arrive	(defend)	raise

Homophones

Identify homophones.

Read each sentence carefully. Choose the correct homophone to fill in the blanks.

1. bored, board

   The boys were ___bored___ so they decided to go outside and skate ___board___ .

2. buy, by

   She went ___by___ the store to ___buy___ some snacks for the party.

3. cent, sent

   I ___sent___ the postcard. It cost 49 ___cent___ s.

4. blew, blue

   Sarah ___blew___ up fifty ___blue___ balloons to decorate the party.

5. hair, hare

   The gray and white ___hair___ ed ___hare___ hopped down the trail.

6. aloud, allowed

   Are you ___allowed___ to say that secret ___aloud___ ?

7. dessert, desert

   We went to the ___desert___ for a hike. On the way home we stopped to get ___dessert___ .

8. sight, site

   The historical ___site___ is now in my ___sight___ .

* Art: Recycled Art

Recycled art is an unusual but very creative art form in which existing materials are reused and recycled to create works of art. This is in contrast to more traditional art forms in which artists use paint, drawing materials, clay, or other mediums associated with artwork creation. Sometimes the materials used in recycled art are essentially garbage, while other materials are created for a purpose other than art and are being given a new lease on life. Recycled art can be made for several reasons. When people have limited materials to work with, it is often created out of necessity. In other cases, as discussed in this lesson, the materials used in the art are deliberately chosen to challenge viewers' perceptions of what is art, what is trash, and what is beautiful and meaningful. Many recycled art artists use their mediums to convey powerful environmental messages.

There are two types of recycled art: upcycled art and downcycled art. These are two complementary approaches that make use of recycled materials in opposing ways. Upcycled art transforms materials that are typically considered trash into beautiful and meaningful art. This practice is considered more common in the recycled art world because it allows artists to make powerful statements about waste. Upcycled art is created by an artist who creates a portrait out of discarded computer parts that would otherwise end up in a landfill.

Downcycled art is the inverse of upcycled art in that artists deconstruct or destroy objects before transforming them into art. Downcycled art is created by an artist who takes an old armchair and rips the stuffing out of it in an installation piece. While downcycled art exists, it is less common because the goal of recycled art is often to elevate materials that are considered worthless by incorporating them into art.

1. Sometimes the materials used in recycled art are essentially _____.
   a. wood
   b. garbage
   c. luxury items

2. _____ art transforms materials that are typically considered trash into beautiful and meaningful art.
   a. Abstract
   b. Acrylic paint
   c. Upcycled

3. _____ art is the inverse of upcycled art in that artists deconstruct or destroy objects before transforming them into art.
   a. Enamel
   b. Fine art
   c. Downcycled

4. There are two types of recycled art: _____ art and _____ art.
   a. decorative and airbrush
   b. upcycled and downcycled
   c. abstract and recycled

Letter "F" Science Spelling Words

	A	**B**	**C**	**D**
1.	Fasett	**Facet**	Facett	Faset
2.	**Farming**	Farmyng	Farrmyng	Farrming
3.	Faullt	**Fault**	Fuallt	Fualt
4.	Fuana	Faona	Foana	**Fauna**
5.	Faldspar	Felldspar	**Feldspar**	Falldspar
6.	Fernment	Ferrnment	**Ferment**	Ferrment
7.	Fermentasion	Ferrmentasion	**Fermentation**	Ferrmentation
8.	**Fission**	Fistion	Fision	Fition
9.	Fisore	**Fissure**	Fiscure	Fisure
10.	**Flood Plain**	Flod Plian	Floud Plain	Flod Plain
11.	Fluding	Floding	**Flooding**	Flouding
12.	Fllura	Fllora	**Flora**	Flura
13.	Flloorish	Fllourish	Floorish	**Flourish**
14.	Flluwstone	Fllowstone	Fluwstone	**Flowstone**
15.	Folliage	Folaige	**Foliage**	Follaige
16.	Fod chian	**Food chain**	Foud chain	Fod chain
17.	Food relasionships	Fod relationships	**Food relationships**	Fod relasionships
18.	Fod Web	**Food Web**	Foud Web	Fud Web
19.	Forradge	Foradge	**Forage**	Forrage
20.	Furrecast	**Forecast**	Furecast	Forrecast
21.	Forrensics	**Forensics**	Furensics	Furrensics
22.	Forrmasions	Formasions	Forrmations	**Formations**
23.	Fosil fuel	Foussil fuel	Fousil fuel	**Fossil fuel**
24.	Francis torbine	Frrancis turbine	Frrancis torbine	**Francis turbine**

Fictional vs. Fictitious vs. Fictive

Fictional is invented as part of a work of fiction

SYNONYMS:
Fabricated
Imaginary

Fictitious is created, taken, or assumed for the sake of concealment; not genuine; false

SYNONYMS:
Bogus
Counterfeit

Fictive - fictitious; imaginary. pertaining to the creation of fiction
- is capable of imaginative creation.

SYNONYMS:

Make-believe
Fabricated

1. He dismissed recent rumors about his private
   life as _____.
   a. fictitious
   b. fictional
   c. fictive

2. I have the impression that this _____
   marriage of ours is like a ghost in a play.
   a. fictional
   b. fictitious
   c. fictive

3. The setting is a _____ island in the
   Chesapeake River.
   a. fictitious
   b. fictional
   c. fictive

4. The writer has _____ talent.
   a. fictitious
   b. fictional
   c. fictive

5. Almost all _____ detectives are unreal.
   a. fictitious
   b. fictional
   c. fictive

6. The names of the shops are entirely _____.
   a. fictive
   b. fictional
   c. fictitious

Introvert vs. Extrovert

Introvert is a person who prefers calm environments, limits social engagement, or embraces a greater than average preference for solitude.

SYNONYMS:
brooder
loner
solitary

Extrovert is an outgoing, gregarious person who thrives in dynamic environments and seeks to maximize social engagement.

SYNONYMS:
character
exhibitionist
show-off
showboat

Fill in the blank with the correct word. [introvert, introverts, extrovert, extroverts]

1. Sue is the __extrovert__ in the family; opinionated, talkative and passionate about politics.

2. He was described as an __introvert__ , a reserved man who spoke little.

3. __Extroverts__ are often described as the life of the party.

4. An __introvert__ is often thought of as a quiet, reserved, and thoughtful individual.

5. __Extroverts__ enjoy being around other people and tend to focus on the outside world.

6. Typically __introverts__ tend to enjoy more time to themselves.

7. Jane is an __introvert__ whose only hobby is reading.

8. I am still not as "outgoing" as an __extrovert__ is.

9. I had been a very __extrovert__ person, living life to the full.

10. I am an __introvert__ , I am a loner.

11. Because Pat is an __extrovert__ who enjoys chatting with others, she is the ideal talk show host.

12. She is basically an __introvert__ , uncomfortable with loud women and confrontations.

Weather Vocabulary Words
Match Up

The weather is simply the state of the atmosphere at any given time, which includes temperature, precipitation, air pressure, and cloud cover. Winds and storms cause daily changes in the weather. Seasonal changes are caused by the Earth's rotation around the sun.

The sun's rays do not fall evenly on the land and oceans because the Earth is round rather than flat. The sun shines more directly near the equator, bringing more warmth to these areas. On the other hand, the polar regions are at such an angle to the sun that they receive little or no sunlight during the winter, resulting in colder temperatures. These temperature differences cause a frantic movement of air and water in great swirling currents, distributing heat energy from the sun across the planet. When the air in one region is warmer than air in another, it becomes less dense and begins to rise, drawing more air in beneath it. Cooler, denser air sinks elsewhere, pushing air outward to flow along the surface and complete the cycle.

Match to the correct answer.

1	H	Anemometer	⇢	meteorological instrument used to measure wind speed
2	F	Barometer	⇢	meteorological instrument used to measure the atmospheric pressure
3	I	Blizzard	⇢	snow storm that has winds of 35 miles per hour or more
4	B	Cloud	⇢	tiny water droplets floating in the atmosphere that you can see
5	G	Coriolis effect	⇢	It affects weather patterns - affects an object that's moving over something that's rotating
6	A	Flash flood	⇢	something that happens quickly usually due to heavy rain
7	D	High-pressure system	⇢	A region with high air pressure and cool, dry air
8	J	Hurricane	⇢	tropical cyclone that formed in the North Atlantic Ocean
9	E	Isobar	⇢	line on a weather map that represents a given barometric pressure
10	C	Low-pressure system	⇢	A region with low air pressure and warm, moist air

* Jobs and Careers

Tip: After you've answered the easy ones, go back and work on the harder ones.

skill	climbing	monetary	professional	hourly
variety	salaried	experience	graduate	achieve

You might have heard that the education you receive and the information you learn in school will help you get a job when you

graduate . Or your abilities and skills will benefit you in your future careers. So, what's the truth? How do people decide whether they

want a job or a career?

There are several common misconceptions regarding the distinctions between a job and a career. Some people believe that a job is

simply an _hourly_ position, whereas a _salaried_ position is a career. Others believe that a career requires a longer educational path

that results in exceptional skills and knowledge. The truth is not what most people believe.

A job is a position or set of duties performed for _monetary_ gain, whereas a career is a focused path or journey that a person takes to

achieve their professional goals. A career can include a variety of jobs along a career path.

Parents and teachers frequently ask their children what they want to be when they grow up. A career is the answer to that question. A

career is a path or _professional_ journey that a person follows throughout their working life. A career can necessitate extensive

education, such as that of a doctor or a lawyer, or it can require extensive _skill_ training, such as that of an electrician or plumber.

The words "career" and "path" are frequently used interchangeably. A career path is a path that people take to _achieve_ their

professional objectives. Many people work for decades on their career paths, which often include a _variety_ of jobs along the way.

With each job, a person gains _experience_ and skills that will help them get a better job and achieve their career goals.

Another term associated with careers is the concept of people _climbing_ a "career ladder". When people climb the metaphorical

career ladder, they progress step by step from one better job to the next. Careers take years to develop and achieve. Sometimes a lot of

education is required at the start of a career before a person can start moving up the ladder, whereas other careers require years of

experience in the field to get to the top.

* Biology: ANIMAL KINGDOM

Animals are the most numerous and diverse of the five kingdoms of living things. Over two million animal species have been identified so far. All animals share certain characteristics. Animals, unlike plants, obtain their energy from food. They are all made up of many cells, and many animals move quickly. Most reproduce sexually and have sense organs that allow them to respond rapidly to their environment.

Jellyfish, for example, has a relatively simple structure. They lack a skeleton, have few muscles, and move in an uncoordinated manner? They float along with the ocean currents. Jellyfish are classified as invertebrates because, like 98% of all animals, they lack a backbone.

Animals with backbones, such as these zebras, are known as vertebrates. Vertebrates include mammals, birds, fish, amphibians, and reptiles. Zebras are classified as mammals. Mammalian animals, which include humans, are the most complex in the animal kingdom.

1. What are 5 examples of a vertebrate?

   fishes, amphibians, reptiles, birds, and mammals.

2. What are 5 examples of invertebrates?

   insects, snail, squids, earthworms and leeches

3. What exactly is a mammal?

   A mammal is an animal that breathes air, has a backbone, and at some point in its life grows hair. Furthermore, all female mammals have milk-producing glands. Mammals are among the most intelligent creatures on the planet. Mammals are a diverse group of animals that include everything from cats to humans to whales.

4. Amphibians are a class of what cold-blooded vertebrates?

   rogs, toads, salamanders, newts, and caecilians

5. Reptiles use a variety of methods to defend themselves such as...

   avoidance, camouflage, hissing and biting

6. What are the 4 types of arthropods?

   insects, myriapods, arachnids, crustaceans

7. Oviparous animals lay eggs where?

   outside their body

8. An herbivore is an organism that mostly feeds on what?

   plants

9. A carnivore is an organism that mostly eats?

   meat, or the flesh of animals

10. An omnivore is an organism that eats?

    plants and animals

* Biology: Excretory System

chloride	pressure	bladder	filtering	bloodstream
molecules	concentrate	urine	muscular	detoxifies
kidneys	substances	glomeruli	reabsorbing	converts

Toxins are present in all animals' bodies and must be eliminated. The human liver __detoxifies__ and modifies dangerous __substances__ so that they can be quickly and easily removed from the body. For example, ammonia is very toxic, so the liver __converts__ it to urea, which is far less toxic and easily removed from the body.

The __kidneys__ are the organs responsible for __filtering__ waste products from the blood and regulating blood composition and pressure. The outer layer of the kidneys contains structures known as __glomeruli__, which are ball-like structures made up of very porous capillaries. Large amounts of water and small molecules, including urea, are forced out through the pores by the blood __pressure__ in these capillaries, but blood cells and larger __molecules__ that are too large to fit through the pores remain in the __bloodstream__.

The glomeruli are surrounded by the ends of the renal tubules, which are long, looping tubes in the kidney that collect blood filtrate and __concentrate__ it into the urine. The filtrate travels through the tubules, __reabsorbing__ nutrients, water, and sodium __chloride__ from the renal tubules and returning them to the blood. Waste products are concentrated in the tubules and become urine as water and nutrients are reabsorbed. Urine is stored in the __bladder__ after the kidneys have concentrated it. Most people can control when they empty their bladder by controlling a __muscular__ valve at the exit point. When this valve is opened and the bladder muscles contract, __urine__ enters the urethra, where it travels before exiting the body.

* Biology: Reading Comprehension Viruses

When we catch a cold or get the flu, we are dealing with the effects of a viral infection. Viruses, despite sharing some characteristics with living organisms, are neither cellular nor alive. The presence of cells, the ability to reproduce, the ability to use energy, and the ability to respond to the environment are all important characteristics of living organisms. A virus cannot perform any of these functions on its own.

A virus, on the other hand, is a collection of genetic material encased in a protective coat, which is typically made of proteins. Viruses are obligate parasites because they must replicate on the host. To replicate itself, a virus must first attach to and penetrate a host cell, after which it will go through the various stages of viral infection. These stages are essentially the virus lifecycle. A virus can enter the host cell via one of several methods by interacting with the surface of the host cell. The virus can then replicate itself by utilizing the host's energy and metabolism.

Bacteriophages, viruses that infect bacteria, either use the lysogenic cycle, in which the host cell's offspring carry the virus, or the lytic cycle, in which the host cell dies immediately after viral replication. Once viral shedding has occurred, the virus can infect additional hosts. Viral infections can be productive in the sense that they cause active infection in the host, or they can be nonproductive in the sense that they remain dormant within the host. These two types of infection can result in chronic infections, in which the host goes through cycles of illness and remission, as well as latent infections, in which the virus remains dormant for a period of time before causing illness in the host.

1. A virus is encased in a protective coat, which is typically made of _____.
   - a. [proteins]
   - b. molecules
   - c. cells

2. To replicate itself, a virus must first attach to and penetrate a ____ cell.
   - a. healthy
   - b. living atom
   - c. [host]

3. Viruses are neither cellular nor __.
   - a. [alive]
   - b. moving
   - c. a threat

4. The virus can replicate itself by utilizing the host's ___ and ___.
   - a. cells and DNA
   - b. molecules and cell
   - c. [energy and metabolism]

5. A virus can remain _____ for a period of time before causing illness in a host.
   - a. metabolized
   - b. [dormant]
   - c. infected

* Spelling Words Word Search

Circle the 12 words listed below. Words appear straight across, back- word straight across, up and down.

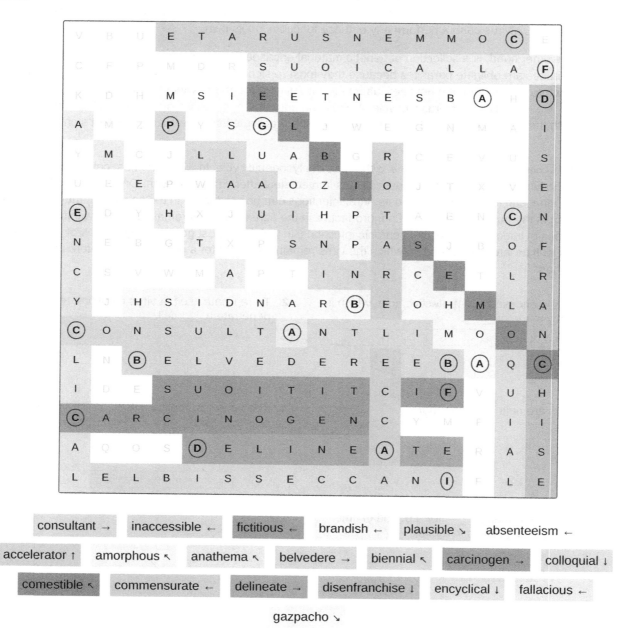

consultant → · inaccessible ← · fictitious ← · brandish ← · plausible ↘ · absenteeism ←

accelerator ↑ · amorphous ↖ · anathema ↖ · belvedere → · biennial ↖ · carcinogen → · colloquial ↓

comestible ↖ · commensurate ← · delineate → · disenfranchise ↓ · encyclical ↓ · fallacious ←

gazpacho ↘

20 words in Wordsearch: 4 vertical, 10 horizontal, 6 diagonal. (11 reversed.)

* Biology Vocabulary Words Crossword

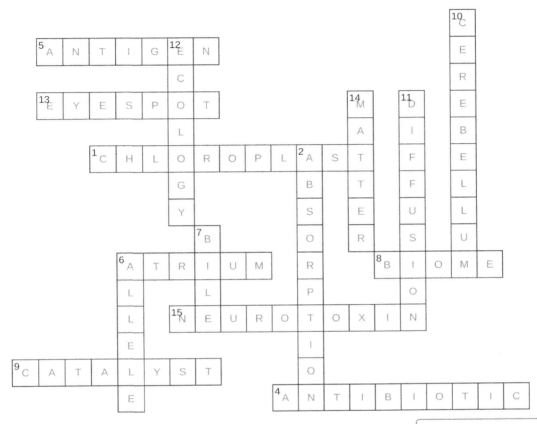

Across

1. organelle in which photosynthesis takes place
4. a substance used to kill microorganisms and cure infections
5. any substance that stimulates an immune response in the body
6. a chamber connected to other chambers or passageways
8. major ecological community with distinct climate and flora
9. substance that initiates or accelerates a chemical reaction
13. an eyelike marking
15. any toxin that affects neural tissues

Down

2. a process in which one substance permeates another
6. any of the forms of a gene that can occupy the same locus
7. a digestive juice secreted by the liver
10. a major division of the vertebrate brain
11. the act of dispersing something
12. the environment as it relates to living organisms
14. that which has mass and occupies space

ATRIUM   BIOME   ANTIGEN
ECOLOGY
CHLOROPLAST   MATTER
ABSORPTION   ANTIBIOTIC
DIFFUSION   ALLELE
EYESPOT   NEUROTOXIN
BILE   CEREBELLUM
CATALYST

* Geometry Reading Comprehension

90-degree	segment	Acute	angles	Obtuse
directions	straight	halves	height	formulas

The study of shapes and space is known as geometry. It provides answers to size, area, and volume questions. The earliest known geometry works date back to 2000 BC and are from Egypt. There were __formulas__ for lengths, areas, and volumes, as well as one for pyramids. Thales of Miletus calculated the __height__ of pyramids in the 7th century BC, and the Greek mathematician Pythagoras proved the well-known Pythagorean Theorem.

Euclid, another Greek mathematician, introduced Euclidean geometry around 300 BC by demonstrating how to prove theorems using basic definitions and truths. We still use Euclidean geometry to prove theorems today.

Geometric terms include points, lines, and __angles__. A point is a non-dimensional object with no length or width. A dot is commonly used to represent it. A line is an object that extends in both __directions__ without end. It is usually depicted with arrowheads to indicate that it continues indefinitely. A line __segment__ is a section of a line that has two ends. A ray is one-half of a line with a single endpoint. Two rays with the same endpoint form an angle. The angle is called a straight angle if the rays are the two __halves__ of a single line. A straight angle is analogous to a book open flat on a desk. A right angle is defined as an angle that is opened half that far.

Angles are expressed in degrees. A right angle is defined as a __90-degree__ angle. __Acute__ angles are those that are less than a right angle. __Obtuse__ angles are those that are larger than a right angle but smaller than a __straight__ angle.

* Biology Vocabulary Words Crossword

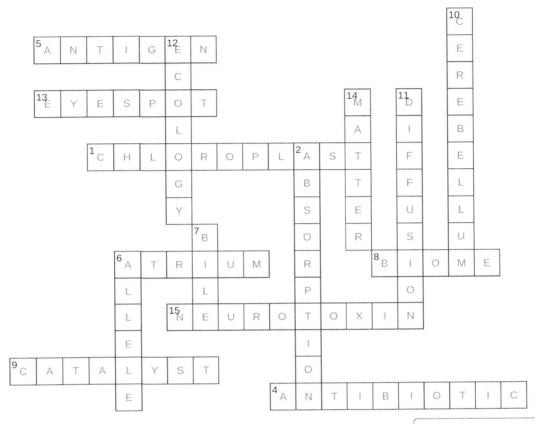

Across

1. organelle in which photosynthesis takes place
4. a substance used to kill microorganisms and cure infections
5. any substance that stimulates an immune response in the body
6. a chamber connected to other chambers or passageways
8. major ecological community with distinct climate and flora
9. substance that initiates or accelerates a chemical reaction
13. an eyelike marking
15. any toxin that affects neural tissues

Down

2. a process in which one substance permeates another
6. any of the forms of a gene that can occupy the same locus
7. a digestive juice secreted by the liver
10. a major division of the vertebrate brain
11. the act of dispersing something
12. the environment as it relates to living organisms
14. that which has mass and occupies space

ATRIUM BIOME ANTIGEN
ECOLOGY
CHLOROPLAST MATTER
ABSORPTION ANTIBIOTIC
DIFFUSION ALLELE
EYESPOT NEUROTOXIN
BILE CEREBELLUM
CATALYST

ANSWERS

Adding and Subtracting Radical Expressions

Simplify the Radical Expressions.

1) $\sqrt{28} + \sqrt{28} - \sqrt{28}$

$2\sqrt{7}$

6) $\sqrt{2} + 6\sqrt{2} + \sqrt{18}$

$10\sqrt{2}$

2) $-3\sqrt{2} - 5\sqrt{2} + 4\sqrt{2}$

$-4\sqrt{2}$

7) $-\sqrt{11} + \sqrt{176}$

$3\sqrt{11}$

3) $\sqrt{45} - \sqrt{45}$

0

8) $4\sqrt{11} + 7\sqrt{44}$

$18\sqrt{11}$

4) $4\sqrt{3} - 2\sqrt{3} - 7\sqrt{3}$

$-5\sqrt{3}$

9) $-\sqrt{18} + \sqrt{63} + \sqrt{8}$

$-\sqrt{2} + 3\sqrt{7}$

5) $\sqrt{80} + \sqrt{80} + \sqrt{80}$

$12\sqrt{5}$

10) $-5\sqrt{3} - 7\sqrt{3} - 2\sqrt{48}$

$-20\sqrt{3}$

ANSWERS

Find the Slope and Y-intercept

1) $y = -\frac{7}{5}x - 3$ slope = $-\frac{7}{5}$

                            y-intercept = -3

2) $y = \frac{1}{5}x + 5$ slope = $\frac{1}{5}$

                            y-intercept = 5

3) $y = 3x + 2$ slope = 3

                            y-intercept = 2

4) $y = \frac{3}{2}x + 3$ slope = $\frac{3}{2}$

                            y-intercept = 3

5) $y = -x + 2$ slope = -1

                            y-intercept = 2

6) $y = 2x - 4$ slope = 2

                            y-intercept = -4

7) $y = -\frac{4}{9}x - 3$ slope = $-\frac{4}{9}$

                            y-intercept = -3

8) $y = -\frac{7}{6}x + 10$ slope = $-\frac{7}{6}$

                            y-intercept = 10

9) $y = \frac{5}{2}x - 4$ slope = $\frac{5}{2}$

                            y-intercept = -4

10) $y = -x + 3$ slope = -1

                            y-intercept = 3

Order of Operations

Evaluate each expression.

1) $(-3)x - (-6) \div (-3) \cdot (-2)x$

   x

2) $3x - (-8)x \cdot 5 - 9x + 3x$

   37x

3) $(-11)x + (-8)x \cdot 4 - (-10)x$

   -33x

4) $60x \div 5 - 5x \cdot 3 + 2x$

   -x

5) $3x - 11x \cdot 2 - 7x$

   -26x

6) $(-11) \cdot (-2)x - (-10)x - (-3)x \cdot (-5)$

   17x

7) $66x \div 11 - 6x \cdot 2$

   -6x

8) $4x \cdot 54x \div 9x - 5x - 9x$

   10x

9) $(-2)x - (-4) \div (-2) \cdot (-12)x$

   22x

10) $8x + 7x \cdot (-2) - (-3)x + 5x$

    2x

11) $(-8)x \cdot (-78)x \div 13x - (-3)x$

    51x

12) $(-6) \cdot (-7)x - (-4)x - (-3)x \cdot (-2)$

    40x

* History: King Tut Reading Comprehension

1. **What was King Tut's real name?**
   a. Tutankhaion
   b. Tutankhaten
   c. Tutankhamun

2. **Tut's father died when he was _____ years old.**
   a. 19 yrs old
   b. Twenty-Two
   c. seven

3. **Tutankhamun died when he was about _____ years old.**
   a. nineteen
   b. 16 years old
   c. 21

4. **Nefertiti was the wife of____.**
   a. Tut
   b. Horemheb
   c. Pharaoh Akhenaten

5. **The tomb of young pharaoh Tut is located in the _____.**
   a. Tuts King Egypt
   b. Maine Valley Sons
   c. Valley of the Kings

* Spelling Words Word Scramble

Look carefully at the jumbled words and unscramble the spelling words below.

1. eenegtl   g e n t e e l

2. luieedbg   b e g u i l e d

3. tramanel   m a t e r n a l

4. ucmuevialt   c u m u l a t i v e

5. dandeut   d a u n t e d

6. lnarabmo   a b n o r m a l

7. geossua   g a s e o u s

8. rirantpiopoap   a p p r o p r i a t i o n

9. iamlemd   d i l e m m a

10. lmaedu   m a u l e d

11. iinnutoti   i n t u i t i o n

12. tiuneaecn   e n u n c i a t e

13. ioeaulgd   d i a l o g u e

14. orecirtd   c r e d i t o r

15. iietdcfne   d e f i c i e n t

16. lntceleie   c l i e n t e l e

17. mtoidte   o m i t t e d

18. inoocslvun   c o n v u l s i o n

19. ietlxpo   e x p l o i t

20. roancgi   o r g a n i c

* Music: Wolfgang Amadeus Mozart

Wolfgang Amadeus Mozart (January 27, 1756 – December 5, 1791; pronounced MOHT-sart) was an Austrian composer, instrumentalist, and music teacher. Johannes Chrysostomus Wolfgangus Theophillus Mozart was his full baptismal name. He was the youngest child of Leopold and Anna Maria Mozart and was born in Salzburg, Austria. The young Mozart displayed exceptional musical talent from an early age. He toured Europe with his parents and older sister "Nannerl," performing for royalty and the aristocratic elite for several years.

Mozart attempted but failed to establish himself as a composer in Paris as a young man. He returned to Salzburg and briefly worked in the Archbishop of Salzburg's court. He was restless, aware of his brilliance, and thought Salzburg was too small for him. He moved to Vienna, where he had some success. He married Constance Weber and had two sons with her.

Mozart composed over 600 musical works, all of which are of the highest quality. The operas, The Marriage of Figaro, Don Giovanni, Cos fan tutte, and The Magic Flute; the symphonies in E-flat major, G minor, and C major ("Jupiter"); concertos for piano, violin, and various wind instruments; and numerous chamber pieces, and the Requiem are among his works. Along with Bach and Beethoven, Mozart is regarded as one of the greatest composers of all time.

There are several stories about Mozart's final illness and death, and it's difficult to know what happened. He was working on The Magic Flute, one of his best works and still a popular opera today. It is written in German rather than Italian, as are the majority of his other operas. It's similar to an English pantomime in some ways. At the same time, he was working on this, he was approached by a stranger and asked to compose a requiem. He was instructed to write this in private. Then he was commissioned to write the Italian opera La Clemenza di Tito, which premiered in Prague in September 1791. The Magic Flute received its first performance at the end of September. The Requiem was then a labor of love for Mozart. He must have realized that he was already gravely ill and that the Requiem (a mass for the dead) was for himself in some ways. He died in Vienna before completing it. Constanze commissioned another composer, Franz Xaver Süssmayr, to complete the work. Mozart was laid to rest in the St. Marx Cemetery.

1. When Mozart returned to Salzburg, he worked in the _____.
   a. Archbishop of Salzburg's court
   b. Salzburg's Music Store
   c. Archbishop High School

2. Mozart was an Austrian _____.
   a. composer, English teacher, singer
   b. science teacher, piano player and composer
   c. composer, instrumentalist, and music teacher

3. Mozart married _____ and had two sons with her.
   a. Constance Weber
   b. Courtney Webber
   c. Countesses Wilson

4. Mozart was laid to rest in the _____.
   a. Mozart family cemetery
   b. Dr. Mary Cemetery
   c. St. Marx Cemetery

* Music Vocabulary Crossword

Music has most likely existed for as long as humans have, which could be over a hundred thousand years! The earliest music is thought to have involved singing and clapping, and then early humans began drumming with sticks or other natural objects. Flutes carved from bones, such as bear and woolly mammoth bones, were among the first known musical instruments. Some of these bone instruments date back to 45,000 years!

Scholars agree that there are no 100% reliable methods for determining the exact chronology of musical instruments across cultures. Comparing and organizing instruments based on their complexity is deceptive, because technological advances in musical instruments have sometimes reduced complexity. Early slit drums, for example, required felling and hollowing out large trees; later slit drums were made by opening bamboo stalks, a much simpler task.

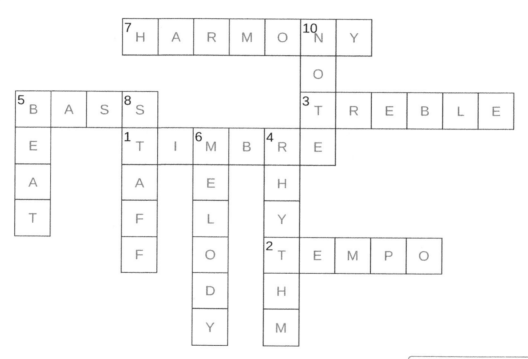

Across

1. the distinctive property of a complex sound
2. the speed at which a composition is to be played
3. having or denoting a high range
5. the lowest part of the musical range
7. compatibility in opinion and action

Down

4. an interval during which a recurring sequence occurs
5. hit repeatedly
6. a succession of notes forming a distinctive sequence
8. a strong rod or stick with a specialized utilitarian purpose
10. a brief written record

BASS   BEAT   STAFF
TIMBRE   HARMONY
TREBLE   MELODY   NOTE
RHYTHM   TEMPO

11th Grade Biography: Helen Keller
Reading Comprehension

Helen Keller was born in Tuscumbia, Alabama, on June 27, 1880. She was a healthy, happy baby. Her father, Arthur, worked for a newspaper, and her mother, Kate, looked after the house and Helen. She grew up on Ivy Green, her family's large farm.

Helen became very ill when she was about one and a half years old. For several days, she had a high fever and a severe headache. Helen survived, but her parents soon discovered that she had lost both her sight and her hearing.

Helen attempted to communicate with those around her. She had a set of motions she used to indicate whether she wanted her mother or father. She would, however, become frustrated. She realized she was unique, and it was challenging for her to communicate her needs to others. In her rage, she would throw tantrums, kicking and hitting others.

Helen's parents quickly realized that she required special assistance. They contacted Boston's Perkins Institute for the Blind. Annie Sullivan, a former student, was suggested by the director. Annie had been blind, but the surgery had restored her vision. Perhaps her unique experience will enable her to assist Helen. On March 3, 1887, Annie started working with Helen and would be her helper and companion for the next 50 years.

Annie started teaching Helen words. She would press word letters into Helen's hand. She would, for example, place a doll in one of Helen's hands and then press the letters D-O-L-L into the other. She taught Helen a few words. Helen would say the words into Annie's hand again and again.

Helen, on the other hand, was oblivious to the significance of the hand gestures. Then, one day, Annie immersed Helen's hand in water from a pump. She then spelled water into Helen's other hand. Something made sense. Helen finally realized what Annie was up to. Helen discovered a whole new world. That day, she picked up a few new words. It was one of the happiest days of her life in many ways.

Annie then taught Helen how to read. Helen must have been very bright, and Annie must have been an excellent teacher because Helen was soon able to read entire books in Braille. Braille is a unique reading system in which letters are formed from small bumps on a page.

What Helen and Annie were able to accomplish is truly amazing. Helen was ten years old when she learned to read and use a typewriter.

Sarah Fuller taught Helen Keller how to speak. Sarah worked as a deaf educator. Helen learned how to feel sound vibrations and how the lips moved to make sounds by resting her hand on Sarah's lips. She began by memorizing a few letters and sounds. She then progressed to words and, finally, sentences. Helen was thrilled to be able to speak.

Helen attended Radcliffe College for Women in Massachusetts when she was sixteen years old. Annie accompanied Helen to school and assisted in signing the lectures into Helen's hand. Helen graduated from Radcliffe with honors in 1904.

Helen began writing about her experiences as a deaf and blind student in college. She began by writing articles for a magazine called the Ladies' Home Journal. These articles were later collected in a book titled The Story of My Life. She published another book, The World I Live In, a few years later, in 1908.

Helen became more interested in assisting others as she grew older. She wished to motivate and encourage them. She became a member of the American Foundation for the Blind and toured the country, giving speeches and raising funds for the organization. Later, during WWII, she visited wounded army soldiers and encouraged them not to give up. Helen dedicated much of her life to raising funds and awareness for people with disabilities, particularly the deaf and blind.

Helen Keller, 87, dies on June 1, 1968, in Easton, Connecticut. Keller, who was born blind and deaf, went on to become a world-renowned writer and lecturer.

She was widely recognized for her work on behalf of the blind and deaf, and President Lyndon B. Johnson awarded her the Presidential Medal of Freedom, the nation's highest civilian honor, in 1964.

"My life has been happy because I have had wonderful friends and plenty of interesting work to do," Helen Keller once wrote, adding, "I seldom think about my limitations, and they never make me sad. Perhaps there is just a touch of yearning at times, but it is vague, like a breeze among flowers. The wind passes, and the flowers are content."

1. **Was Helen born a healthy baby?**
   a. Yes, she was happy and healthy.
   b. Yes. But had some health issues.

2. **Helen Keller was born in _____.**
   a. Tallahassee, Alabama
   b. Tuscumbia, Alabama

3. **Helen's dad worked for a _____.**
   a. bank
   b. newspaper

4. **Helen became very ill when she was about _____.**
   a. 2-3 years old
   b. 1-2 years old

5. **Who was Annie?**
   a. Helen's mom
   b. Helen's helper and companion

6. **When did Helen parent's realize she lost her sight and hearing?**
   a. After she became ill with a high fever and headache.
   b. They received a call from Helen's doctor.

7. **Helen could read entire books in _____.**
   a. Braille
   b. Spanish

8. **When did Helen's parents realize that she needed some special help?**
   a. After Helen was unable to communicate with people and became frustrated.
   b. After the teacher sent a note home about Helen's bad grades.

9. **Who was Sarah?**
   a. Sarah was a teacher for the deaf.
   b. Sarah was Helen's nurse.

10. **At 16 years old Helen attended _____ in Massachusetts.**
    a. High School
    b. Radcliffe College

11. **A number of Helen's articles were published for a magazine called the _____.**
    a. Ladies' Home Journal
    b. Deaf Ladies of Today

12. **Helen died on ____ in ____.**
    a. July 1, 1968, in Easton, Cincinnati
    b. June 1, 1968, in Easton, Connecticut

11th Grade English Refresher: 4 Types of Sentences

Declarative, imperative, interrogative, and exclamatory sentences are all types of sentences. Identifying and classifying sentences is easy once you know why each sort of sentence exists, how many there are, and how they are constructed. Each of these phrases' aims contributes to the uniqueness of the English language. The structure of conversation and written communication would be drastically different if these phrases were not used.

As the name implies, declarative phrases make statements. In most cases, they are expressed in a non-emotional, neutral manner. These sentences are used to state facts, describe things, and explain things.

Imperative sentences are used to express a command or a demand. Rather than being stated directly, the subjects of these sentences are frequently implied to be the listener.

Exclamatory sentences get their name from the fact that they exclaim something. Although exclamatory phrases can be classified in different ways, they are easily distinguished by the presence of intense emotions. An exclamation point marks the end of the sentence.

Interrogative sentences ask questions and are always followed by a question mark. Interrogative sentences frequently begin with "question words" such as who, what, where, when, how, or why. That is not always the case, however.

1. Which type of sentence might have an implied subject?
   a. interrogative
   b. declarative
   c. imperative

2. What end mark is used for interrogative sentences?
   a. period
   b. question mark
   c. exclamation mark

3. Which is an imperative sentence?
   a. What movie do you want to go see?
   b. Can you wash the car today?
   c. Please wash my car.

4. Which type of sentence shows strong emotion?
   a. interrogative
   b. declarative
   c. exclamatory

5. The sunset is beautiful tonight. This is what type of sentence?
   a. declarative
   b. imperative
   c. interrogative

6. Do not touch the stove! This is what type of sentence?
   a. exclamatory
   b. declarative
   c. imperative

7. Do you feel okay? This is what type of sentence?
   a. declarative
   b. Interrogative
   c. exclamatory

8. Declarative sentences make statements and end in _____.
   a. periods
   b. question mark
   c. exclamation mark

9. Imperative sentences make _____ or _____.
   a. commands or demand
   b. commands or thoughts
   c. commands or question

10. Interrogative sentences ask _____ and end in _____.
   a. commands and requests
   b. demand and exclamation mark
   c. questions and question marks

11th Grade English Refresher:
Simple, Compound & Complex

Score: _____

Date: _____

A **clause** is a collection of related words that includes a subject and a verb. Clauses are classified into two types: **independent clauses** and **dependent clauses**. **Independent clauses** constitute a complete thought and can function independently. **Dependent clauses** contain a subject and a verb but do not function as a complete thought. Clauses are important to understand because they are the foundation of all sentence types. Now we'll look at the three different types of sentences.

Simple sentences are made up of a single independent clause. That's how easy they are! It has a subject and a verb. It completes the thought.

Compound sentences contain at least two independent clauses and no dependent clauses. To put it another way, a compound sentence is formed by combining at least two simple sentences.

Complex sentences have at least one independent clause and one dependent clause.

Clauses, which are written expressions that contain a subject and a verb, are the building blocks of all sentences. Dependent clauses cannot stand on their own, whereas independent clauses can. Sentences are classified into three types: simple, compound, and complex. Simple sentences are made up of a single independent clause. Compound sentences are also made up of two or more independent clauses. Complex sentences contain an independent clause as well as one or more dependent clauses.

1. 'Darkness cannot drive out darkness; only light can do that.' - Martin Luther King Jr.
   a. Compound sentence
   b. Complex sentence
   c. Dependent clause

2. 'Beauty is in the heart of the beholder.' - H.G. Wells
   a. Dependent clause
   b. Independent clause
   c. Simple sentence

3. Their robot can follow a simple path through a maze.
   a. compound sentence
   b. simple sentence
   c. complex sentence

4. Kristina was late because she the traffic was terrible.
   a. compound sentence
   b. complex sentence
   c. simple sentence

5. He won the prize, but he was not happy.
   a. complex sentence
   b. compound sentence
   c. simple sentence

6. 'Silence is golden when you can't think of a good answer.' - Muhammad Ali
   a. Complex sentence
   b. Dependent clause
   c. Independent clause

7. Although it was cold, we played the match.
   a. Complex sentence
   b. Independent clause
   c. Dependent clause

8. 'People won't have time for you if you are always angry or complaining.' - Stephen Hawking
   a. Simple sentence
   b. Independent clause
   c. Complex sentence

11th Grade History: Age of Discovery

Score: _____

Date: _____

Tip: After you've answered the easy ones, go back and work on the harder ones.

valuable	Navigator	Middle	Discovery	Columbus
voyage	Africa	tobacco	sugar	sailed

Early in the 14th century, the Age of _____ (also known as the Age of Exploration) began. It lasted until the mid-1600s.

European nations began to explore the globe during this time period. A large part of the Far East and the Americas were found as well

as new routes to India and the _____ East. The Renaissance occurred at the same time as the Age of Exploration.

The process of preparing for an expedition can be costly and time-consuming. Many ships _____ away and never came

back. So what was it about exploration that piqued the interest of Europeans? Answering this question is as easy as saying "money."

Despite the fact that some explorers went on expeditions to acquire notoriety or to have an exciting experience, the primary goal of an

organization was to make money.

New trade routes discovered by expeditions brought quite a lot of money for their countries. Many traditional routes to India and China

were closed after the Ottoman Empire took Constantinople in 1453. Spices and silk were brought in via these trading routes, making

them extremely _____. New explorers were seeking oceangoing routes to India and the Far East. Gold and silver were

discovered by some journeys, including the Spanish ones to the Americas, which made them wealthy. They also found fresh territory to

create colonies and cultivate crops like _____, cotton, and _____.

Henry the _____, a Portuguese explorer, kicked off the Age of Exploration in the country. Henry dispatched a fleet of ships

to map and investigate the continent's western coast. They explored a large portion of west _____ for the Portuguese after

traveling further south than any previous European expedition had. Portuguese explorer Bartolomeu Dias discovered the southern tip of

Africa and into the Indian Ocean in 1488

The Spanish urgently needed a trade route to Asia. The famed European explorer, Christopher _____, believed he might

reach China by sailing west over the Atlantic Ocean. He turned to the Spanish for funding after failing to secure it from the Portuguese.

Isabella and Ferdinand, the monarchs of Spain, agreed to foot the bill for Columbus' _____. Columbus made his voyage to

the New World in 1492 and discovered the Americas.

11th Grade Financial: Checking Accounts

Financial literacy is the integration of financial, credit, and debt management knowledge required to make financially responsible decisions—choices that are essential in our daily lives. Understanding how a checking account works, what using a credit card really means, and how to avoid debt are all examples of financial literacy. To summarize, financial literacy has a tangible impact on families as they attempt to balance their budgets, purchase a home, fund their children's education, and save for retirement.

A checking account is a type of financial account that allows you to easily access and secure your money for daily transactions. It will enable you to deposit your paychecks and withdraw funds for vacations, dining out, or whatever else you want to spend your money on. To use a debit card or withdraw cash from an ATM, you must first open a checking account with a financial institution. These accounts, which usually have a low or no fee, are essential for most people's financial lives.

Checking accounts come in a variety of options or packages to help meet the needs of different people. To make the best decision, it's critical to understand the various types of checking accounts and some of their unique features.

Some checking accounts are completely free.

This is a popular type of checking account for obvious reasons. There are no monthly service fees or additional fees with free checking accounts, regardless of balance, the number of checks written, or other activity. You can use these accounts to make direct deposits, pay bills online, and write checks, just like a regular checking account. However, when compared to other accounts, these accounts usually pay the least amount of interest.

Basic Checking

These accounts, as the name suggests, provide the fundamentals. If you want to use a debit card, get cash from an ATM once in a while, and write a few checks, this is the account for you. These accounts will most likely have a small monthly or yearly fee that can be waived if you maintain a minimum balance or direct deposit your check every month. These types of accounts typically pay little to no interest.

Summary

A checking account is a financial account that allows you to easily access your money for daily transactions. Basic, free, interest-bearing, or money market, student, and joint accounts are among the most common types of checking accounts. Checking accounts have several advantages over other types of accounts or simply carrying cash. They support direct deposit, which expedites the receipt of your paycheck, and they are a more secure way to store your money. They can also make bill paying more accessible and less expensive, save you money on check-cashing fees, and simplify tracking monthly expenses. They can also help you avoid carrying cash by allowing you to use a debit card, and they're highly liquid, so you can get your money the same day you need it.

1. These types of accounts will most likely have a small monthly or yearly fee.
   a. Basic Checking
   b. Free Checking

2. You must first open a checking account with a _____ to withdraw cash from an ATM.
   a. financial institution
   b. employer

3. There are no monthly service fees or additional fees with _____ checking accounts.
   a. Basic
   b. Free

4. _____enables you to deposit your paychecks and withdraw funds for vacations.
   a. A checking account
   b. Stocks and bonds

5. Financial literacy has a tangible impact on_____.
   a. the bank
   b. families

6. Financial literacy is the integration of financial, credit, and _____.
   a. debt management
   b. checking accounts

11th Grade Math: Pre-Calculus Functions

We call something a "function" of another if it is dependent on another, such as the area of a circle is dependent on the radius. When the radius changes, the area changes. The radius affects the circle's area and vice versa.

If a rule that connects two variables, commonly x and y, assigns only one value of y to each of the x values, then the rule is termed a function.

When this is true, we say that y is a function of x.

Do you require any other assistance? Try looking for instructional videos on Pre-Calculus Functions on YouTube.

1. Given f(x) = x - 7, what will f(12) be equal to?
   a. 21
   b. 7
   c. 5

2. If h(x) = x +2, which of the following interpretation is incorrect?
   a. using the above relation, h(4) = 6
   b. h multiplied by g is equal to x+2
   c. h of x is equal to x+2

3. Given f(x) = (2,6), (-7,4), (9,2), (-5,1), and (7,2), the corresponding domain and range for f(x) are:
   a. Domain = {9, 4, 2, 1, 2} Range = {4, -7, 2, -5, 7}
   b. Domain = {6, 4, 2, 1, 2} Range = {2, -7, 9, -5, 7}
   c. Domain = {2 , -7, 9, -5, 7} Range = {6, 4, 2, 1, 2}

4. Identify which of the following statements about functions is incorrect.
   a. A function may have one input and generate multiple corresponding outputs.
   b. A function may never have multiple outputs for a single input.
   c. A function may have one input corresponding to one output.

5. Which of the following is the name given to the collection of all the outputs of a function?
   a. Inputs
   b. Range
   c. Domain

6. Which direction will the graph shift if the graph of f(x - 1) + 3 is changed to the graph of f(x + 1) + 3?
   a. 2 units to the right
   b. 2 units up
   c. 2 units to the left

7. Find the inverse of the following function: f(x) = 2x + 1
   a. 2x-1+f
   b. (x - 1)/2
   c. 2f-x

8. What is the symmetry line, or axis, of the following equation? y= (x+2)^2 + 10
   a. x=10
   b. x=-2
   c. x=2

9. If f(x) = 5 + 3x and g(x) = 5 - 9x, find f(g(2)).
   a. -44
   b. -13
   c. -34

10. Which type of transformation stretches or shrinks the function's graph?
    a. Translation
    b. Reflection
    c. Dilation

Score: _____

11th Grade Math: Inequalities

Date: _____

Mathematics isn't always about "equals"; sometimes all we know is that something is greater or less than another. An inequality is a mathematical equation that uses greater or less than symbols and is useful in situations where there are multiple solutions.

For example: Alexis and Billy compete in a race, and Billy wins!

What exactly do we know?

We don't know how fast they ran, but we do know Billy outpaced Alexis.

Billy was quicker than Alexis. That can be written down as follows: b > a

(Where "b" represents Billy's speed, ">" represents "greater than," and "a" represents Alexis's speed.)

Do you require any other assistance? Try looking for instructional videos on YouTube.

1. A truck is driving across a bridge that has a weight limit of 50,000 pounds. The front of the truck weighs 19,800 pounds when empty, and the back of the truck weighs 12,500 pounds. How much cargo (C), in pounds, can the truck carry and still cross the bridge?
   a. C ≤ 10000
   b. C ≤ 17700
   c. C ≤ 7700

2. Monica wants to buy a phone, and the cheapest one she's found so far is $15. Monica has $4.25 set aside for a cell phone. How many hours (H) will Monica have to work to afford a mobile phone if she earns $2.15 per hour?
   a. H ≥ 3.75
   b. H ≥ 5.50
   c. H ≥ 5

3. Solve the inequality 4x + 8 > 5x +9
   a. x < 8
   b. x > 2
   c. x < -1

4. Solve the following inequality - 4|2 - x| - 4 < -28
   a. x > 8 or x < -4
   b. x < 8 or x > -4
   c. x > 4 or x < 28

5. Which of the following best describes the appearance of these two inequalities when graphed together? 2y - 9 ≥ 4x and 4 < x + y
   a. both boundary lines will be solid or dotted
   b. both boundary lines will be dotted
   c. one boundary line will be solid and one will be dotted

6. Which compound inequality has the solution x < -8 ?
   a. x + 2 > 16 OR x + 6 < 8
   b. 6 - 2x > 22 OR 3x + 14 < -10
   c. 4x + 2 > 7 AND 2 - 6x > -1

7. If 2x - 8 ≥ 2, then
   a. x ≤ 4
   b. x ≥ 5
   c. x ≤ 8

8. Which of the following is an example of an inequality?
   a. 70 - 2(15) = 88
   b. 60 + 2x < 120
   c. 70 + 3x = 80

11th Grade Math: Linear Equation

Score: _____

Date: _____

What exactly is a linear equation?

First, consider the word equation. An equation is a mathematical statement containing the equals sign. Of course, linear means "in a straight line."

A linear equation is an equation with degree 1 -, which means that the highest exponent on all variables in the equation is 1. It turns out that if you plot the solutions to a linear equation in a coordinate system, they form a straight line.

A linear equation resembles an equation (there must be an equals sign) with variables that all have an exponent of one (in other words, no variable is raised to a higher power, and no variable is under a square root sign).

These equations are linear: $y=2x+9$ or $5x=6+3y$

1. Which of the following is a solution to both $y - 3x = 6$ and $y - 6x = 3$?
   a. (6,9)
   b. (3,6)
   c. (1,9)

2. Different plans are available from two cellphone carriers. AT&K charges a monthly flat rate of $100 plus $10 for each gigabyte of data used. Verikon Communications does not have a flat rate, but instead charges $40 for each gigabyte of data used. Let c represent your total cost and d represent the data used. What is the equation system that represents these two plans?
   a. $V = 100 + 10d$ and $A = 40d$
   b. $A = 100d$ and $V = 40d$
   c. $c = 100 + 10d$ and $c = 40d$

3. Solve the following system of equations $3x + y = 1$ and $-x + 2y = 2$
   a. (2, 1)
   b. (3, 1)
   c. (0, 1)

4. What is the slope of a line with a graph that moves one place to the right by going up three places on a coordinate plane?
   a. -3
   b. 3
   c. 2

5. Find the slope of the line $2x - y = 6$.
   a. 6
   b. 2
   c. -2

6. Which of the following linear equations has a y-intercept of 3 and a graph that slopes upward from left to right?
   a. $-4x + 2y - 6 = 0$
   b. $-4x + 2y + 6 = 0$
   c. $4x + y + 3 = 0$

7. What are the x and y-intercepts of $3x + 4y = 12$?
   a. (0, 12) and (3, 0)
   b. (4, 0) and (0, 3)
   c. (12, 4) and (4, 3)

8. Which linear equation has the solutions (1, 3) and (3, 9)?
   a. $x = 1y$
   b. $y = 9x + 2$
   c. $y = 3x$

11th Grade Math: Geometry and Trigonometry

We all know that geometry is the study of various shapes, sizes, and positions of various shapes based on the number of sides, angles, etc. On the other hand, trigonometry is a subset of geometry that deals with the properties of one of geometry's shapes called "Triangle." Both trigonometry and geometry appear to be related, but they are not the same thing.

Trigonometry is primarily concerned with the study of various properties of triangles, lengths, and angles. It does, however, deal with waves and oscillations. We primarily study the relationships between the side lengths and angles of a right-angle triangle in trigonometry. Six trigonometric relationships exist. Secant, Cosecant, and Cotangent are subsets of the three fundamental ones, Sine, Cosine, and Tangent.

Geometry is defined as the study of various sizes, shapes, and properties of empty spaces with a given number of dimensions, such as 2D or 3D. Plane geometry involves two-dimensional geometric objects like points, lines, curves, and various plane figures like circles, triangles, and polygons. Solid geometry is the study of three-dimensional objects such as polyhedra, spheres, cubes, prisms, and pyramids. Spherical geometry is also concerned with three-dimensional objects such as spherical triangles and polygons.

_____

Do you require any other assistance? Try looking for instructional videos on YouTube.

_____

1. A right triangle's hypotenuse is 10 feet long. It has a 6-foot-long side. What is the value on the third side?
   a. 6 ft.
   b. 8 ft.
   c. 8.1 ft.

2. In order to form a right triangle, which of the following measurements must be taken?
   a. 6, 8, 10
   b. 3, 4, 5
   c. All of these will produce a right triangle.

3. There are six and eight-inch sides to an abc right triangle. Third side length is how many feet?
   a. 8.0 in
   b. 10.0 in.
   c. 9.5 in.

4. A right triangle's two shorter sides are 12 feet and 14 feet long, respectively. What's the hypotenuse measured at?
   a. 10.85 ft.
   b. 18.43 ft.
   c. 20.24 ft.

5. What's the volume of a 5-inch cube with straight sides?
   a. 125 square inches
   b. 125 cubic inches
   c. 25 cubic inches

6. The height of a square pyramid is two feet. Calculate the pyramid's volume if the base has a 4 foot side.
   a. 5.6 cubic feet
   b. 6 cubic feet
   c. 10.7 cubic feet

Absolute value is an important concept for numbers, whether real or complex. Remember that the absolute value |x| of a real number x is itself if it is positive or zero; however, if x is negative, its absolute value |x| is its negation –x, that is, the corresponding positive value. For example, |3| equals 3, but |–4| equals 4. The absolute value function removes the sign from a real number.

The absolute value of a complex number a + bi, also known as its modulus, is its distance from the origin on the complex number plane. The complex number a + bi is represented as a point (a, b) on the complex plane, and the coordinate of the origin is (0, 0). Simply calculate the distance between (0,0) and (a,b). The distance formula can be used to calculate the absolute value of a complex number.

Determine each complex number's absolute value.

1) $| \ 3 + 3i \ |$

$3 \sqrt{2}$ EXAMPLE

2) $| \ 4 + 7i \ |$

3) $| \ -1 + 6i \ |$

4) $| \ 4 - 6i \ |$

5) $| \ 5 - i \ |$

6) $| \ 6 - i \ |$

7) $| \ -1 + i \ |$

8) $| \ 8 - i \ |$

9) $| \ -1 + i \ |$

10) $| \ -7 - 5i \ |$

Do you require any other assistance? Try looking for instructional videos on YouTube.

Score : _____

Date : _____

An **infinite geometric series** is the sum of an infinite geometric sequence. The sum of all finite geometric series can be found. When the common ratio in an infinite geometric series is greater than one, the terms in the sequence grow larger and larger, and adding the larger numbers yields no final answer. Infinity is the only possible answer. As a result, we do not consider the common ratio greater than one for an infinite geometric series.

Infinite Geometric Series

Determine whether each series converges or diverges.

1) $4.70 + 0.47 + 0.05 + 0.00...$

2) $\sum\limits_{n=1}^{\infty} -2.70 \cdot \left(2.1 \right)^{n-1}$

3) $\sum\limits_{n=1}^{\infty} 1.90 \cdot \left(0.3 \right)^{n-1}$

4) $\sum\limits_{n=1}^{\infty} 6.80 \cdot \left(2.3 \right)^{n-1}$

Evaluate each series.

5) $a_1 = -4.40, r = 0.5$

6) $2.30 + 5.75 + 14.37 + 35.94...$

7) $a_1 = -3.10, r = 0.7$

8) $-4.60 - 12.42 - 33.53 - 90.54...$

Determine the common ratio of each series.

9) $-4.30 - 12.04 - 33.71 - 94.39...$

10) $a_1 = 2.10, S = 1.91$

11) $a_1 = 5.00, S = 4.17$

12) $\sum\limits_{n=1}^{\infty} -5.70 \cdot \left(-0.3 \right)^{n-1}$

11th Grade Math: Domain and Range

Score: _____

Date: _____

The collection of all input values on which a function is defined is known as the domain. If a value is entered into the function, the function will remain defined regardless of what value is entered. A function's range is defined as the set of all possible output values for the function. It can also be thought of as the collection of all possible values that the function will accept as input.

1. Which of the following describes a collection of a function's outputs?

    a. Domain

    b. Inputs

    c. Range

2. What is the range of the function: $g(x) = |x| + 1$

    a. $R = \{1 \geq x\}$

    b. $R = \{x \geq 1\}$

    c. $R = \{y \geq 1\}$

3. A set of ordered pairs is called what?

    a. the domain

    b. a function

    c. a relation

4. What is the domain of a relation?

    a. the set of all y-values

    b. the set of all y + x values

    c. the set of all x-values

5. Which is the set of all y-values or the outputs?

    a. Domain

    b. Function

    c. Range

6. For the function {(0,1), (1,-3), (2,-4), (-4,1)}, write the domain and range.

    a. D:{0, 1, 2, -4} R:{1, -3, -4}

    b. D: {1, -3, -4,} R: {0, 1, 2, -4}

    c. D:{0, 1, 2, 3, 4} R:{1, -3, -4}

7. Identify the range of the following function when given the domain { 2, 3, 10}: y = 4x - 12

    a. -10, 0, 28

    b. -4, 0, 28

    c. 4, 5, 20

8. Which set of ordered pairs is not a function?

    a. (-9, 4), (-6, 3), (-2, 8), (0, 21)

    b. (1, 2), (3, 5), (6, 9), (7, 11)

    c. (2, 3), (4, 9), (3, 8), (4, 15)

9. What variable does Domain represent?

    a. Range

    b. X

    c. output

10. Which is the set of all y-values or the outputs?

    a. Range

    b. Domain

    c. Relation

11th Grade Word of The Day

Use the dictionary to write the definition
and divide the words for each day
below into syllables.

○ **MONDAY** WORD: *UNICYCLE*
EXAMPLE:
A unicycle is a vehicle that touches the
ground with only one wheel.

u–ni–cy–cle

TUESDAY **WORD: arthropods**

WEDNESDAY **WORD: mollusks**

THURSDAY **WORD: accelerator**

FRIDAY **WORD: kefir**

SATURDAY / SUNDAY **WORD: opacity**

Write Words In ABC Order

_____
_____
_____
_____
_____
_____
_____

For each word, find one
synonym & one antonym. (if
none: write word + none)

_____
_____
_____
_____
_____
_____
_____
_____
_____
_____
_____
_____
_____

11th Grade Word of The Day

Use the dictionary to write the definition
and divide the words for each day
below into syllables.

MONDAY WORD: **autonomous**

Write Words In ABC Order

_____

_____

_____

_____

_____

TUESDAY **WORD: cacophony**

_____

_____

_____

_____

WEDNESDAY **WORD: comestible**

For each word, find one
synonym & one antonym. (if
none: write word + none)

_____

THURSDAY **WORD: concierge**

_____

_____

_____

_____

_____

FRIDAY **WORD: encyclical**

_____

_____

_____

_____

SATURDAY / SUNDAY **WORD: fallacious**

_____

_____

_____

_____

11th Grade Word of The Day

Use the dictionary to write the definition
and divide the words for each day
below into syllables.

MONDAY WORD: **gimmicky**

Write Words In ABC Order

_____

_____

_____

TUESDAY **WORD: imperturbable**

_____

_____

_____

_____

_____

WEDNESDAY **WORD: knickknack**

For each word, find one
synonym & one antonym. (if
none: write word + none)

THURSDAY **WORD: incontrovertible**

_____

_____

_____

_____

_____

FRIDAY **WORD: filibuster**

_____

_____

_____

_____

SATURDAY / SUNDAY **WORD: gazetteer**

_____

_____

_____

11th Grade Word of The Day

Use the dictionary to write the definition
and divide the words for each day
below into syllables.

MONDAY WORD: **concierge**

Write Words In ABC Order

TUESDAY **WORD: encyclical**

WEDNESDAY **WORD: fungible**

For each word, find one
synonym & one antonym. (if
none: write word + none)

THURSDAY **WORD: ignominy**

FRIDAY **WORD: largesses**

SATURDAY / SUNDAY **WORD: intransigence**

11th Grade Word of The Day

Use the dictionary to write the definition
and divide the words for each day
below into syllables.

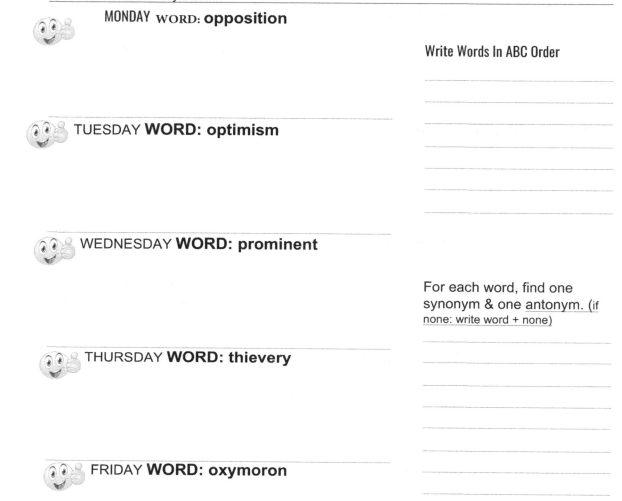

MONDAY WORD: **opposition**

Write Words In ABC Order

_____

_____

_____

_____

_____

_____

TUESDAY WORD: optimism

WEDNESDAY WORD: prominent

For each word, find one
synonym & one antonym. (if
none: write word + none)

_____

_____

THURSDAY WORD: thievery

_____

_____

_____

_____

FRIDAY WORD: oxymoron

_____

_____

_____

SATURDAY / SUNDAY WORD: nuisance

_____

_____

_____

_____

11th Grade Word of The Day

Use the dictionary to write the definition
and divide the words for each day
below into syllables.

MONDAY WORD: **neckerchief**

Write Words In ABC Order

TUESDAY **WORD: myrrh**

WEDNESDAY **WORD: recalcitrant**

For each word, find one
synonym & one antonym. (if
none: write word + none)

THURSDAY **WORD: invertebrate**

FRIDAY **WORD: viviparous**

SATURDAY / SUNDAY **WORD: oviparous**

GRADE_____

DATE_____   **RESEARCH:** Friedrich Clemens Gerke

Occupation _____

BORN DATE:_____   Nationality_____

DEATH DATE:_____   Education_____   #Children_____

Childhood and Family Background Facts

Work and Career Facts

Children, Marriage and or Significant Relationships

Friends, Social Life and Other Interesting Facts

Did you enjoy researching this person?

Give a Rating: ☆ ☆ ☆ ☆ ☆

DATE_____   **RESEARCH: Ken Kutaragi**

Occupation _____

BORN DATE: _____   Nationality _____

DEATH DATE: _____   Education _____   #Children _____

Childhood and Family Background Facts

Work and Career Facts

Children, Marriage and or Significant Relationships

Friends, Social Life and Other Interesting Facts

Did you enjoy researching this person?

Give a Rating: ☆ ☆ ☆ ☆ ☆

GRADE_____

DATE_____   **RESEARCH: Charles Macintosh**

Occupation _____

BORN DATE:_____   Nationality_____

DEATH DATE:_____   Education_____   #Children _____

Childhood and Family Background Facts

Work and Career Facts

Children, Marriage and or Significant Relationships

Friends, Social Life and Other Interesting Facts

Did you enjoy researching this person?

Give a Rating: ☆ ☆ ☆ ☆ ☆

GRADE_____

DATE_____

RESEARCH: Ilya Ilyich Mechnikov

Occupation _____

BORN DATE: _____   Nationality _____

DEATH DATE: _____   Education _____   #Children _____

Childhood and Family Background Facts

Work and Career Facts

Children, Marriage and or Significant Relationships

Friends, Social Life and Other Interesting Facts

Did you enjoy researching this person?

Give a Rating: ☆ ☆ ☆ ☆

GRADE_____

DATE_____

RESEARCH: Daniel David Palmer

Occupation _____

BORN DATE:_____ Nationality _____

DEATH DATE:_____ Education _____ #Children _____

Childhood and Family Background Facts

Work and Career Facts

Children, Marriage and or Significant Relationships

Friends, Social Life and Other Interesting Facts

Did you enjoy researching this person?

Give a Rating: ☆ ☆ ☆ ☆ ☆

GRADE_____

DATE_____

RESEARCH: Adolphe Sax

Occupation _____

BORN DATE: _____ Nationality _____

DEATH DATE: _____ Education _____ #Children _____

Childhood and Family Background Facts

Work and Career Facts

Children, Marriage and or Significant Relationships

Friends, Social Life and Other Interesting Facts

Did you enjoy researching this person?

Give a Rating: ☆ ☆ ☆ ☆ ☆

11th Grade Language: Spanish

Use Google to help translate.

1. You would answer: ¡Muy bien! to which of the following questions in Spanish?
   a. 'Cómo te llamas?
   b. 'De dónde eres?
   c. 'Cómo estás?

2. What does Soy de Virginia means?
   a. I am from Virginia
   b. My name is Virginia
   c. I am Virginia

3. Buenas tardes is a Spanish greeting for which time of the day?
   a. Good night
   b. Good morning
   c. Afternoon

4. You would answer: Me llamo Antonio to which of the following questions in Spanish?
   a. 'A quién llamas?
   b. 'Cómo te llamas?
   c. 'Cuándo llamas?

5. You would answer: Soy de Carolina to which of the following questions in Spanish?
   a. 'De dónde eres?
   b. 'Dónde vas?
   c. 'Cómo te llamas?

6. How would you say 'Good morning' to a store clerk?
   a. Buenos días
   b. Hola
   c. My llamo

7. 'Soy de California.
   a. 'She from California.
   b. 'I am from California.
   c. 'I live in California.

8. Which of the following persons would you address by using the pronoun 'Tú'?
   a. a teacher
   b. Your aunt
   c. Your sibling

9. What would be the best greeting for the nighttime?
   a. Buenas tardes
   b. Soy
   c. Buenas noches

10. Which of the following is NOT a way to tell someone your name?
    a. Soy de...
    b. Me llamo...
    c. Mi nombre es...

11. Which two words mean 'you?'
    a. Tú and Usted
    b. Yo and Cómo
    c. Usted and Nónde

12. Buenos días, señor. ?
    a. Good night sir. ?
    b. Good morning sir. ?
    c. Good afternoon sir. ?

13. Cómo se llama ud.?'
    a. What's your name.?'
    b. What time is it.?'
    c. Where are you?

14. Where it is?'
    a. Me rónde es?'
    b. De dónde es?'
    c. Re dónde see?'

11th Grade Biography: Daniel Boone

Score: _____

Date: _____

wildlife	acres	chopping	legendary	Appalachian
construction	herd	hunter	Appalachian	defeated
Creek	blacksmith	British	foxes	eleven
Shawnee	Rebecca	rifle	furs	Indians

One of America's first folk heroes was Daniel Boone. As a woodsman, his exploits were _____.

He was a highly skilled _____, marksman, and tracker. He was in charge of Kentucky's exploration and

settling.

Daniel grew up in a Pennsylvania Quaker household. He had _____ brothers and sisters, and his father

was a farmer. Daniel put in long hours on his father's farm. By the age of five, he was _____ wood

and caring for his father's cows, and by the age of ten, he was managing his father's _____. Daniel was a big

fan of being outside. He will do anything to avoid being trapped within. He would hunt small _____

and learn to find their trails in the woods while monitoring his father's cowherd. He also made acquaintances with

the Delaware _____ in the area. They taught him everything he knew about survival in the wild,

including how to track, trap, and hunt. Daniel quickly began to dress in Indian garb.

Daniel bought his first _____ when he was thirteen years old. He had a natural talent for shooting and soon

became the family's primary hunter. He used to go hunting alone for days at a time. He'd go for _____,

beavers, deer, and wild turkeys.

The Boones relocated to North Carolina's Yadkin Valley in 1751. Daniel gathered enough animal hides to assist

his family in purchasing 1300 _____ of property. He became renowned as the best sniper in the country,

winning every competition he entered.

In 1754, the French-Indian War began. This was a conflict between the _____ colonies and a French-Indian coalition. Daniel joined the British army and served as a _____ and a supply wagon driver. He was present at the Battle of Turtle _____, in which French-Indian forces easily _____ British forces. Daniel was able to flee on horseback.

Daniel moved back to North Carolina, where he married _____. They'd have a total of ten children. Daniel encountered a man named John Findley, who told him about Kentucky west of the _____ Mountains.

Daniel Boone led an expedition into Kentucky in 1769. The Cumberland Gap, a tiny gap through the _____ Mountains, was found by him. Daniel, on the other hand, discovered a region that he regarded as a paradise. There were lots of farming meadows and wild wildlife to hunt. Daniel stayed in Kentucky with his brother John to hunt and trap furs and pelts. The _____ Indians, however, quickly grabbed them. The Shawnee and England had agreed that the territory west of the Appalachians belonged to them. Daniel's _____, firearms, and horses were taken from him, and he was instructed never to return.

Daniel made a second trip to Kentucky in 1775. He and a group of men assisted in the _____ of the Wilderness Trail, a road leading to Kentucky. They felled trees and even constructed little bridges to allow wagons to pass through.

11th Grade Art: Pablo Picasso

French	angles	depressed	life	collaborated
painting	Spanish	sand	Barcelona	influence
painter	Carlos	blue	circuses	suicide
newspapers	dream	Madrid	historians	prestigious
recovered	died	classical-style	greatest	features

Tip: First, read the entire passage. After that, go back and fill in the blanks. You can skip the blanks you're unsure about and finish them later.

Pablo Picasso was born on October 25, 1881, in Spain and grew up there. His father was a _____ who also taught art. Pablo has always enjoyed drawing since he was a child. According to legend, his first word was "piz," which is _____ for "pencil." Pablo quickly demonstrated that he had little interest in school but was an extremely talented artist. Pablo enrolled in a _____ art school in _____ when he was fourteen years old. He transferred to another school in _____ a few years later. Pablo, on the other hand, was dissatisfied with the traditional art school teachings. He didn't want to paint in the manner of people from hundreds of years ago. He wished to invent something new.

Pablo's close friend _____ Casagemas committed _____ in 1901. Pablo became _____. He began painting in Paris around the same time. For the next four years, the color _____ dominated his paintings. Many of the subjects appeared depressed and solemn. He depicted people with elongated _____ and faces in his paintings. Poor People on the Seashore and The Old Guitarist are two of his paintings from this time.

Pablo eventually _____ from his depression. He also had feelings for a _____ model. He began to use warmer colors such as pinks, reds, oranges, and beiges in his paintings. The Rose Period is a term used by art _____ to describe this period in Pablo's life. He also started painting happier scenes like _____. The Peasants and Mother and Child are two of his paintings from this time period.

Picasso began experimenting with a new _____ style in 1907. He _____ with another artist, Georges Braque. By 1909, they had developed a completely new painting style known as Cubism. Cubism analyzes and divides subjects into different sections. The sections are then reassembled and painted from various perspectives and

_____.

Picasso began combining Cubism and collage in 1912. He would use _____ or plaster in his paint to give it texture in this area. He would also add dimension to his paintings by using materials such as colored paper, _____, and wallpaper. Three Musicians and the Portrait of Ambroise Vollard are two of Picasso's Cubism paintings.

Although Picasso continued to experiment with Cubism, he went through a period of painting more _____ paintings around 1921. He was influenced by Renaissance painters such as Raphael. He created strong characters that appeared three-dimensional, almost like statues. The Pipes of Pan and Woman in White are two of his works in this style.

Pablo became interested in the Surrealist movement around 1924. Surrealist paintings were never meant to make sense. They frequently resemble something out of a nightmare or a _____. Although Picasso did not join the movement, he did incorporate some of its ideas into his paintings. This period was dubbed "Monster Period" by some. Guernica and The Red Armchair are two examples of surrealism's _____ on Picasso's art.

Pablo Picasso is widely regarded as the greatest artist of the twentieth century. Many consider him to be one of the _____ artists in all of history. He painted in a variety of styles and made numerous unique contributions to the world of art. He painted several self-portraits near the end of his _____. Self-Portrait Facing Death, a self-portrait done with crayons on paper, was one of his final works of art. He _____ a year later, on April 8, 1973, at the age of 91.

11th Grade Financial: Money, Stocks and Bonds

Tip: First, read the entire passage. After that, go back and fill in the blanks. You can skip the blanks you're unsure about and finish them later.

prices	obligation	currency	issued	barter
stake	coins	exchange	principal	economy
profits	piece	conditions	valuable	gold
NASDAQ	bankruptcy	golden	services	symbols
goods	shareholders	monetary	value	

Three important _____ must be met in order for something to qualify as a financial asset. It has to be:

Something you can have

Something monetary in nature

A contractual claim provides the basis for that monetary value

That last condition may be difficult to grasp at first, but it will become clear in a few minutes.

As a result, financial assets differ from physical assets such as land or _____. You can touch and feel the actual physical asset with land and gold, but you can only touch and feel something (usually a _____ of paper) that represents the asset of value with financial assets.

Money is a government-defined official medium of _____ that consists of cash and _____. Money, _____, cash, and legal tender all refer to the same thing. They are all _____ of a central bank's commitment to keep money's value as stable as possible. Money is a financial asset because its value is derived from the faith and credit of the government that issued it, not from the paper or metal on which it is printed.

Money is obviously a _____ financial asset. We would all have to _____ with one another without a common medium of exchange, trading whatever _____ and _____ we have for something else we need, or trade what we have for something else we could then trade with someone else who has what we need. Consider how complicated that can become!

Stock is another crucial financial asset in the US _____. Stock, like money, is simply a piece of paper that represents something of value. The something of value' represented by stock is a _____ in a company. Stock is also known as 'equity' because you have a stake in its _____ when you own stock in a company.

Consider little Jane's lemonade stand as the most basic example. Jane only has $4 to begin her business, but she requires $10. Jane's parents give her $3 in exchange for 30% of her business, a friend gives her $1 for 10%, and her brother gives her $2 in exchange for 20%. Jane, her parents, a friend, and her brother are now all _____ in her company.

That example, as simple as it is, accurately describes stock. The complexities arise when we attempt to assign a _____ value to that stock. A variety of factors determines a stock's _____. One share of stock in one company does not equal one share of stock in another. The number of shares issued by each company, as well as the size and profitability of each company, will affect the value of your share. Anything that has an impact on a business, good or bad, will affect the stock price.

These are the most basic and fundamental factors that can influence the value of a share of stock. Individual stock _____ are affected by macroeconomic trends as well. Thousands of books have been written in an attempt to discover the _____ rule that determines the exact value of a share of stock.

The value of a stock can fluctuate from minute to minute and even second to second. The New York Stock Exchange and _____ were the world's two largest stock exchanges in 2014. (both located in the United States).

Bonds are the final financial asset we'll look at. Bonds are, in essence, loans. When an organization, such as a company, a city or state, or even the federal government, requires funds, bonds can be _____. Bonds come in various forms, but they are all debt instruments in which the bondholder is repaid their _____ investment, plus interest, at some future maturity date.

The only way a bondholder's money is lost is if the entity that issued the bond declares _____. Bonds are generally safer investments than stocks because they are a legal _____ to repay debt, whereas stocks represent ownership, which can make or lose money.

11th Grade Financial: Vocabulary Crossword

Score: _____

Date: _____

Across

1. The profit or loss on an investment over a one-year period.
2. The cost of borrowing money on a yearly basis, expressed as a percentage rate.
5. Twice a month.
6. To receive something on loan with the understanding that you will return it.
8. The loss that comes from selling an investment for less than you paid for it.

Down

3. An item with economic value, such as stock or real estate.
4. Stands for "automated teller machine
7. The profit that comes from selling an investment for more than you paid for it.
9. An individual who signs a loan, credit account, or promissory note of another person
10. Borrowing money, or having the right to borrow money, to buy something.

ANNUAL RETURN
CAPITAL LOSS   ATM
CAPITAL GAIN   COSIGNER
BORROW   CREDIT
BIMONTHLY   ASSET   APR

Cursive Writing Practice

Score: _____   Date: _____

Why did the teacher wear

sunglasses? (Because her

students were bright!) Why

was the teacher cross-eyed?

(She couldn't control her

pupils!) How do bees get to

school? (By school buzz!)

What did the paper say to

the pencil? (Write on!) How

do you get straight As? (Use

Cursive Writing Practice

Score: _____ Date: _____

a ruler!) What building has

the most stories? (The

library!) What do you get

when you throw a million

books into the ocean? (A

title wave!) What is my

favorite subject? (His-tory!)

Why did the teacher write on

the window? (To make the

lesson very clear!)

11th Grade Science: Protists

First, read the entire passage. After that, go back and fill in the blanks. You can skip the blanks you're unsure about and finish them later.

Amoebas	scoot	oxygen	molds	reproduce
enormous	color	unclassifiable	energy	acellular
tiny	cell	consume	tail	cellular

Protists are organisms that are classified under the biological kingdom protista. These are neither plants, animals, bacteria, or fungi, but rather _____ organisms. Protists are a large group of organisms with a wide variety of characteristics. They are essentially all species that do not fit into any of the other categories.

Protists as a group share very few characteristics. They are eukaryotic microorganisms with eukaryote _____ structures that are pretty basic. Apart from that, they are defined as any organism that is not a plant, an animal, a bacteria, or a fungus.

Protists can be classified according to their mode of movement.

Cilia - Certain protists move with _____ hair called cilia. These tiny hairs can flap in unison to assist the creature in moving through water or another liquid.

Other protists have a lengthy _____ known as flagella. This tail can move back and forth, aiding in the organism's propulsion.

Pseudopodia - When a protist extends a portion of its cell body in order to _____ or ooze. Amoebas move in this manner.

Different protists collect _____ in a variety of methods. Certain individuals consume food and digest it internally. Others digest their food through the secretion of enzymes. Then they _____ the partially digested meal. Other protists, like plants, utilize photosynthesis. They absorb sunlight and convert it to glucose.

Algae is a main form of protist. Algae are photosynthesis-capable protists. Algae are closely related to plants. They contain chlorophyll and utilize _____ and solar energy to generate food. They are not called plants, however, because they lack specialized organs and tissues such as leaves, roots, and stems. Algae are frequently classified according on their _____, which ranges from red to brown to green.

Slime _____ are distinct from fungus molds. Slime molds are classified into two types: cellular and plasmodial. Slime molds of Plasmodium are formed from a single big cell. They are also referred to as _____. Even though these organisms are composed of only one cell, they can grow quite _____, up to several feet in width. Additionally, they can contain several nuclei inside a single cell. Cellular slime molds are little single-celled protists that can form a single organism when combined. When combined, various _____ slime molds will perform specific activities.

_____ are single-celled organisms that move with the assistance of pseudopods. Amoebas have no structure and consume their food by engulfing it with their bodies. Amoebas _____ by dividing in two during a process called mitosis.

11th Grade Science: Black Hole
Reading Comprehension

Black holes are one of the universe's most mysterious and powerful forces. A black hole is a region of space where gravity has become so strong that nothing, not even light, can escape. A black hole's mass is so compact or dense that the force of gravity is so strong that even light cannot escape.

Black holes are entirely invisible. Because black holes do not reflect light, we cannot see them. Scientists can detect black holes by observing light and objects in their vicinity. Strange things happen in the vicinity of black holes due to quantum physics and space-time. Even though they are authentic, they are a popular subject for science fiction stories.

When giant stars explode at the end of their lives, black holes form, this type of explosion is known as a supernova. If a star has enough mass, it will collapse in on itself and shrink to a tiny size. Because of its small size and massive mass, the gravity will be so strong that it will absorb light and turn into a black hole. As they continue to absorb light and mass around them, black holes can grow enormously large. They can absorb other stars as well. Many scientists believe that supermassive black holes exist at the centers of galaxies.

An event horizon is a special boundary that exists around a black hole. At this point, everything, including light, must gravitate toward the black hole. Once you've crossed the event horizon, there's no turning back!

In the 18th century, two scientists, John Michell and Pierre-Simon Laplace, proposed the concept of a black hole. The term "black hole" was coined in 1967 by physicist John Archibald Wheeler.

1. Black holes are _____.
   a. can be seen with telescope
   b. invisible
   c. partial visible

2. Black holes are one of the most mysterious forces in the _____.
   a. near the moon
   b. under the stars
   c. universe

3. A black hole is where _____ has become so strong that nothing around it can escape.
   a. black dust
   b. gravity
   c. the sun

4. We can't actually see black holes because they don't _____.
   a. need sun
   b. reflect light
   c. have oxygen

5. Black holes are formed when _____ explode at the end of their lifecycle.
   a. giant stars
   b. planets
   c. Mars

6. Black holes can grow incredibly huge as they continue to absorb_____.
   a. stars
   b. other planets
   c. light

11th Grade Biology: Life on Earth

First, read the entire passage. After that, go back and fill in the blanks. You can skip the blanks you're unsure about and finish them later.

ancient	volcanic	metabolize	transmit	droplets
scientists	microbes	energy	billion	reproduce
ammonia	oceans	amino	produce	molecules

One of the most intriguing aspects of Earth's history is how life came to be there. To learn how life came to be on

Earth, many _____ have committed their careers to do so. We'll look at a few significant tests to

better understand how scientists have proposed how life began on Earth, but first, let's go back in time, around

four _____ years.

The environment on primitive Earth was vastly different from what it is today. Numerous _____ and

seas had hot vents at their bottoms, and the land also had plenty of _____ activity. Unlike our

current atmosphere, which is primarily composed of nitrogen and oxygen, the _____ atmosphere

was likely to contain water, methane, _____, and hydrogen.

Now that we know what Earth may have looked like in the distant past, let's look at the processes that lead to the

emergence of life on the planet.

Creating tiny organic compounds like _____ acids for proteins and nucleotides for DNA is the first

stage. Even while these organic _____ are present in living things, they are not live creatures in and

of themselves. Instead, they are merely combinations of different elements that happen to be found in living

things.

The next stage was the joining of these small organic molecules to _____ larger ones. Due to their single unit composition, tiny molecules are referred to as monomers. As a result of combining, they form polymers that include several repeating units. To be clear, the word "mono" refers to a single thing, such as monorail or monocle, while the term "poly" refers to numerous things. It's similar to making a big chain out of paper clips. To put it another way, the long chain of paper clips is one polymer.

Things start to become dicey in the third stage of Earth's early history. Protobionts were made from the polymers generated from the monomers. The study of protozoa is critical for gaining a better understanding of the earliest stages of life. Protobionts are microscopic _____ with membranes that can regulate their own internal environment. Cells can proliferate, _____, and even adjust to their environs as these _____ can. These pre-cell formations have formed spontaneously, according to numerous studies.

The basic protobionts evolved a fourth step: the ability to _____ genetic information. To put it another way, protobionts have the ability to self-replicate, which means they can create new ones. A cell's ability to _____ and pass on genetic information from one generation to the next and digest matter and _____ sets it apart from other living things. A vast range of life forms has arisen from these primitive cells, which were derived from more complicated molecules, which themselves originated from simpler ones.

11th Grade Language: Technology

Match the English and German words. Use Google translate.

1	☐	mouse	Nachricht	A
2	☐	touch	Handy	B
3	☐	screen	Maus	C
4	☐	Wi-Fi	Schoß	D
5	☐	message	Spiel	E
6	☐	game	berühren	F
7	☐	website	Rechner	G
8	☐	mobile	Bildschirm	H
9	☐	smart	Schreibtischplatte	I
10	☐	computer	Tastatur	J
11	☐	desktop	klug, intelligent	K
12	☐	lap	WLAN	L
13	☐	net	Netz	M
14	☐	app(lication)	App, Anwendung	N
15	☐	keyboard	Webseite	O

11th Grade Geography: Australia

Captain Arthur Phillip led a fleet of 11 British ships carrying convicts to the colony of New South Wales on January 26, 1788, effectively founding Australia. After overcoming a period of adversity, the fledgling colony began to commemorate this date with great fanfare, and it eventually became known as Australia Day. Australia Day has become increasingly contentious in recent years. It marks the beginning of the process by which the continent's Indigenous people were gradually evicted from their land as white colonization spread across the continent.

Australia, formerly known as New South Wales, was intended to be a penal colony. The British government appointed Arthur Phillip captain of the HMS Sirius in October 1786, and commissioned him to establish an agricultural work camp for British convicts there. Phillip had difficulty assembling the fleet that was to make the journey because he had no idea what to expect from the mysterious and distant land. His requests for more experienced farmers to help the penal colony were repeatedly denied, and he was both underfunded and underequipped. Nonetheless, Phillip led his 1,000-strong party, of which more than 700 were convicts, around Africa to the eastern side of Australia, accompanied by a small contingent of Marines and other officers. The voyage lasted eight months and claimed the lives of 30 men.

_____

Unscramble the words and then identify which capital city goes with each state/territory.

Victoria	Canberra	Western Australia	Adelaide	New South Wales	Perth
Australia Capital Territory	Hobart	Brisbane	South Australia	Sydney	Northern Territory
Tasmania	Darwin	Queensland	Melbourne		

1. rcotviia   _ _ _ _ _ _ i a

2. ldenneusaq Q u _ _ _ _ _ _ _ d

3. amsatani   T _ _ _ _ n _ _

4. rnrotenh etityrror   _ o _ _ h _ _ n T _ r _ _ _ _ _ _

5. tohsu lairustaa   _ _ _ t _ A _ _ t _ _ _ _ a

6. rteewns tlraaisua   _ e s _ _ _ _ _ _ _ _ _ _ _ i _

7. ratisaaul tcpiala oterytrri   _ _ _ _ _ a l _ _ _ a _ i _ a _ T _ _ _ _ t _ _ _

8. wne ohtus lswea   _ _ w _ _ _ t _ _ _ _ _ s

9. racnaebr   C _ _ _ _ _ r _

10. nyeyds   _ _ d n _ _

11. banibesr   _ _ _ s _ _ n _

12. aaleeddi   A _ _ _ _ _ d _

13. htepr   _ e _ _ _

14. bmlunroee _ _ _ _ _ u r _ _

15. batrho   _ _ _ a _ t

16. randiw   D a _ _ _ _

11th Grade Grammar: Preposition

Prepositional phrases are collections of words that contain prepositions. Remember that prepositions are words that indicate the relationships between different elements in a sentence, and you'll have no trouble identifying prepositional phrases.

Another way to look at it, a prepositional phrase is a group of words that function as a unified part of speech despite the absence of a verb or a subject. It is usually made up of a preposition and a noun or a preposition and a pronoun.

Under the rock is an example of a prepositional phrase. In this example, the preposition is "under," and the prepositional phrase is "under the rock."

_____

Choose the correct preposition.

up	up	off	out	through
down	on	away	together	off
about	out	upon	off	across

1. He pulled _____ his cancer treatment very well.

2. We must pull _____ to make this work.

3. Why don't you put _____ the yellow dress?

4. I have put _____ my holidays until later this year.

5. I don't know how she puts _____ with noisy children all day.

6. The CFS put _____ six fires today.

7. I feel quite run _____ since I got my cold.

8. I might go to Hobart to run _____ from this heat.

9. Coles has run _____ of bread today.

10. You need to set _____ writing your resume.

11. You will never guess who I ran _____ today!

12. I will go to the airport to see _____ my best friend.

13. He set _____ for Paris last Saturday.

14. The little dog was set _____ by a big dog.

15. Many students want to set _____ their own business.

11th Grade Geography Multiple Choice: Passport

Score: _____

Date: _____

Select the best answer for each question.

1. When traveling abroad, the most important item to take along is the _____.
   a. passport
   b. ticket
   c. ID

2. Passports usually expire after a period of _____ and thus need to be extended in time prior to your travels.
   a. five years
   b. six years
   c. ten years

3. The most powerful passport in the world is from which country?
   a. United Kingdom
   b. United Arab Emirates
   c. United States of America

4. In _____, _____ ordered the first US passports to be printed.
   a. 1901, John Edward Briscoe
   b. 15th century, King Henry V
   c. 1783, Benjamin Franklin

5. Standard passports contain _____ in most countries.
   a. 32 pages
   b. 52 pages
   c. 60 pages

6. The Emirati passport allows travel to _____ countries without visa.
   a. 38
   b. 157
   c. 179

7. The most expensive passports are from _____ in 2019.
   a. United States of America
   b. Australia
   c. United Arab Emirates

8. Citizens of the _____ state in Italy (the smallest country in the world!) carry passports, but there are no immigration control or border posts.
   a. Borogna
   b. Vatican
   c. Rome

9. In the UK, one passport is printed every ____! This allows for 5 million passports to be printed each year in the UK.
   a. 5 seconds
   b. 2.5 seconds
   c. 10 seconds

10. The _____ allows the visitor to remain in the foreign nation for a specific length of time.
    a. passport
    b. visas
    c. re-entry permit

11. US passports are valid for _____ for adults, but only _____ for persons under 16 years of age.
    a. 10 years ; 7 years
    b. 5 years ; 3 years
    c. 10 years ; 5 years

12. In what year did the United States also began producing a passport card, which, for less than the cost of a traditional passport book?
    a. 2002
    b. 1783
    c. 2008

11th Grade Geography Multiple Choice Quiz: 7 Continents

Select the best answer for each question.

1. **The continents are the huge landmasses that separated by the _____ of the oceans.**
    a. waters
    b. glaciers
    c. ice

2. **60% - 70% of the world's freshwater supply is stored in _____.**
    a. Antarctica
    b. Europe
    c. Asia

3. **It is the largest continent in size and has the biggest land area.**
    a. Asia
    b. Europe
    c. Africa

4. **The _____ continent has the most populous cities, where almost _____ people lived here.**
    a. Europe ; 5.3 billion
    b. Asian ; 4.6 billion
    c. Africa ; 1.4 billion

5. **What is the smallest continent on the planet?**
    a. Antarctica
    b. Australia/Oceania
    c. Asia

6. **This is the continent with the most countries which consists of 54 countries.**
    a. North America
    b. Australia
    c. Africa

7. **North America is a continent that is located entirely in the _____ and _____ hemispheres.**
    a. southern and western
    b. northern and western
    c. northern and eastern

8. **What continent is considered to be the wealthiest and richest continent?**
    a. Africa
    b. Europe
    c. North America

9. **_____ is a continent of many natural superlatives.**
    a. Antarctica
    b. South America
    c. North America

10. **What is the smallest continent by population numbers?**
    a. Australia
    b. Africa
    c. Antarctica

11. **This continent has the largest number of people who speak English either as their first language or as their second language fluently.**
    a. North America
    b. South America
    c. Europe

12. **_____ is the most active volcano in Antarctica.**
    a. Mount Melbourne
    b. Deception Island
    c. Mount Erebus

11th Grade Geography Multiple Choice Quiz: Argentina

Score: _____

Date: _____

Select the best answer for each question.

1. **Argentina is located on the _____ continent and borders Bolivia, Brazil, Chile, Paraguay, and Uruguay.**
   a. South American
   b. North American
   c. Central America

2. **About _____ people live in Argentina.**
   a. 46 million
   b. 460 million
   c. 55 million

3. **What type of government does Argentina have?**
   a. Oligarchy, Democracy
   b. Democracy, Republic
   c. Monarchy, Republic

4. **Argentina gained independence from _____ in 1816.**
   a. France
   b. Spain
   c. Portugal

5. **Argentina is the _____ country in South America after Brazil.**
   a. second largest
   b. third largest
   c. seventh largest

6. **The original flag of Argentina was adopted in _____.**
   a. 1816
   b. 1817
   c. 1812

7. **The name 'Argentina' comes from the _____ word 'argentum' which means silver.**
   a. British
   b. Latin
   c. Greek

8. **_____ of the people live in urban centres, which means cities and towns.**
   a. 92%
   b. 95%
   c. 91%

9. **This is the second largest city in Argentina and it is also one of the oldest cities in Argentina.**
   a. Rosario
   b. Córdoba
   c. Buenos Aires

10. **The official language used in Argentina is _____.**
   a. Spanish
   b. Italian
   c. French

11. **The _____, Argentina's longest river, forms a natural border between Paraguay and Argentina.**
   a. Uruguay River
   b. Negro River
   c. Paraná River

12. **The _____ is the second biggest wetland in the world after the Pantanal in Brazil.**
   a. Grand Affluents
   b. Okavango Delta
   c. Ibera Wetlands

11th Grade Geography
Multiple Choice Quiz: Costa Rica

Score: _____

Date: _____

Select the best answer for each question.

1. **The population of Costa Rica is _____.**
   a. 3.2 million people
   b. 5.1 million people
   c. 5.5 million people

2. **_____ is the official language of Costa Rica.**
   a. French
   b. Spanish
   c. Italian

3. **Costa Rica is a country on the _____ continent and is one of the countries in the region called Central America.**
   a. South American
   b. North American
   c. Central America

4. **_____ was the first European to set foot in Costa Rica.**
   a. Miguel Mora Porras
   b. José María Castro Madriz
   c. Christopher Columbus

5. **Costa Rica remained a _____ colony for almost 300 years.**
   a. Spanish
   b. English
   c. French

6. **In year _____, Costa Rica became an independent country.**
   a. 1563
   b. 1821
   c. 1838

7. **The total population of Costa Rica in 2021 is _____.**
   a. 5,047,561
   b. 5,470,561
   c. 5,740,615

8. **The capital of Costa Rica is _____ with _____ people.**
   a. Heredia with 356,000
   b. Limon with 63,081
   c. San José with 1.4 million

9. **The name Costa Rica comes from the _____ for Rich Coast**
   a. Greek
   b. Spanish
   c. Latin

10. **The climate of Costa Rica from December to April is _____.**
    a. summer season
    b. dry season
    c. rainy season

11. **Costa Rica's natural resources comes from _____.**
    a. Biomass
    b. Coal and petroleum
    c. Hydropower

12. **What is the standard currency in Costa Rica?**
    a. Costa Rican Colon
    b. Costa RIcan Dollar
    c. Costa Rican Peso

11th Grade Geography Multiple Choice Quiz: World Flags

Score: _____

Date: _____

Select the best answer for each question.

1. **The first flags were flown in the _____ to tell others that we own a piece of land and that we rule over the people and land.**
   a. 17th century
   b. 16th century
   c. 18th century

2. **_____ was the first man to set foot on the moon, taking the first steps in 1969 and erecting an American flag.**
   a. Wing Commander Rakesh Sharma AC
   b. Astronaut Buzz Aldrin
   c. Neil Armstrong

3. **The _____ flag is one of the only two square flags in the world.**
   a. Argentina
   b. Tunisia
   c. Swiss

4. **In ancient times and in the 4th century, the _____ symbolized the different points of the compass and later as the symbol of faith.**
   a. square
   b. cross
   c. sun

5. **The flag of _____, is the only world flag that is not rectangular or square shaped.**
   a. Vatican
   b. Nepal
   c. Switzerland

6. **This country uses a maple leave in its flag which shows that the country is caring for its nature and environment.**
   a. Belize
   b. Canada
   c. Cyprus

7. **The first men to climb and reach the top of the world's highest mountain, Mount Everest, put up the _____ when they reached the summit of Mount Everest in May 1953.**
   a. Swiss flag
   b. Five-starred Red Flag
   c. British 'Union Jack'

8. **When was the first flag raised on the moon?**
   a. June 20, 1699
   b. July 20, 1969
   c. August 20, 1969

9. **In combination with a star, the _____ represents divinity and especially the Islam.**
   a. moon
   b. triangle
   c. sun

10. **The triangle in a flag often also symbolizes _____ and _____.**
    a. energy and love
    b. strength and power
    c. unity and faith

11. **The three points of a triangle in flag represent the Trinity (Father, Son and Holy Spirit) in _____.**
    a. Christianity
    b. Islam
    c. Judaism

12. **The _____ color is a strong color in Islam, while in China, it is associated with good luck.**
    a. green
    b. red
    c. blue

11th Grade Health Multiple Choice Quiz: Heart

Select the best answer for each question.

1. **The human heart has _____ chambers or closed spaces.**
   - a. two
   - b. three
   - c. four

2. **The heart of a grown-up person weighs about _____.**
   - a. 8 to 12 ounces
   - b. 6 to 8 ounces
   - c. 8 to 10 ounces

3. **The heart is made up of _____ layers.**
   - a. five
   - b. three
   - c. four

4. **The _____ is the inner layer of the heart. This is the smooth, thin lining of the heart chambers.**
   - a. pericardium
   - b. endocardium
   - c. myocardium

5. **The _____ is the outer covering of the heart and is a strong sack that protects it.**
   - a. pericardium
   - b. endocardium
   - c. myocardium

6. **_____ occurs when the heart muscle contracts (pushes in).**
   - a. Diastole
   - b. Ventricular systole
   - c. Systole

7. **_____ is when the heart muscle relaxes (stops pushing in).**
   - a. Systole
   - b. Diastole
   - c. Ventricular systole

8. **_____ refers to the heart muscle.**
   - a. Myocardium
   - b. Endocardium
   - c. Pericardium

9. **The heart muscle beats at a rate of ___ beats per minute on average.**
   - a. 80
   - b. 70
   - c. 60

10. **The two bottom chambers of the heart are the _____ and the _____. These pump blood out of the heart to the body and lungs.**
    - a. right atrium, left atrium
    - b. right ventricle, left ventricle
    - c. pulmonary valve, aortic valve

11. **The two top chambers are the _____ and the _____. They receive the blood entering the heart.**
    - a. superior vena cava, aorta
    - b. right ventricle, left ventricle
    - c. right atrium, left atrium

12. **The main artery going out of the right ventricle is the _____.**
    - a. pulmonary artery
    - b. aorta
    - c. superior vena cava

11th Grade Science Multiple Choice Quiz: Noble Gases

Select the best answer for each question.

1. The noble gases are located to the far right of the periodic table and make up the _____.
   a. 16th column
   b. 18th column
   c. 17th column

2. Noble gases are _____, meaning each molecule is a single atom and almost never react with other elements.
   a. diatomic
   b. polyatomic
   c. monoatomic

3. The six noble gases are:
   a. Chlorine, bromine, iodine, astatine, tennessine
   b. Helium, hydrogen, radon, lithium, krypton, neon
   c. helium, neon, argon, krypton, xenon, and radon.

4. Helium is the second most abundant element in the universe after _____.
   a. radon
   b. hydrogen
   c. Argon

5. Xenon gets its name from the _____ word "xenos" which means "stranger or foreigner."
   a. Greek
   b. Latin
   c. Spanish

6. _____ has the lowest melting and boiling points of any substance.
   a. Neon
   b. Radon
   c. Helium

7. All of the noble gases except for _____ have stable isotopes.
   a. radon
   b. argon
   c. neon

8. This element is non-flammable and it is much safer to use in balloons than hydrogen.
   a. Krypton
   b. Helium
   c. Xenon

9. Many of the noble gases were either discovered or isolated by _____ chemist _____.
   a. Scottish, Sir William Ramsay
   b. Russian, Dmitri Mendeleev
   c. German, Robert Bunsen

10. Krypton gets its name from the _____ word "kryptos" meaning "_____".
    a. Greek; "sweet"
    b. Greek; "the hidden one."
    c. Greek; "lazy"

11. _____ , mixed with nitrogen, is used as a filler gas for incandescent light bulbs.
    a. Carbon monoxide
    b. Hydrogen
    c. Argon

12. _____, a highly radioactive element and is only available in minute amounts, is utilized in radiotherapy.
    a. Radon
    b. Carbon
    c. Uranium

11th Grade Science Multiple Choice Quiz: Alkali Metals

Select the best answer for each question.

1. The elements of the alkali metals include _____,
   ____, ____, ____, ____, and ____.
   a. magnesium, calcium, Radium, beryllium,
      silicon,and lithium
   b. lithium, sodium, potassium, rubidium, cesium,
      and francium
   c. radium, beryllium, lithium, sodium, calcium, and
      francium

2. The alkali metals are all in the _____ of the
   periodic table except for hydrogen.
   a. 1st column
   b. 2nd column
   c. 16th column

3. Alkali Metals have a _____ when compared to
   other metals.
   a. high density
   b. low density
   c. light density

4. The word "alkali" comes from the ____ word
   meaning "ashes."
   a. German
   b. Arabic
   c. Greek

5. ____ is the most important alkali metal.
   a. lithium
   b. sodium
   c. potassium

6. Alkali metals are generally stored in _____.
   a. oil
   b. soil
   c. water

7. All alkali metals have ____ atomic numbers.
   a. even
   b. odd
   c. prime

8. Potassium's atomic number is ___ and its symbol
   is ____.
   a. 19 and P
   b. 19 and K
   c. 11 and Na

9. Alkali metals are the ____in group one of the
   periodic systems.
   a. non metals
   b. chemical elements
   c. late transition metals

10. _____ is the lightest known metal.
    a. Sodium
    b. Lithium
    c. Francium

11th Grade Organisms Multiple Choice Quiz: Domestic Pig

Score: _____

Date: _____

Select the best answer for each question.

1. Domestic pigs are often _____ but small pigs kept as pets (pot-bellied pigs) are often other colors.
   a. white
   b. black
   c. pink

2. The dental formula of adult pigs is 3.1.4.3/3.1.4.3, giving a total of _____ teeth.
   a. 36
   b. 44
   c. 50

3. Pigs are_____ in the genus Sus
   a. reptiles
   b. amphibians
   c. mammals

4. _____ of piglet fatalities are due to the mother attacking, or unintentionally crushing, the newborn pre-weaned animals.
   a. 60%
   b. 50%
   c. 30%

5. The ancestor of the domestic pig is the _____, which is one of the most numerous and widespread large mammals.
   a. wild boar
   b. babirusa
   c. warthog

6. Pigs are _____, which means that they consume both plants and animals.
   a. omnivores
   b. herbivores
   c. carnivores

7. Pigs need a _____, _____ under a roof to sleep, and they should not be crowded.
   a. warm, muddy area
   b. warm, clean area
   c. cold, clean area

8. Piglets weigh about _____ at birth, and usually double their weight in one week.
   a. 1.5 kilograms
   b. 2.2 kilograms
   c. 1.1 kilograms

9. Pigs often roll in _____ to protect themselves from sunlight.
   a. water
   b. mud
   c. grass

10. Pigs are among the smartest of all domesticated animals and are even smarter than _____.
   a. dogs
   b. cats
   c. birds

11th Grade History Multiple Choice Quiz: The Emancipation Proclamation

Select the best answer for each question.

1. The Emancipation Proclamation was an order given on _____ by 16th US president to free the slaves.
   a. January 1, 1863
   b. December 6, 1865
   c. September 22, 1862

2. Only about _____ of the 4 million slaves were immediately set free.
   a. 60,000
   b. 50,000
   c. 39,000

3. The proclamation gained the Union the support of international countries such as _____ and _____ where slavery had already been abolished.
   a. Great Britain and France
   b. Missouri and Kentucky
   c. Delaware, and Maryland

4. The Emancipation Proclamation was an edict issued by U.S. President _____ that freed the slaves of the Confederate states in rebellion against the Union.
   a. James Madison
   b. George Washington
   c. Abraham Lincoln

5. When was the Thirteenth Amendment adopted and became part of the United States Constitution?
   a. September 17, 1862
   b. December 6, 1865
   c. December 18, 1864

6. _____ arrived on Virginia's shores in 1619, only a dozen years after the first white settlers.
   a. African Americans
   b. Latino Americans
   c. European Americans

7. The Emancipation Proclamation was _____.
   a. a constitutional order
   b. a formal order
   c. an executive order

8. The Emancipation Proclamation pave the way for the _____.
   a. 14th Amendment
   b. 12th Amendment
   c. 13th Amendment

9. Around _____ black soldiers fought on the side of the Union Army helping the North win the war.
   a. 100,000
   b. 150,000
   c. 200,000

10. Which states still had slavery after the Emancipation Proclamation?
    a. Virginia and Texas
    b. Delaware and Kentucky
    c. North Carolina and Ohio

11th Grade History Multiple Choice Quiz: The Battle of Fort Sumter

Score: _____

Date: _____

Select the best answer for each question.

1. **The Battle of Fort Sumter was the _____ of the American Civil War and signaled the start of the war.**
   a. second battle
   b. first battle
   c. third battle

2. **The Battle of Fort Sumter took place over two days from _____.**
   a. April 12–13, 1861.
   b. February 8-9, 1861
   c. August 28-29, 1861

3. **Fort Sumter is an island in _____ not far from Charleston.**
   a. Virginia
   b. California
   c. South Carolina

4. **The main commander from the North was Major _____.**
   a. Ulysses S. Grant
   b. Harriet Tubman
   c. Robert Anderson

5. **He was a student of Major Anderson's at the army school of West Point and the leader of the Southern forces.**
   a. Jefferson Davis
   b. General P. T. Beauregard
   c. Major Robert Anderson

6. **How many people died in the Battle of Fort Sumter?**
   a. 618,222
   b. 0
   c. 504

7. **Who is the former U.S. senator who'd pledged to drink the blood of casualties?**
   a. Stephen A. Douglas
   b. James Chesnut, Jr.,
   c. Charles Sumner

8. **8. The Northern states fell in behind Lincoln, while _____, _____ and _____ duly tumbled into the Confederacy.**
   a. Texas, North Carolina, and Pennsylvania
   b. Virginia, North Carolina, and Tennessee
   c. Virginia, Tennessee, and Massachusetts

9. **After many hours of bombardment, _____ realized that he had no chance to win the battle.**
   a. Harriet Tubman
   b. Robert Anderson
   c. General P. T. Beauregard

10. **How many states were there in the Confederate States of America?**
    a. 9
    b. 11
    c. 5

11. **Who was the president of the Confederate States of America during the American Civil War?**
    a. Andrew Johnson
    b. Abraham Lincoln
    c. Jefferson Davis

12. **What was the site of the Confederacy's largest prison camp for captured Union soldiers?**
    a. Rock Island
    b. Andersonville
    c. Attica

11th Grade History Multiple Choice Quiz: Siege of Vicksburg

Select the best answer for each question.

1. **Which army surrounded the city of Vicksburg, Mississippi during the siege and eventually took control?**
   a. Union Army
   b. South Army
   c. North Army

2. **The siege began on _____.**
   a. May 18, 1863
   b. April 26, 1865
   c. July 4, 1863.

3. **Who was the overall commander of the Confederate Army during the siege?**
   a. John Clifford Pemberton
   b. Theodore R. Davis
   c. John McClernand

4. **Around _____ people live in the city of Vicksburg today.**
   a. 36,000
   b. 17,000
   c. 24,000

5. **Which state did the Siege of Vicksburg took place?**
   a. Texas
   b. Mississippi
   c. California

6. **Around how long did the Siege of Vicksburg last?**
   a. Over 1 month
   b. Over one week
   c. One year

7. **The people of Vicksburg were _____ by the time they surrendered.**
   a. starving
   b. dehydrated
   c. sick

8. **Which side won the Siege of Vicksburg?**
   a. Neither side won
   b. North
   c. South

9. **Vicksburg was an important port city in which major river?**
   a. Mississippi River
   b. Missouri River
   c. Ohio River

10. **What other major battle did the Union won around the same time as the Siege of Vicksburg?**
    a. Battle of Gettysburg
    b. Battle of Ford Sumter
    c. Battle of the Ironclads

11. **Who was the overall commander of the Union Army in the battle?**
    a. Ulysses S. Grant
    b. Theodore R. Davis
    c. John Pemberton

12. **On what day did Vicksburg finally surrender to the Union army?**
    a. July 4, 1863
    b. July 21, 1863
    c. April 26, 1865

11th Grade History Multiple Choice Quiz: Renaissance

Score: _____

Date: _____

Select the best answer for each question.

1. Renaissance began in the 1300s, during the late _____.
   a. Ancient History
   b. Middle Ages
   c. Modern Eras

2. _____ and others from Spain and Portugal discovered two continents that had been unknown to Europeans.
   a. Christopher Columbus
   b. John Cabot
   c. Amerigo Vespucci

3. Renaissance is a French word meaning _____.
   a. resurrection
   b. rebirth
   c. renacimiento

4. The Age of Exploration, also called the _____, began in the 1400s and continued through the 1600s.
   a. Age of Investigation
   b. Age of Discovery
   c. Age of Enlightenment

5. The Age of Exploration began in the nation of _____ under the leadership of _____.
   a. Spain ; Francisco Pizarro
   b. Portugal ; Henry the Navigator
   c. Mexico ; Vasco da Gama

6. The early leaders in the Age of Exploration are _____ and ___.
   a. Portugal and Spain
   b. Mexico and China
   c. Africa and India

7. The Age of Exploration was one of the most important times in the history of _____.
   a. Philology
   b. world geography
   c. world historiography

8. Which technique was used by Leonardo da Vinci to add additional perspective and dimension to paintings?
   a. Use of light and dark
   b. Sfumato
   c. Balance and proportion

9. The main religion of Renaissance Europe was _____ and the main church was the _____.
   a. Confucianism; Confucian church
   b. Buddhism; Buddhist monastery
   c. Christianity; Catholic Church

10. _____ and _____ were popular forms of entertainment and a big part of Renaissance daily life.
   a. Reading and drawing
   b. Music and dancing
   c. Dancing and reading

11. The renaissance architecture style was taken from _____ and _____ and then altered to fit their current lifestyle.
   a. Ancient Roman Architecture and Egypt
   b. Ancient Rome and Greece
   c. Germany and India

12. What year did Johannes Gutenberg, a German, invented the printing press?
   a. 1458
   b. 1450
   c. 1374

11th Grade History Multiple Choice Quiz: American Civil War Weapons

Score: _____

Date: _____

Select the best answer for each question.

1. At the start of the war, many soldiers used old-style guns called _____.
   a. rifle
   b. lorenz rifle
   c. muskets

2. The _____ was a type of bullet that was used throughout the Civil War.
   a. cannonballs
   b. Enfield bullet
   c. Minie ball

3. The Civil War, and the major events leading up to the war, lasted from _____ to _____.
   a. 1853 to 1860
   b. 1950 to 1869
   c. 1860 to 1865

4. The Civil War was the first major war that involved _____.
   a. ironclad ships
   b. cannons
   c. submarines

5. The Civil War was the deadliest war in American history. There were around _____ soldiers killed in action and _____ total dead.
   a. 201,000 ; 657,000
   b. 210,000 ; 625,000
   c. 2,100,000 ; 1,064,000

6. What does Virginia's State Motto "Sic semper tyrannis" means?
   a. Public sentiment is everything
   b. Prelude to war
   c. Thus always to tyrants

7. Who was the 16th US president at the time of the American civil war?
   a. Ulysses S. Grant
   b. Abraham Lincoln
   c. James Buchanan

8. Which form of communication was popular on the home front during the civil war that people used to find out news of loved ones who were in the army?
   a. newspapers
   b. radio
   c. tabloid

9. The war began in Charleston, S.C., when Confederate artillery fired on Fort Sumter on _____.
   a. April 12, 1861
   b. February 15, 1862
   c. July 12, 1861

10. _____ was a famous nurse to the Union Troops. She was called the "Angel of the Battlefields" and founded the American Red Cross.
    a. Bull Run
    b. Dorethea Dix
    c. Clara Barton

11. Which of the following is best at destroying enemy fortification?
    a. bayonets
    b. swords
    c. cannons

12. Future steel tycoon _____ was in charge of the U.S. Military Telegraph Corps during the war.
    a. Andrew Carnegie
    b. Robert E. Lee
    c. Ulysses S. Grant

11th Grade Health Multiple Choice: Small Intestine

Select the best answer for each question.

1. The small intestine is between the _____ and the _____.
   a. stomach, large intestine
   b. gallbladder, pancreas
   c. liver, stomach

2. What are the three regions of small Intestine?
   a. cecum, colon, and the rectum
   b. duodenum, jejunum, and ileum
   c. ileum, colon, cecum

3. The _____ is the small intestine's final section. It is around 3m long and has villi comparable to the jejunum.
   a. cecum
   b. duodenum
   c. ileum

4. The _____ receives bile and juice from the pancreas and it is where most digestion takes place.
   a. ileum
   b. jejunum
   c. duodenum

5. The _____ is where digested products (sugars, amino acids, and fatty acids) are absorbed into the bloodstream.
   a. jejunum
   b. duodenum
   c. ileum

6. A small intestine can be ___ to ___ meters long in adults over the age of five.
   a. four to five meters
   b. five to six meters
   c. three to four meters

7. Food enters the small intestine after it leaves the _____.
   a. large intestine
   b. bile
   c. stomach

8. The ileum absorbs _____, bile salts, and any digestive products that were not absorbed by the jejunum.
   a. vitamin B12
   b. Iron
   c. vitamin B6

9. The small intestine is _____ to _____ long and coils like a maze.
   a. 35 to 37 feet
   b. 22 to 25 feet
   c. 18 to 20 feet

10. The_____ break down proteins and bile emulsifies fats into micelles.
    a. gastric juice
    b. digestive enzymes
    c. saliva

Reading Comprehension: Law Enforcement Dogs

Score: _____

Date: _____

Police dogs are dogs that assist cops in solving crimes. In recent years, they have grown to be an essential part of law enforcement. With their unique abilities and bravery, police dogs have saved many lives. They are often regarded as an important and irreplaceable part of many police departments because they are loyal, watchful, and protective of their police officer counterparts.

Today, police dogs are trained in specific areas. They could be considered experts in their field. Some of the particular police dog roles are as follows:

Tracking: Tracking police dogs use their keen sense of smell to locate criminal suspects or missing people. Tracking dogs are trained for years and can track down even the most elusive criminal. Without police tracking dogs, many suspects would be able to elude capture.

Substance Detectors: Like tracking dogs, these police dogs use their sense of smell to assist officers. Substance dogs are trained to detect a specific substance. Some dogs are trained to detect bombs or explosives. These brave dogs are trained not only to detect explosives but also to respond (very carefully!) and safely alert their officer partner to the explosive location. Other dogs may be drawn to illegal drugs. By quickly determining whether an illegal substance is nearby, these dogs save officers from searching through luggage, a car, or other areas by hand.

Public Order - These police dogs assist officers in keeping the peace. They may pursue a criminal suspect and hold them until an officer arrives, or they may guard an area (such as a jail or prison) to prevent suspects from fleeing.

Cadaver Dogs: Although it may sound disgusting, these police dogs are trained to locate dead bodies. This is a critical function in a police department, and these dogs perform admirably.

A police dog is not just any dog. Police dogs require very special and specialized training. There are numerous breeds of dogs that have been trained for police work. What breed they are often determined by the type of work they will do. German Shepherds and Belgian Malinois are two of the most popular breeds today, but other dogs such as Bloodhounds (good for tracking) and Beagles (good for drug detection) are also used. Police dogs, regardless of breed, are typically trained to do their job from the time they are puppies.

Typically, police dogs are regarded as heroes. They frequently go to live with their human partner police officer. They've known this person for years and have grown to consider them family, which works out well for both the officer and the dog.

1. Tracking police dogs use their _____ to locate criminal suspects or missing people.
   a. keen sense of training
   b. keen sense of taste
   c. keen sense of smell

2. Some substance dogs are trained to detect _____.
   a. runaway children
   b. bombs or explosives
   c. metal and iron

3. Police dogs are trained in ___ areas.
   a. many
   b. a few
   c. specific

4. Police dogs are dogs that assist cops in solving _____.
   a. littering
   b. homelessness
   c. crimes

5. Substance dogs are trained to detect a specific ____.
   a. substance
   b. person
   c. other police dogs

6. What type of police dog is trained pursue a criminal suspect and hold them until an officer arrives?
   a. Crime Fighting dog
   b. Tracking dog
   c. Public Order dog

7. These police dogs are trained to locate dead bodies
   a. Law and Order dogs
   b. Cadaver dogs
   c. Deadly Substance dogs

8. What are the two most popular police dogs used today?
   a. German Shepherds and Belgian Malinois
   b. Bloodhounds and German Shepherds
   c. Belgian Malinois and Rottweiler

English: Tenses

Verbs are classified into three tenses: past, present, and future. The term "past" refers to events that have already occurred (e.g., earlier in the day, yesterday, last week, three years ago). The present tense is used to describe what is happening right now or what is ongoing. The future tense refers to events that have yet to occur (e.g., later, tomorrow, next week, next year, three years from now).

borrowed	went	eat	play	go	giving
read	give	gave	will eat	yelled	seeing
will have	had	reading	will go	do	will borrow
playing	doing	yelling	did	will yell	will do
will give	fight	borrow	yell	will fight	will play
borrowing	played	fighting	read	have	will see
going	see	will read	fought	eating	ate
saw	having				

Simple Present (11)	Present Progressive (IS/ARE +) (11)	Past (11)	Future (11)

Music: Jimi Hendrix

Score: _____

Date: _____

First, read the entire passage. After that, go back and fill in the blanks. You can skip the blanks you're unsure about and finish them later.

guitar	odd	acoustic	mother	Animals
guitarist	stage	Seattle	rock	childhood

Jimi Hendrix, a _____, singer, and songwriter, wowed audiences in the 1960s with his outrageous electric guitar skills and experimental sound.

Jimi Hendrix began playing guitar as a teenager and grew up to become a _____ legend known for his innovative electric guitar playing in the 1960s. His performance of "The Star-Spangled Banner" at Woodstock in 1969 was one of his most memorable. Hendrix died of drug-related complications in 1970, leaving his imprint on the world of rock music and remaining popular to this day.

On November 27, 1942, in _____, Washington, Hendrix was born Johnny Allen Hendrix (later changed by his father to James Marshall). He had a difficult _____, living in the care of relatives or acquaintances at times.

When Hendrix was born, his _____, Lucille, was only 17 years old. She had a rocky relationship with his father, Al, and eventually left the family after the couple had two more sons, Leon and Joseph. Hendrix only saw his mother on rare occasions before her death in 1958.

Music became a haven for Hendrix in many ways. He was a fan of blues and rock and roll and taught himself to play the _____ with the help of his father.

When Hendrix was 16, his father bought him his first _____ guitar, and the following year, his first electric guitar - a right-handed Supro Ozark that he had to play upside down because he was naturally left-handed. Soon after, he started performing with his band, the Rocking Kings. In 1959, he dropped out of high school and worked _____ jobs while pursuing his musical dreams.

In mid-1966, Hendrix met Chas Chandler, bassist for the British rock band the _____, who agreed to become Hendrix's manager. Chandler persuaded Hendrix to travel to London, where he formed the Jimi Hendrix Experience with bassist Noel Redding and drummer Mitch Mitchell.

While performing in England, Hendrix amassed a cult following among the country's rock royalty, with the Beatles, Rolling Stones, Who, and Eric Clapton all praising his work. According to one critic for the British music magazine Melody Maker, he "had great _____ presence" and appeared to be playing "with no hands at all" at times.

According to one journalist in the Berkeley Tribe, "Nobody could get more out of an electric guitar than Jimi Hendrix. He was the ultimate guitarist."

History: The Mayflower

Score: _____

Date: _____

First, read the entire passage. After that, go back and fill in the blanks. You can skip the blanks you're unsure about and finish them later.

ship	sail	voyage	assist	settlers
passengers	illness	load	leaking	Cape

In 1620, a _____ called the Mayflower transported a group of English colonists to North America. These people established New England's first permanent European colony in what is now Plymouth, Massachusetts. Later, they were named the Pilgrims.

The Mayflower was approximately 106 feet long, 25 feet wide, and had a tonnage of 180. The deck of the Mayflower was about 80 feet long, roughly the length of a basketball court. The ship had three masts for holding sails:

The fore-mast (in front)

The main-mast (in the middle)

The mizzen mast (in the back) (back)

On August 4, 1620, the Mayflower and the Speedwell set sail from Southampton, England. They had to come to a halt in Dartmouth, however, because the Speedwell was leaking. They left Dartmouth on August 21, but the Speedwell began _____ again, and they came to a halt in Plymouth, England. They decided to abandon the Speedwell at Plymouth and _____ as many passengers as possible onto the Mayflower. On September 6, 1620, they set sail from Plymouth.

The Mayflower set _____ from Plymouth, England, west across the Atlantic Ocean. The ship's original destination was Virginia, but storms forced it to change course. On November 9, 1620, more than two months after leaving Plymouth, the Mayflower sighted _____ Cod. The Pilgrims decided to stay even though they were north of where they had planned to settle.

It is estimated that around 30 children were on board the Mayflower during the epic _____ to America, but little is known about many of them.

They were children of passengers, some traveled with other adults, and some were servants - but having young people among the _____ was critical to the Plymouth Colony's survival.

It is believed that when the colonists faced their first harsh winter of _____ and death in a new land, the children would _____ the adults by tending to the sick, assisting in the preparation of food, and fetching firewood and water.

While nearly half of the ship's _____ died during the winter of 1620/1621, it is believed that there were fewer deaths among the children, implying that the struggling colony had a better chance of thriving.

Health: The Food Groups

First, read the entire passage. After that, go back and fill in the blanks. You can skip the blanks you're unsure about and finish them later.

produce	consume	yogurt	stored	bones
repair	water	portion	vitamins	fiber

Eating healthy foods is especially important for children because they are still developing. Children's bodies require nutrition to develop strong, healthy _____ and muscles. You will not grow as tall or as strong as you could if you do not get all the _____ and minerals you require while growing.

Healthy food includes a wide variety of fresh foods from the five healthy food groups:

Dairy: Milk, cheese, and _____ are the most critical dairy foods, which are necessary for strong and healthy bones. There aren't many other foods in our diet that have as much calcium as these.

Fruit: Fruit contains vitamins, minerals, dietary fiber, and various phytonutrients (nutrients found naturally in plants) that help your body stay healthy. Fruits and vegetables provide you with energy, antioxidants, and _____. These nutrients help protect you against diseases later in life, such as heart disease, stroke, and some cancers.

Vegetables and legumes/beans: Vegetables should account for a large _____ of your daily food intake and should be encouraged at all meals (including snack times). To keep your body healthy, they supply vitamins, minerals, dietary fiber, and phytonutrients (nutrients found naturally in plants).

Grain (cereal) foods: choose wholegrain and/or high _____ bread, cereals, rice, pasta, noodles, and so on. These foods provide you with the energy you require to grow, develop, and learn. Refined grain products (such as cakes and biscuits) can contain added sugar, fat, and sodium.

Protein from lean meats and poultry, fish, eggs, tofu, nuts and seeds, and legumes/beans is used by our bodies to _____ specialized chemicals such as hemoglobin and adrenalin. Protein also helps to build, maintain, and _____ tissues in our bodies. Protein is the primary component of muscles and organs (such as your heart).

Calories are a unit of measurement for the amount of energy in food. We gain calories when we eat, which gives us the energy to run around and do things. If we _____ more calories than we expend while moving, our bodies will store the excess calories as fat. If we burn more calories than we consume, our bodies will begin to burn the previously _____ fat.

Art: J. M. W. Turner

Joseph Mallord William Turner, also known as William Turner, was an English Romantic painter, printmaker, and watercolorist. He is well-known for his expressive colorizations, imaginative landscapes, and turbulent, often violent sea paintings.

On April 23, 1775, J. M. W. Turner was born above his father's barbershop in London, England. When Joseph was a child, he began to draw pictures. He enjoyed drawing outside scenes, particularly buildings. His father's shop sold some of his drawings.

He began attending the Royal Academy of Art in London when he was fourteen years old. He kept sketching and painting with watercolors. Many of his sketches were published in magazines. While he mostly drew buildings and architecture, he also began to draw some seascapes.

In 1796, Turner completed his first oil painting. Fishermen at Sea was the title. Turner gained a national reputation as a talented artist as a result of the painting's critical acclaim. Many people compared his work to that of other well-known painters.

Turner was captivated by the power of God in natural scenes, particularly the ocean and the sun. He would make numerous sketches in numbered notebooks, which he would then reference when painting in his studio. He frequently included people in his paintings, but they were small and insignificant compared to the power of nature around them.

Turner's work evolved, with less emphasis on detail and more emphasis on the energy of the natural phenomenon he was painting, such as the sea, a storm, a fire, or the sun. The paintings' objects became less recognizable.

The painting Rain, Steam, and Speed is an example of this. Light and mist are used to power the train engine as it moves down the track in this landscape of a locomotive crossing a bridge. The focus is on the color and changing light as the train passes through the landscape.

Many of Turner's later works are reminiscent of the Impressionist style of painting that would emerge in France in the coming years. Turner's work undoubtedly influenced artists like Monet, Degas, and Renoir.

Many art historians regard J. M. W. Turner as the most incredible landscape painter of all time. His artwork had a significant influence on many artists who came after him, including many impressionists.

1. Turner's later works are reminiscent of the _____ style of painting.
   a. Impressionist
   b. Watercolor

2. In 1796, Turner completed his first _____painting.
   a. colored
   b. oil

3. Turner began attending the _____ of Art in London.
   a. Royal State University
   b. Royal Academy

4. Turner was born above his father's _____.
   a. mechanic shop
   b. barbershop

5. J. M. W. Turner was an English Romantic painter, _____, and watercolorist.
   a. teacher
   b. printmaker

6. Turner frequently included _____ in his painting.
   a. animals
   b. people

Weather and Climate

The difference between weather and climate is simply a matter of time. Weather refers to the conditions of the atmosphere over a short period of time, whereas climate refers to how the atmosphere "behaves" over a longer period of time.

When we discuss climate change, we are referring to changes in long-term averages of daily weather. Today's children are constantly told by their parents and grandparents about how the snow was always piled up to their waists as they trudged off to school. Most children today have not experienced those kinds of dreadful snow-packed winters. The recent changes in winter snowfall indicate that the climate has changed since their parents were children.

Weather is essentially the atmosphere's behavior, particularly in terms of its effects on life and human activities. The distinction between weather and climate is that weather refers to short-term (minutes to months) changes in the atmosphere, whereas climate refers to long-term changes. Most people associate weather with temperature, humidity, precipitation, cloudiness, brightness, visibility, wind, and atmospheric pressure, as in high and low pressure.

Weather can change from minute to minute, hour to hour, day to day, and season to season in most places. However, the climate is the average of weather over time and space. A simple way to remember the distinction is that climate is what you expect, such as a very hot summer, whereas weather is what you get, such as a hot day with pop-up thunderstorms.

Use the word bank to unscramble the words!

Pressure	Density	Cloudy	Latitude	Elevation	Weather
Absorb	Humid	Precipitation	Windy	Forecast	Climate
Sunshine	Temperature				

1. IUMHD   _ u _ _ _

2. UDLOYC   _ l _ u _ _

3. FSEATOCR   _ _ _ _ _ a _ t

4. UDLTITAE   L _ _ _ _ u _ _

5. IEOCAIIPPTRNT   _ _ _ _ _ _ t _ _ _ o n

6. TEEERPAURMT   T _ _ _ e _ _ t _ _ _

7. RSEREUPS   _ r e _ _ _ _ _

8. LEICATM   _ _ i _ _ t _

9. SNNIEHUS   S _ _ _ _ i _ _

10. OBBASR   _ b s _ _ _

11. VETIEOANL   _ _ _ _ a t _ _ _

12. EATWRHE   W _ _ _ _ e _

13. NDWIY   _ _ _ _ y

14. TYNEIDS   _ _ _ _ i _ y

Science: Vertebrates

To begin, all animals are classified as either vertebrates or invertebrates. Invertebrates lack a backbone, whereas vertebrates do. Scientists can't stop there, because each group contains thousands of different animals! As a result, scientists divide vertebrates and invertebrates into increasingly smaller groups. Let's talk about vertebrates and some of their classifications.

Vertebrates range in size from a frog to a blue whale. Because there are at least 59,000 different types of vertebrates on the planet, they are further classified into five major groups: mammals, birds, fish, amphibians, and reptiles. Remember that animals are classified into these groups based on what they have in common. Why is an elephant classified as a mammal while a crocodile is classified as a reptile? Let's go over some of the characteristics of each vertebrate group.

Warm-blooded animals are mammals. This means that their bodies maintain their temperature, which is usually higher than the temperature of the surrounding air. They also have hair or fur; they have lungs to breathe air; that they feed milk to their babies; and that most give birth to live young, rather than laying eggs, as a dog does.

- Birds have feathers, two wings (though not all birds, such as the ostrich and penguin, can fly), are warm-blooded, and lay eggs.
- Fish have fins or scales, live in water, and breathe oxygen through gills.
- Like salamanders and frogs, Amphibians have smooth, moist skin (amphibians must keep their skin wet); lay eggs in water; most breathe through their skin and lungs.
- Reptiles have scales (imagine a scaly lizard), are cold-blooded (their body temperature changes as the temperature around them changes), breathe air. Most reptiles, including the crocodile and snake, lay hard-shelled eggs on land.

Vertebrates play several vital roles in an ecosystem. Many predator species are large vertebrates in ecosystems. Lions, eagles, and sharks are examples of predatory vertebrates. Many prey species in ecosystems are also vertebrates. Mice, rabbits, and frogs are examples of these animals. Many vertebrates serve as scavengers in ecosystems. They are significant because they remove dead animals from the environment. Turkey vultures and hyenas, for example, are both vertebrate scavengers. Furthermore, many vertebrates serve as pollinators in ecosystems. Bats and monkeys, for example, may aid in pollen spread by visiting various trees and plants.

Humans value vertebrates for a variety of reasons. Vertebrates are domesticated animals used by humans. These animals are capable of producing milk, food, and clothing. They can also help with work. Agricultural animals are usually vertebrates. Humans also hunt a variety of wild vertebrate animals for food.

1. Vertebrates range in _____ from a frog to a blue whale.
   a. age
   b. size

2. Fish have fins or scales, live in water, and breathe ___ through gills.
   a. oxygen
   b. water

3. Invertebrates lack a _____, whereas vertebrates _____.
   a. skin, whereas vertebrates do
   b. backbone, whereas vertebrates do

4. Warm-blooded animals are _____.
   a. mammals
   b. producers

5. Some vertebrates serve as _____, they remove dead animals from the environment.
   a. scavengers
   b. invertebrates

6. Lions, eagles, and sharks are examples of _____ vertebrates.
   a. ecofriendly
   b. predatory

7. _____ animals are capable of producing milk, food, and clothing.
   a. Non-producing
   b. Domesticated

8. Many vertebrates serve as _____ in ecosystems, they may aid in pollen spread by visiting various trees and plants.
   a. water lilies
   b. pollinators

Science: Organelles

Do you and your dog have a similar appearance? We are all aware that people and dogs appear to be very different on the outside. However, there are some similarities on the inside. Cells make up all animals, including humans and dogs.

All animal cells appear to be the same. They have a cell membrane that contains cytoplasm, which is a gooey fluid. Organelles float in the cytoplasm. Organelles function as tiny machines that meet the needs of the cell. The term organelle refers to a "miniature organ." This lesson will teach you about the various organelles found in animal cells and what they do.

The nucleus of the cell is the cell's brain. It is in charge of many of the cell's functions. The nucleus is where DNA, the genetic instructions for building your body, is stored. DNA contains vital information! Your nucleus has its membrane to protect this essential information, similar to the membrane that surrounds the entire cell.

Your cells require energy. Energy is produced by mitochondria, which are oval-shaped organelles. Mitochondria convert the nutrients that enter the cell into ATP. Your cells use ATP for energy. Because they are the cell's powerhouses, you might think of these organelles as the mighty mitochondria.

The nutrients must be digested before they can be converted into energy by the mitochondria. Digestion is carried out by a group of organelles known as lysosomes. Digestive enzymes are found in lysosomes. Enzymes can sometimes be released into the cell. Because the enzymes kill the cell, lysosomes are known as "suicide bags."

Use Google or your preferred source to help match each term with a definition.

1		nucleus	responsible for chromosome segregation	A
2		lysosomes	degradation of proteins and cellular waste	B
3		Golgi Apparatus	protein synthesis	C
4		Mitochondria	lipid synthesis	D
5		SER	site of photosynthesis	E
6		RER	stores water in plant cells	F
7		Microtubules	prevents excessive uptake of water, protects the cell (in plants)	G
8		ribosomes	degradation of H2O2	H
9		peroxysomes	powerhouse of the cell	I
10		cell wall	modification of proteins; "post-office" of the cell	J
11		chloroplast	protein synthesis + modifications	K
12		central vacuole	where DNA is stored	L

Science: Invertebrates

Invertebrates can be found almost anywhere. Invertebrates account for at least 95% of all animals on the planet! Do you know what one thing they all have in common? Invertebrates lack a backbone.

Your body is supported by a backbone, which protects your organs and connects your other bones. As a result, you are a vertebrate. On the other hand, invertebrates lack the support of bones, so their bodies are often simpler, softer, and smaller. They are also cold-blooded, which means their body temperature fluctuates in response to changes in the air or water around them.

Invertebrates can be found flying, swimming, crawling, or floating and provide essential services to the environment and humans. Nobody knows how many different types of invertebrates there are, but there are millions!

Just because an invertebrate lacks a spinal column does not mean it does not need to eat. Invertebrates, like all other forms of animal life, must obtain nutrients from their surroundings. Invertebrates have evolved two types of digestion to accomplish this. The use of intracellular digestion is common in the most simple organisms. The food is absorbed into the cell and broken down in the cytoplasm at this point. Extracellular digestion, in which cells break down food through the secretion of enzymes and other techniques, is used by more advanced invertebrates. All vertebrates use extracellular digestion.

Still, all animals, invertebrates or not, need a way to get rid of waste. Most invertebrates, especially the simplest ones, use the process of diffusion to eliminate waste. This is merely the opposite of intracellular digestion. However, more advanced invertebrates have more advanced waste disposal mechanisms. Similar to our kidneys, specialized glands in these animals filter and excrete waste. But there is a happy medium. Even though some invertebrates do not have complete digestive tracts like vertebrates, they do not simply flush out waste through diffusion. Instead, the mouth doubles as an exit.

Scientists have classified invertebrates into numerous groups based on what the animals have in common. Arthropods have segmented bodies, which means that they are divided into sections. Consider an ant!

Arthropods are the most numerous group of invertebrates. They can live on land, as spiders and insects do, or in water, as crayfish and crabs do. Because insects are the most numerous group of arthropods, many of them fly, including mosquitoes, bees, locusts, and ladybugs.

They also have jointed legs or limbs to help them walk, similar to how you have knees for your legs and elbows for your arms. The majority of arthropods have an exoskeleton, tough outer skin, or shell that protects their body. Have you ever wondered why when you squish a bug, it makes that crunching sound? That's right; it's the exoskeleton!

Mollusks are the second most numerous group of invertebrates. They have soft bodies and can be found on land or in water. Shells protect the soft bodies of many mollusks, including snails, oysters, clams, and scallops. However, not all, such as octopus, squid, and cuttlefish, have a shell.

1. Invertebrates lack a _____.
   a. backbone
   b. tailbone

2. Invertebrates are also ____.
   a. cold-blooded
   b. warm-blooded

3. _____ can live on land, as spiders and insects do, or in water, as crayfish and crabs do.
   a. Vertebrates
   b. Arthropods

4. All animals, invertebrates or not, need a way to get rid of ____.
   a. their skin
   b. waste

5. _____ have soft bodies and can be found on land or in water.
   a. Arthropods
   b. Mollusks

6. Just because an invertebrate lacks a _____ column does not mean it does not need to eat.
   a. spinal
   b. tissues

7. Your body is supported by a backbone, which protects your ____ and connects your other bones.
   a. organs
   b. muscles

8. Invertebrates lack the support of bones, so their bodies are often simpler, ___, and smaller.
   a. softer and bigger
   b. softer and smaller

Score: _____

Music: Musical Terms

Date: _____

Complete the crossword by filling in a word that fits each clue. Fill in the correct answers, one letter per square, both across and down, from the given clues. There will be a gray space between multi-word answers.

Tip: Solve the easy clues first, and then go back and answer the more difficult ones.

Across

2. the highest adult male singing voice; singing falsetto
4. the part of a song that transitions between two main parts
5. a combination of three or more tones sounded simultaneously
8. making up the song or melody as you play
11. a song written for one or more instruments playing solo
12. the highest of the singing voices
13. is a poem set to music with a recurring pattern of both rhyme and meter
14. timing or speed of the music

Down

1. singing without any instruments
3. low, the lowest of the voices and the lowest part of the harmony
6. to play a piece of music sweetly, tender, adoring manner
7. the sound of two or more notes heard simultaneously
9. is a musical interval; the distance between one note
10. played by a single musical instrument or voice
15. a range of voice that is between the bass and the alto
16. the repeating changing of the pitch of a note

CHORD BRIDGE ALTO
HARMONY SOPRANO
IMPROVISATION DOLCE
OCTAVE VIBRATO STANZA
SONATA A CAPPELLA TEMPO
BASS SOLO TENOR

History: The Vikings

Score: _____

Date: _____

First, read the entire passage. After that, go back and fill in the blanks. You can skip the blanks you're unsure about and finish them later.

sail	settle	North	Christianity	raided
Middle	defeated	shallow	cargo	Denmark

During the _____ Ages, the Vikings lived in Northern Europe. They first settled in the Scandinavian lands that are now Denmark, Sweden, and Norway. During the Middle Ages, the Vikings played a significant role in Northern Europe, particularly during the Viking Age, which lasted from 800 CE to 1066 CE.

In Old Norse, the word Viking means "to raid." The Vikings would board their longships and _____ across the seas to raid villages on Europe's northern coast, including islands like Great Britain. In 787 CE, they first appeared in England to raid villages. When the Vikings _____, they were known to attack defenseless monasteries. This earned them a bad reputation as barbarians, but monasteries were wealthy and undefended Viking targets.

The Vikings eventually began to _____ in areas other than Scandinavia. They colonized parts of Great Britain, Germany, and Iceland in the ninth century. They spread into northeastern Europe, including Russia, in the 10th century. They also established Normandy, which means "Northmen," along the coast of northern France.

By the beginning of the 11th century, the Vikings had reached the pinnacle of their power. Leif Eriksson, son of Erik the Red, was one Viking who made it to _____ America. He established a brief settlement in modern-day Canada. This was thousands of years before Columbus.

The English and King Harold Godwinson _____ the Vikings, led by King Harald Hardrada of Norway, in 1066. The defeat in this battle is sometimes interpreted as the end of the Viking Age. The Vikings stopped expanding their territory at this point, and raids became less frequent.

The arrival of Christianity was a major factor at the end of the Viking age. The Vikings became more and more a part of mainland Europe as Scandinavia was converted to _____ and became a part of Christian Europe. Sweden's, Denmark's, and Norway's identities and borders began to emerge as well.

The Vikings were perhaps best known for their ships. The Vikings built longships for exploration and raiding. Longships were long, narrow vessels built for speed. Oars primarily propelled them but later added a sail to help in windy conditions. Longships had a shallow draft, which allowed them to float in _____ water and land on beaches.

The Vikings also built _____ ships known as Knarr for trading. The Knarr was wider and deeper than the longship, allowing it to transport more cargo.

Five recovered Viking ships can be seen at the Viking Ship Museum in Roskilde, _____. It's also possible to see how the Vikings built their ships. The Vikings used a shipbuilding technique known as clinker building. They used long wood planks that overlapped along the edges.

Fun Facts:

- The Viking is the mascot of the Minnesota Vikings of the National Football League.
- Certain Vikings fought with monstrous two-handed axes. They are capable of easily piercing a metal helmet or shield.

Geography: Canada

Canada is the world's second-largest country, covering 10 million square kilometers. Canada's borders are bounded by three oceans: the Pacific Ocean to the west, the Atlantic Ocean to the east, and the Arctic Ocean to the north. The Canada-United States border runs along Canada's southern border.

Queen Victoria, Queen Elizabeth II's great-great-grandmother, chose Ottawa, which is located on the Ottawa River, as the capital in 1857. It is now the fourth largest metropolitan area in Canada. The National Capital Region, which encompasses 4,700 square kilometers around Ottawa, preserves and improves the area's built heritage and natural environment.

Canada is divided into ten provinces and three territories. Each province and territory has a separate capital city. You should be familiar with the capitals of your province or territory, as well as those of Canada.

Below are some of Canada's Territories, Provinces, and Capital Cities. Draw a line through each word you find.

```
R  L  U  G  M  A  N  I  T  O  B  A  N  K  M  E  X  L  S  P
W  K  A  K  B  B  H  A  L  B  E  R  T  A  G  D  K  P  R  R
Q  M  N  Y  N  X  W  I  S  Z  L  X  B  Q  E  K  B  T  X  I
I  Q  A  L  U  I  T  E  G  I  R  T  O  R  O  N  T  O  Y  N
A  B  R  I  T  I  S  H  C  O  L  U  M  B  I  A  E  C  E  C
V  N  N  R  S  Q  H  G  I  W  I  N  N  I  P  E  G  H  L  E
S  O  G  X  Z  G  A  O  N  T  A  R  I  O  F  B  R  A  L  E
T  V  Q  Z  E  D  M  O  N  T  O  N  C  D  F  W  Q  R  O  D
.  A  V  H  B  E  F  R  E  D  E  R  I  C  T  O  N  L  W  W
J  S  V  P  O  Q  U  E  B  E  C  C  I  T  Y  N  W  O  K  A
O  C  Y  J  R  W  S  H  V  C  V  Q  H  W  W  U  L  T  N  R
H  O  E  L  E  E  B  A  A  Z  O  U  Q  G  H  N  V  T  I  D
N  T  W  X  G  A  Q  L  S  T  J  E  F  H  I  A  I  E  F  I
·  I  K  M  I  D  C  I  L  X  L  B  U  V  T  V  C  T  E  S
S  A  C  P  N  C  O  F  T  Z  M  E  U  E  E  U  T  O  N  L
P  Q  Y  F  A  P  L  A  G  P  Y  C  F  M  H  T  O  W  B  A
I  W  S  D  R  Y  W  X  G  W  P  U  E  U  O  G  R  N  M  N
Y  N  E  W  B  R  U  N  S  W  I  C  K  T  R  P  I  C  R  D
R  X  B  T  E  R  V  Y  J  B  H  H  M  K  S  W  A  J  N  Z
G  F  S  A  S  K  A  T  C  H  E  W  A  N  E  Y  U  K  O  N
```

Yukon	Nunavut	Nova Scotia	Prince Edward Island	New Brunswick
Quebec	Ontario	Manitoba	Saskatchewan	Alberta
British Columbia	Victoria	Edmonton	Regina	Winnipeg
Toronto	Quebec City	Fredericton	Charlottetown	Halifax
St. John's	Iqaluit	Yellowknife	Whitehorse	

Environmental Health: Water Pollution

First, read the entire passage. After that, go back and fill in the blanks. You can skip the blanks you're unsure about and finish them later.

naturally	spills	toxic	crops	causes
streams	Gulf	wastewater	Acid	ill

Water pollution occurs when waste, chemicals, or other particles cause a body of water (e.g., rivers, oceans, lakes) to become _____ to the fish and animals that rely on it for survival. Water pollution can also disrupt and hurt nature's water cycle.

Water pollution can occur _____ due to volcanoes, algae blooms, animal waste, and silt from storms and floods.

Human activity contributes significantly to water pollution. Sewage, pesticides, fertilizers from farms, wastewater and chemicals from factories, silt from construction sites, and trash from people littering are some human _____.

Oil _____ have been some of the most well-known examples of water pollution. The Exxon Valdez oil spill occurred when an oil tanker collided with a reef off the coast of Alaska, causing over 11 million gallons of oil to spill into the ocean. Another major oil spill was the Deepwater Horizon oil spill, which occurred when an oil well exploded, causing over 200 million gallons of oil to spill into the _____ of Mexico.

Water pollution can be caused directly by air pollution. When sulfur dioxide particles reach high altitudes in the atmosphere, they can combine with rain to form acid rain. _____ rain can cause lakes to become acidic, killing fish and other animals.

The main issue caused by water pollution is the impact on aquatic life. Dead fish, birds, dolphins, and various other animals frequently wash up on beaches, killed by pollutants in their environment. Pollution also has an impact on the natural food chain. Small animals consume contaminants like lead and cadmium.

Clean water is one of the most valuable and essential commodities for life on Earth. Clean water is nearly impossible to obtain for over 1 billion people on the planet. They can become _____ from dirty, polluted water, which is especially difficult for young children. Some bacteria and pathogens in water can make people sick to the point of death.

Water pollution comes from a variety of sources. Here are a few of the main reasons:
Sewage: In many parts of the world, sewage is still flushed directly into _____ and rivers. Sewage can introduce dangerous bacteria that can make humans and animals very sick.

Farm animal waste: Runoff from large herds of farm animals such as pigs and cows can enter the water supply due to rain and large storms.

Pesticides: Pesticides and herbicides are frequently sprayed on _____ to kill bugs, while herbicides are sprayed to kill weeds. These potent chemicals can enter the water through rainstorm runoff. They can also contaminate rivers and lakes due to unintentional spills.

Construction, floods, and storms: Silt from construction, earthquakes, and storms can reduce water oxygen levels and suffocate fish.

Factories: Water is frequently used in factories to process chemicals, keep engines cool, and wash things away. Sometimes used _____ is dumped into rivers or the ocean. It may contain pollutants.

Health Spelling Words:
Healthy Routines

Write the correct word for each sentence.

Reading	overeat	Eating	read	fat
fresh	fruit	health	glass	chair
floss	Breakfast	Staying	daily	Sleep
fiber	enough	burn	Walking	body

1. Creating a healthy _____ routine is simple.

2. _____ hydrated is vital for our health.

3. Exercise has tremendous _____ benefits.

4. Exposure to the sun enables the _____ to produce vitamin D.

5. _____ is one of the most underrated healthy habits you can do.

6. Vegetables are low in calories, yet high in vitamins, minerals, and _____.

7. _____ has benefits to both your physical and mental health.

8. _____ is the only time during the day where our bodies are able to relax, unwind and recover.

9. _____ a variety of good foods.

10. _____ is the most important meal of the day.

11. Drink a _____ of water.

12. Sitting in your _____ all day long isn't good for you.

13. Excess body _____ comes from eating more than we need.

14. Cooking the right amount makes it easier to not _____.

15. Physical activity helps us _____ off the extra calories.

16. Eat _____ instead of eating a candy bar.

17. Make time to _____ every day.

18. Don't forget to _____.

19. Swap sugary desserts for _____ fruit.

20. Get _____ sleep.

Science: Titanium (Ti) Element

Titanium is the first element in the periodic table's fourth column. It is a transition metal. Titanium atoms contain 22 protons and 22 electrons.

Titanium is a complex, light, silvery metal under normal conditions. It can be brittle at room temperature, but it becomes more bendable and pliable as the temperature rises.

Titanium's high strength-to-weight ratio is one of its most desirable properties. This means it is both extremely strong and lightweight. Titanium is double the strength of aluminum but only 60% heavier. It is also as strong as steel but weighs a fraction of the weight.

Compared to other metals, titanium is relatively non-reactive and highly resistant to corrosion caused by different metals and chemicals such as acids and oxygen. As a result, it has relatively low thermal and electrical conductivity.

Titanium is not found in nature as a pure element but rather as a compound found in the Earth's crust as a component of many minerals. According to the International Atomic Energy Agency, it is the ninth most prevalent element in the Earth's crust. Rutile and ilmenite are the two most essential minerals for titanium mining. Australia, South Africa, and Canada are the top producers of these ores.

Titanium is mostly used in the form of titanium dioxide (TiO2). Tio2 is a white powder used in various industrial applications such as white paint, white paper, white polymers, and white cement.

Metals like iron, aluminum, and manganese are combined with titanium to create strong and lightweight alloys that can be utilized in spacecraft, naval vessels, missiles, and armor plating. Due to its corrosion resistance, it is particularly well-suited for seawater applications.

The biocompatibility of titanium is another valuable property of the metal. This indicates that the human body will not reject it. Together with its strength, durability, and lightweight, titanium is a good material for medical applications. It is utilized in various applications, including hip and dental implants. Titanium is also utilized in the manufacture of jewelry, such as rings and watches.

Reverend William Gregor recognized titanium as a new element for the first time in 1791. As a hobby, the English clergyman was fascinated by minerals. He coined the term menachanite for the element. M.H. Kalproth, a German chemist, eventually altered the name to titanium. M. A. Hunter, an American scientist, was the first to create pure titanium in 1910.

Titanium is named after the Greek gods Titans.

Titanium has five stable isotopes: titanium-46, titanium-47, titanium-48, titanium-49, and titanium-50. The isotope titanium-48 accounts for the vast bulk of titanium found in nature.

1. Titanium has five stable _____.
   a. isotopes
   b.

2. Titanium is the first element in the periodic table's _____ column.
   a. 4rd
   b. fourth

3. Titanium is a transition _____.
   a. metal
   b.

4. Titanium is mostly used in the form of _____ (TiO2).
   a. titanium dioxide
   b. dioxide oxygen

Proofreading Skills: Volunteering

In this activity, you'll see lots of grammatical *errors*. Correct all the grammar mistakes you see.

There are **10** mistakes in this passage. 3 capitals missing. 4 unnecessary capitals. 3 incorrect homophones.

Your own life can be changed and the lives of others, through volunteer work. to cope with the news that there has been a disaster, you can volunteer to help those in need. Even if you can't contribute financially, you can donate you're time instead.

Volunteering is such an integral part of the American culture that many high schools require their students to participate in community service to graduate.

When you volunteer, you have the freedom to choose what you'd like to do and who or what you think is most deserving of your time. Start with these ideas if you need a little inspiration. We've got just a few examples here.

Encourage the growth and development of young people. Volunteer as a Camp counselor, a Big Brother or Big Sister, or an after-school sports program. Special Olympics games and events are excellent opportunities to know children with special needs.

Spend the holidays doing good deeds for others. Volunteer at a food bank or distribute toys to children in need on Thanksgiving Day, and you'll be doing your part to help those in need. your church, temple, mosque, or another place of worship may also require your assistance.

You can visit an animal shelter and play with the Animals. Volunteers are critical to the well-being of shelter animals. (You also get a good workout when you walk rescued dogs.)

Become a member of a political campaign. Its a great way to learn more about the inner workings of politics if your curious about it. If you are not able To cast a ballot, you can still help elect your preferred candidate.

Help save the planet. Join a river preservation group and lend a hand. Participate in a park cleanup day in your community. Not everyone is cut out for the great outdoors; if you can't see yourself hauling trees up a hill, consider working in the park's office or education center instead.

Take an active role in promoting health-related causes. Many of us know someone afflicted with a medical condition (like cancer, HIV, or diabetes, for example). a charity that helps people with a disease, such as delivering meals, raising money, or providing other assistance, can make you Feel good about yourself.

Find a way to combine your favorite things if you have more than one. For example, if you're a fan of kids and have a talent for arts and crafts, consider volunteering at a children's hospital.

Jackie Robinson: The First African-American Player In MLB

First, read over the entire passage(s). Then go back and fill in the blanks. You can skip the blanks you're unsure about and come back to them later.

Roosevelt	general	Pasadena	paved	Dodgers
honorable	Rookie	major	Texas	enthusiast
League	prejudice	batting	military	football

On January 31, 1919, in Cairo, Georgia, Jack _____ Robinson was born. There were five children in the family, and the youngest one was him. After Jackie was born, Jackie's father left the family, and he never returned. His mother, Millie, took care of him and his three brothers and one sister when they were young.

The family moved to _____, California, about a year after Jackie was born. Jackie was awed by his older brothers' prowess in sports as a child. Meanwhile, his brother Mack rose to prominence as a track star and Olympic silver medalist in the 200-meter dash.

Jackie was an avid sports _____. Like his older brother, he competed in track and field and other sports like football, baseball, and tennis. Football and baseball were two of his favorite sports to play. Throughout high school, Jackie was subjected to racism daily. Even though white teammates surrounded him, he felt like a second-class citizen off the field.

After high school, Jackie went to UCLA, where he excelled in track, baseball, _____, and basketball. To his credit, he was the first player at UCLA to receive all four varsity letters in the same season. The long jump was another event where he excelled at the NCAA level.

With the outbreak of World War II, Robinson's football career was over before it began. He was called up for _____ service. Jackie made friends with the legendary boxing champion Joe Lewis at basic training. Robinson was accepted into officer training school thanks to Joe's assistance.

After completing his officer training, Jackie was assigned to the 761st Tank Battalion at Fort Hood, _____. Only black soldiers were assigned to this battalion because they could not serve alongside white soldiers. When Jackie refused to move to the back of an army bus one day, he got into trouble. In 1944, he was discharged with an _____ discharge after nearly being expelled from the military.

Robinson began his professional baseball career with the Kansas City Monarchs soon after he was discharged from the military. The Negro Baseball _____ was home to the Monarchs. Black players were still not allowed to play in Major League Baseball at this time. Jackie performed well on the field. He was an outstanding shortstop, hitting .387 on average.

While playing for the Monarchs, Branch Rickey, the Dodgers' _____ manager, approached Jackie. Branch hoped that the Dodgers could win the pennant by signing an African-American player. Branch warned Robinson that he would encounter racial _____ when he first joined the Dodgers. Branch was looking for a person who could take insults without reacting. This famous exchange between Jackie and Branch occurred during their first conversation:

Jackie: "Are you looking for a Negro who is afraid to fight back, Mr. Rickey?"
Jackie: "Are you looking for a Negro who is afraid to fight back, Mr. Rickey?" Robinson, I'm looking for a baseball player who has the guts not to fight back."

For the Montreal Royals, Jackie first played in the minor leagues. He was constantly confronted with racism. Because of Jackie, the opposing team would occasionally fail to show up for games. Then there were the times when people would verbally abuse or throw objects at him. In the midst of all this, Jackie remained calm and focused on the game. He had a .349 batting average and was named the league's most valuable player.

Robinson was called up to play for the Brooklyn _____ at the start of the 1947 baseball season, and he did. On April 15, 1947, he became the first African-American to play in the sport's major leagues. Racially charged taunts were once again directed at Jackie from both fans and fellow players alike. Death threats were made against him. But Jackie had the courage not to fight back. He kept his word to Branch Rickey and dedicated himself solely to the game of baseball. The Dodgers won the pennant that year, and Jackie was named the team's _____ of the Year for his achievements.

Jackie Robinson was one of the best _____ league baseball players for the next ten years. During his lengthy career, his _____ average stood at.311, and he hit 137 home runs while also stealing 197 bases. Six times he was selected to the All-Star team, and in 1949 he was named the National League MVP.

Because of Jackie Robinson's groundbreaking work, other African-American players could play in the major leagues. He also _____ the way for racial integration in different facets of American life. He was inducted into the Baseball Hall of Fame in 1962. On October 24, 1972, Robinson suffered a heart attack and died.

Flamingo Bird Facts

First, read over the entire passage(s). Then go back and fill in the blanks. You can skip the blanks you're unsure about and come back to them later.

females	algae	vivid	coast	diet
prey	theory	top-heavy	wading	mudflats

Flamingos are the show stoppers of the avian world. Their long legs, bending beaks, and _____ orange hue make them a sight to behold. They're a popular attraction at zoos and nature preserves because they are fascinating to see up close.

Phoenicopterus ruber is the scientific name for the American Flamingo. They reach a height of 3 to 5 feet and a weight of 5 to 6 pounds at maturity. Males tend to be larger than _____ in general. Feathers of the common flamingo are typically pinkish red. Additionally, their pink feet and pink and white bill, which has a black tip, distinguish them.

Central and South America and the Caribbean are home to the American Flamingo. It can also be found in the Bahamas and Cuba, and the Yucatan Peninsula of Mexico's Caribbean coast. As far as Brazil, there are some that can be found on the northern _____. In addition, the Galapagos Islands have a population.

Lagoons and low-lying _____ or lakes are the preferred environments for the Flamingos. They like seeking food by wading across the water. They form enormous flocks, sometimes numbering in the tens of thousands.

Flamingos come in a variety of colors, including pink and orange. Carotenoids are responsible for the orange hue of several foods, such as carrots. Carrots would turn your skin and eyes orange if you just ate them. Flamingoes appear pink or orange because they eat _____ and small shellfish rich in carotenoids. They would lose their vibrant hue if they switched to a different _____.

Is it possible for flamingoes to fly? Yes. Flamingos can fly, even though we usually associate them with _____ in the water. Before they can take off, they have to run to build up their speed. They often fly in big groups.

Scientists don't know why Flamingos stand on one leg, but they have a few ideas. There is a rumor that it is to keep one leg warm. Because it's cold outside, they can keep one leg near their body to keep it warm. Another _____ is that they are drying out one leg at a time. A third idea argues that it aids them in deceiving their _____, as one leg resembles a plant more than two.

It doesn't matter the reason; these _____ birds can stand on one leg for long periods. They even sleep with one leg balanced on the ground!

Boston Tea Party

First, read over the entire passage(s). Then go back and fill in the blanks. You can skip the blanks you're unsure about and come back to them later.

cargo	Indians	protest	hefty	leader
Parliament	displeasure	favorite	Harbor	pounds

Was it a big, boisterous tea party? Not at all. There was tea in the mix, but no one was drinking it. It was a _____ by the American Colonists against the British government that resulted in the Boston Tea Party. They boarded three trade ships in Boston _____ and threw the ships' _____ of tea into the ocean to show their anger at the government. Into the water, they threw 342 chests of tea. Some of the colonists dressed up as Mohawk _____, but they fooled no one. The British knew who had thrown away the tea.

First, it might seem like a silly idea to throw tea into the ocean dressed as Mohawks. But the people who lived in colonial America knew why they did this. Among the British, tea was a _____ drink. People who worked for the East India Trading company made a lot of money from it. They were told they could only buy tea from this one company in the colonies. This was a British company. They were also informed that the tea would be taxed at a _____ rate. The Tea Act was the name given to the tax that was levied on the sale of tea.

People in the colonies didn't think this was fair because they weren't represented in British _____ and didn't say how taxes were done. They asked that the tea be returned to Great Britain since they refused to pay taxes on it. As a result, they decided to toss the tea into the ocean as a form of protest against Britain's excessive taxes.

Historians wouldn't know for sure if the protest was planned or not. People in the town had met earlier that day to talk about the tea taxes and fight them. Samuel Adams was in charge of the meeting, which was significant. Samuel Adams was a key revolutionary _____ in Boston. Many people liked him because he could use public _____ with Parliament's power to tax the colonies to do good things for the country. The tea was destroyed, but no one is sure if Samuel Adams planned to do this. Instead, a group of people did it on their own because they were angry. In the future, Samuel Adams said that it was people defending their rights, not a group of people who were mad at each other. Although Adams did not participate in the Boston Tea Party, he was undoubtedly one of its planners.

It was, in fact, a lot of tea. The 342 containers had 90,000 _____ of tea in them! In today's money, that would be equivalent to around one million dollars in tea.

Littering

First, read the entire passage. After that, go back and fill in the blanks. You can skip the blanks you're unsure about and finish them later.

butts	jail	negative	neighborhood	amount
suspension	recreational	streets	fine	community

The annual cost of cleaning up litter in the nation's _____, parks, and coastal areas is estimated to be in the millions of dollars. The cleanup of trash has a direct expense, but it also has a _____ impact on the surrounding environment, the value of property, and other economic activity. Food packaging, bottles, cans, plastic bags, and paper are the most common sources of litter. Did you know cigarette _____ remain the most littered item in the U.S. and across the globe? One of the many strategies that states can use to reduce the amount of litter in their communities is to enact and strictly adhere to laws that carry criminal penalties for the behavior. The penalties for littering vary significantly from state to state, depending on the _____, nature, and location of the litter. The seriousness of the offense is determined by the weight or volume of litter in 10 states, for example. For instance, several states penalize people for disposing of large goods like furniture or major appliances in public places. Legislation addressing trash on public roadways, along the beaches, and in _____ areas has been passed in several states due to these concerns.

In situations that are considered to be relatively small, the courts will typically impose a fine. They may also compel the defendant to perform _____ service, such as picking up garbage. In Massachusetts, for instance, the minimum _____ is $25, whereas, in the state of Maryland, the maximum penalty is $30,000. When a crime is more serious, the offender may be sentenced to up to six years in _____, depending on the state. In addition, the laws in the states of Maryland, Massachusetts, and Louisiana all include provisions that allow the _____ of a driver's license for those who violate the laws. In almost every state, a person's sentence worsens with each subsequent conviction.

It doesn't matter if someone throws trash out on purpose or accidentally; either way, they're contributing to pollution by doing so. Our city's parks, sidewalks, roads, and private property and parks are all impacted by litter. Research has shown that litter leads to the accumulation of even more garbage. A clean _____, on the other hand, lowers the incidence of littering and enhances both the local living standards and the quality of life.

STATE BIKE LAWS

There are two levels of enforcement for bicycle laws: state and local. However, while bikers are generally required to adhere to the same traffic laws as cars, most jurisdictions also have legislation specifically for people operating bicycles on public roads. Other bicycle-specific rules and regulations can be found in state and local legislation, such as those prohibiting riding a bike on the sidewalk or while intoxicated.

Biker (and pedestrian) safety has been called into question due to some local bicycle regulations, such as those requiring bicyclists to ride on the sidewalk or walk their bikes across intersections. Bicyclists should familiarize themselves with the laws along frequently traveled routes because they can vary from municipality to municipality and are not always straightforward. Continue reading to find out more about the operation of bicycle legislation.

Violations of the law when operating a bicycle are treated the same as any other type of moving offense. There is no effect on your motor insurance when you receive a traffic ticket that specifies whether the infraction occurred while riding a bicycle.

Rules for Bicyclists on the Road

Bicyclists are expected to use hand signals when turning, changing lanes, or stopping, even if their bicycles have turn signals. A traffic penalty can be issued if a cyclist fails to indicate while riding in traffic:

Right Turn/Lane Change: The right hand extended straight out
Left Turn/Lane Change: The right hand at the elbow bent 90 degrees.
Stop: Right hand bent down 90 degrees at the elbow
Mandatory wear of a helmet

Children under the age of 16 or 18 are generally required to wear bicycle helmets in most states and the District of Columbia. Even though there are no state laws that require cyclists of any age to wear helmets, many local laws do. For example, Washington state has no law about helmets, but many cities, like Seattle, require cyclists of all ages to wear helmets.

Reflectors and Lights

Red lights on back and white lights on the front are required in nearly every state, as well as white and red reflectors on the front and back. Depending on the legislation in each state and locality, the specifics can be somewhat different.

Bike Riding on the Sidewalk

Most state and local laws say that people over a certain age (13 in San Francisco, for example) can't ride their bikes on sidewalks, but bikers always have to give way to pedestrians. On the other hand, some municipal rules make it legal to bicycle on sidewalks, while others make it illegal to ride bicycles on particular streets.

Not Stopping at a Red Light or Stop Sign

Bicyclists, like motorists, are not permitted to ride through a stop sign or stoplight without first stopping entirely. It may not seem practical to come to a complete stop when riding a bicycle, especially if you are stopping while going uphill. Yet, failure to do so could result in a citation being issued to the rider.

1. **State laws and local ordinances often include measures requiring cyclists to wear _____.**
   a. headlights
   b. helmets

2. **A bicycle violation will not affect your automobile insurance.**
   a. True
   b. False

3. **Bicyclists are expected to use the appropriate _____ while turning, changing lanes, or stopping, even though some bicycles come equipped with turn signals.**
   a. motion sensors
   b. hand signals

4. **Rules pertaining to the use of bicycles are enforced at the _____ levels, just like other traffic laws.**
   a. state and local
   b. state and countrywide

5. **Bicyclists are prohibited from proceeding through a _____ or _____ without first coming to a complete stop, just like vehicles are.**
   a. stop sign, stoplight
   b. yield sign, yellow light

6. **_____ on back and _____ lights on the front are required in nearly every state, as well as white and red reflectors on the front and back.**
   a. Red lights, white
   b. White lights, flashing

TODAY IS RESEARCH DAY!   GRADE_____

DATE_____   **RESEARCH: Buddha**

    Occupation _____

BORN DATE:_____   Nationality _____

DEATH DATE:_____   Education _____   #Children _____

Childhood and Family Background Facts

Work and Career Facts

Children, Marriage and or Significant Relationships

Friends, Social Life and Other Interesting Facts

Did you enjoy researching this person?

Give a Rating:

GRADE_____

DATE_____   **RESEARCH: Martin Cooper**

Occupation _____

BORN DATE:_____   Nationality _____

DEATH DATE:_____   Education _____   #Children _____

Childhood and Family Background Facts

Work and Career Facts

Children, Marriage and or Significant Relationships

Friends, Social Life and Other Interesting Facts

Did you enjoy researching this person?

Give a Rating: ☆ ☆ ☆ ☆ ☆

GRADE_____

DATE_____   **RESEARCH: Aristotle**

Occupation _____

BORN DATE:_____   Nationality _____

DEATH DATE:_____   Education _____   #Children _____

Childhood and Family Background Facts

Work and Career Facts

Children, Marriage and or Significant Relationships

Friends, Social Life and Other Interesting Facts

Did you enjoy researching this person?

Give a Rating: ☆ ☆ ☆ ☆ ☆

GRADE_____

DATE_____   **RESEARCH: Francis Beaufort**

Occupation _____

BORN DATE:_____   Nationality _____

DEATH DATE:_____   Education _____   #Children _____

Childhood and Family Background Facts

Work and Career Facts

Children, Marriage and or Significant Relationships

Friends, Social Life and Other Interesting Facts

Did you enjoy researching this person?

Give a Rating: ☆ ☆ ☆ ☆ ☆

DATE_____   **RESEARCH:** Alan Archibald Campbell-Swinton

Occupation _____

BORN DATE: _____   Nationality _____

DEATH DATE: _____   Education _____   #Children _____

Childhood and Family Background Facts

Work and Career Facts

Children, Marriage and or Significant Relationships

Friends, Social Life and Other Interesting Facts

Did you enjoy researching this person?

Give a Rating: ☆ ☆ ☆ ☆ ☆

GRADE_____

DATE_____

RESEARCH: Nicolaus Copernicus

Occupation _____

BORN DATE:_____ Nationality_____

DEATH DATE:_____ Education_____ #Children_____

Childhood and Family Background Facts

Work and Career Facts

Children, Marriage and or Significant Relationships

Friends, Social Life and Other Interesting Facts

Did you enjoy researching this person?

Give a Rating: ☆ ☆ ☆ ☆ ☆

Identification (ID Only) License

In this activity, you'll see lots of grammatical *errors*. Correct all the grammar mistakes you see.

There are **8** mistakes in this passage. 2 capitals missing. 2 unnecessary capitals. 4 incorrectly spelled words.

For the sole purpose of proving your identity, you can get one of two types of identificatoin licenses. No testing is needed. All candidates, however, Must meet the same conditoins for verification of identification, legal presence, and residency as any other license. IDs are not valid for driving a car. A parent or legal guardian must sign a portion of the Minor/Teen-age Affidavit and Cancellation form at the time of application if the applicant is under the age of 18.

One ID-only license is called an "Expiring Identification License," and it can be provided to anyone who does not currently have a valid driver's license and can show that They meet all of the other requirements for obtaining one.

The second form is a "permanent identification license" that anyone with intellectual or physical disabilities can obtian. a positive proof of identity is required, and in addition to that, a certified declaration from a licensed physician declaring that the individual is unable to operate a vehicle must also be submitted. Those who meet the eligibility requirements can get this iD for free. The ID licenses iscued in this manner do not expire.

History of the Driving Age Part 2

Score: _____

Date: _____

First, read the entire passage. After that, go back and fill in the blanks. You can skip the blanks you're unsure about and finish them later.

ownership	discussions	issued	National	Code
minimum	legislation	strict	policies'	daily

As the driver's license became highly common, many were compelled to ask: who may apply for a license? It was not a simple question. For some families, especially those in rural areas, having younger teens who could drive was essential to _____ living. Others questioned whether or not youngsters were capable of handling the responsibility of driving. In 1909, Pennsylvania was the first state to impose a _____ driving age limit of 18 years. The age ranged from 14 in California to 15, 16, 17, or even 18 in other states. It wasn't until 1921 that Connecticut _____ the first graduated licenses, allowing sixteen-year-olds to drive in the company of an adult driver who was also licensed, while the first learner's permit was issued in New York in 1925.

More Americans were able to purchase automobiles, and more permits were awarded throughout the 1920s. This sparked _____ regarding the necessity for a national driving age standard. This resulted in the First _____ Conference on Street Highway Safety in 1924. Two years later, in 1926, the second national conference established the Uniform Vehicle _____, which mandated that the _____ driving age be 16. This was merely a model law that states were encouraged to adopt. By the decade's conclusion, most states in the United States had adopted a minimum driving age of 16 in their state _____.

After World War II, the argument over the driving age resumed. The growing middle class in the United States in the postwar years of the 1950s made automobile _____ even more feasible for the typical American. It wasn't until the 1950s and 1960s that the average American teenager could anticipate having access to a car and a license. With more young drivers on the road, more teen accidents and fatalities led to new _____ emergence.

History of the Driving Age Part 1

In this activity, you'll see lots of grammatical *errors*. Correct all the grammar mistakes you see.

There are **20** mistakes in this passage. 4 capitals missing. 3 unnecessary capitals. 2 unnecessary apostrophes. 3 punctuation marks missing or incorrect. 8 incorrectly spelled words.

In the United States, reaching the age of sixteen is a significant milestone. You are not a legal adult, but you have taken the first critical step toward freedom because you are now of driving age. it is a crucial moment for many teens. In the United States, the minimum driving age is 16. Still, there is also a graduated licensing program in which teens learn to drive with a learner's permit, then advance to a full license with restrictions such as the number of passengers After a period those restrictions are lifted. the fact that the United State's and many other countries have only lately embraced this practice illustrates that the Argument over the appropriate age to began driving is far from being settled. Cars weren't a concern for the country's founding fathers in 1776; therefore this is a problem unique to the 20th century that has never been faced before. How did America handle this debate? Let's embark on a journey through history to find oot.

Starting at the turn of the century is an excellent place to begin our adventure. In the late 19th century, automobiles were only beginning to enter society. It's vital to remember that Henry ford's assembly line production, which made cars affordable and accessible, didn't start untal 1913; therephore, automobiles were relatively uncommon before this time. Local governments at the time began to consider requiring drivers to regaster to generate revenue for the stite government and hold drivers accountable For vehicle-related damages. According to most exparts, the first driver's license was awarded to a man in Chicago in 1899. The license wasn't actually for a car, but for some kind of "steam-powered vehicle."

As the United State's entered the 20th century, registration of Both automobiles and drivers became the norm. In 1903, New York was the first stite to require auto registration, followed by Massachusetts and missouri. The method quickly gained popularity and spread throughout the United States.

Teen Drinking and Driving

Just Say NO!

Every year, thousands of drunk driving accidents and fatalities are caused by impaired driving. According to statistics, the nation's fatal crashes involved an intoxicated driver. Drinking and driving is dangerous. Even a few drinks can render you unsafe behind the wheel and endanger your life and the lives of others.

Due to a lack of driving experience, teenagers are less adept at identifying and responding to driving hazards, controlling the vehicle, and altering the rate of speed according to varying road conditions. The driving habits of adolescents are also influenced by peer pressure, emotions, and other stressors.

Teenagers are four times more likely to be killed in a car accident at night than during the day because night driving is more challenging. Also, teens are less likely to wear safety belts, making them more likely to get hurt and their injuries worsen. More than three times as many teens are injured in car crashes if they are not buckled up.

Driving under the influence, driving while intoxicated, drunk driving, or impaired driving are all terms used by different states, but generally, a baseline blood alcohol content (BAC) of .08 grams per deciliter (g/dL) or above is considered alcohol-impaired. Driving with even trace levels of alcohol in your system is illegal under zero-tolerance legislation, which applies to drivers younger than 21. States may also impose harsher punishments for drivers with high BACs, vehicle minors, and repeat offenders.

There will be signs of legal impairment, including:

Slur speech
Memory and motor skills limitations
Reduced visual and verbal awareness
Decreased judgment or control
Impaired vision
Nausea

The legal drinking age in the United States is 21 years. Therefore, a minor detected drinking will have committed a misdemeanor of the first degree. In some areas, a student can be detained for a maximum of six months or receive a fine of up to $1,000. The court may decide to impose both of the maximum punishments on you.

Some states combat the problem of underage drinking behind the wheel by applying the same maximum penalties to those caught providing alcohol to someone less than 21 years old. If a police officer has adequate evidence, the student's driver's license may be suspended immediately and revoked on the spot.

Colleges use a code of student conduct to punish students who engage in off-campus behavior that has a significant negative impact on the health or property of members of the university community. Therefore, if a student is convicted of DUI/OVI, he or she may be suspended or expelled from school.

The acronyms DUI, DWI, OMVI, and OVI all refer to the same thing: Driving under the influence of alcohol or drugs is referred to as driving DUI, driving while intoxicated (DWI), operating a motor vehicle while impaired (OMVI), and operating a vehicle while impaired (OVI).

You can:

- Choose never to drink and drive.

- Refuse to ride with a teen driver who has consumed alcohol.
- Knowing and abiding by the state's laws.
- Adhere to the "rules of the road" outlined in their parent-teen driving agreement.
- Wear a seat belt on every trip, regardless of length.
- Observe posted speed restrictions.
- Never text or use a cell phone while driving.

1. Even just a few beers can put your life and the lives of others in jeopardy if you get behind the wheel of a vehicle while _____.
   a. intoxicated
   b. incinerated
   c. indecencies

2. Teenagers, because of their lack of driving experience, are less skilled at recognizing and reacting to driving _____.
   a. legislation
   b. hazards
   c. stressors

3. BAC stands for _____.
   a. blood alcohol content
   b. blood alcohology confinement
   c. blood alcoholic nonattainment

4. Under the _____ law, which applies to drivers younger than 21, it is against the law to get behind the wheel with any amount of alcohol in your system, even traces of it.
   a. zero-tolerance
   b. zero-non-impaired
   c. zero-alcohol and beverages

5. (BAC) of _____ per deciliter (g/dL) or higher is considered to be alcohol-impaired.
   a. .02 grams
   b. .08 grams
   c. .3% grams

6. When a police officer has _____, a student's privilege to drive a vehicle can be instantly withdrawn and suspended.
   a. parent's permission
   b. a court order
   c. sufficient evidence

7. If a student is found guilty of driving under the influence of alcohol or another controlled substance, the student faces the possibility of being _____ from school.
   a. given a warning
   b. enrolled
   c. expelled

8. Driving under the influence of alcohol or drugs is referred to as driving _____.
   a. DIU
   b. DWI
   c. DUI

9. Signs of legal impairment
   a. Nausea, Diarrhea, Coughing
   b. Nausea, Slur speech, Impaired vision
   c. Slur speech, Workaholic, Laughing a lot

10. Always fasten your _____, no matter how _____ the drive may be.
    a. seat belt, short
    b. belt buckle, fast
    c. seat belt, long

A Community Garden Letter

First, read the questions. Then read the letter. Answer the questions by circling the correct letter.

Jill Kindle
780 Billings St.
Riverstide, MB
J9K 5G9

June 5, 2018

Dear Andrew,

Thank you for your letter asking about gardening plots in a community garden. There are two plots available in the Greendale Community Garden at 678 Warren Drive. The fee for the 10 x 10 plot is $45.00 per year and the 10 x 12 plot is $55.00 per year. The water is included. There are a couple gardening tools, but it is best to bring your own. I suggest you talk to Dawn Clover to get a key for the shed. You can write your name on your tools and keep them in the shed. Dawn is the coordinator and her phone number is 693-555-9009. Please send your cheque to:

Greendale Community Garden
c/o Dawn Clover
789 Gibbons St.
Riverstide, MB
J8K 4G9

Thank you for your interest in the community garden program. We hope you have a fun time gardening this season.

Please let me know if you have any more questions.

Best regards,

Jill Kindle

Director of Community Gardens
City of Riverstide

A Community Garden Letter
Questions

1. Who sent this letter?
   a. Andrew Fitzgerald
   b. Jill Kindle
   c. Dawn Clover

2. Who is the letter for?
   a. Jill Kindle
   b. Dawn Clover
   c. Andrew Fitzgerald

3. How much is the 10 x 12 plot per year?
   a. $90.00
   b. $45.00
   c. $55.00

4. What is Dawn Clover's phone number?
   a. 693-555-9006
   b. 963-555-9669
   c. 693-555-9009

5. What job does Jill Kindle have?
   a. Community Garden Person
   b. Director of Community Gardens
   c. Garden Coordinator

6. What town or city is this community garden in?
   a. Gibbons
   b. Billings
   c. Riverstide

7. Where is the Greendale Community Garden?
   a. 678 Warren Drive
   b. 780 Billings St.
   c. 789 Gibbons St.

8. How many plots are available?
   a. 2
   b. 10
   c. 12

9. The water costs extra.
   a. True
   b. False

10. When was this letter written?
    a. June 5, 2018
    b. June 5, 2019
    c. June 9, 2015

History Reading Comprehension: George Washington

You've probably seen him on a one-dollar bill. The capital of the United States is named after him.

George Washington was born on February 22, 1732, and died on December 14, 1799. As the son of wealthy plantation owners, he grew up in Colonial Virginia. A plantation is a large farm that is tended by a large number of people. George's father died when he was 11 years old, so he was raised primarily by his older brother, who ensured he received a basic education and learned how to be a gentleman. George's teeth had deteriorated over time, necessitating the use of dentures (fake teeth). They eventually turned a dingy brown color, and many people assumed they were made of wood, but they weren't. Imagine attempting to eat corn on the cob with wooden teeth.

George married the widow Martha Custis, who had two children from her previous marriage when he was an adult. A widow is someone whose husband has died, which is why she was able to marry George later in life. George became a plantation owner while also serving in the Virginia legislature, which meant he helped write and pass laws in Virginia. He was a very busy man!

The United States had not yet been formed at this point, and the British still ruled and owned the colonies. George and his fellow plantation owners became enraged because they felt they were being treated unfairly by their British rulers. A group of people from each town or colony met and decided that the colonies would fight the British together.

George Washington was elected as the first President of the United States of America in 1789. He had the option of becoming king, but he believed that no one should be in power for too long. A president in the United States is elected or chosen by popular vote, and George Washington decided not to run for reelection after his second term. Almost all American presidents followed in his footsteps, but the two-term (or eight-year) limit was not established until the 1950s.

George Washington served as president during peaceful times, and he was instrumental in establishing the new government and leadership of the United States. He was also a member of the leadership that aided in the adoption of the Constitution. The United States Constitution is the law of the land, and it guarantees the people of our country basic freedoms. However, freedom does not imply the ability to do whatever you want. Even free countries have laws and rules that must be followed.

Washington caught a cold just a few years after leaving the presidency. He became ill quickly with a cold and died on December 14, 1799.

Fun Facts

He was the only president who was elected unanimously.

He never served as president in the capital named after him, Washington, D.C. The capital was in New York City during his first year, then moved to Philadelphia, Pennsylvania.

He stood six feet tall, which was unusual for the 1700s.

George Washington did not have wooden teeth, but he did wear ivory dentures.

In his will, Washington freed his slaves.

1. George Washington was born on _____.
   a. 02-22-1732
   b. February 24, 1732

2. The United States Constitution is the law of the
   ____.
   a. land
   b. world

3. George's _____ had deteriorated.
   a. teeth
   b. feet

4. George Washington can be seen on a _____.
   a. one-dollar bill
   b. five-dollar bill

5. George's father died when he was 20 years old.
   a. True
   b. False

6. George was a plantation owner.
   a. True
   b. False

7. George married the widow _____.
   a. Martha Custis
   b. Mary Curtis

8. In his will, Washington freed his _____.
   a. children
   b. slaves

9. George served in the _____ legislature.
   a. Virginia
   b. Maryland

10. George Washington was elected as the _____
    President of the USA.
    a. forth
    b. first

11. A widow is someone whose husband has died.
    a. True
    b. False

12. George died on December 14, 1699.
    a. True
    b. False

13. George grew up in _____.
    a. Washington DC
    b. Colonial Virginia

14. The capital of the United States is named after
    George.
    a. True
    b. False

15. A plantation is a town that is tended by a large
    number of officials.
    a. True
    b. False

16. Washington caught a ____ just a few years after
    leaving the presidency.
    a. cold
    b. flight

Health: Immune System

Score: _____

Date: _____

white	defends	cell-mediated	cells	Immune
external	Macrophages	signals	foreign	invading

Your immune system _____ you against harmful intruders. _____ responses occur when your body's immune system detects threats.

Your immune system, which detects and eliminates _____ invaders, provides this tremendous service. An immunological reaction occurs when your body's immune system detects _____ intruders. Your immune system is a great asset that selflessly protects you from antigens, or foreign intruders.

Immunity by Cells

Antibody-mediated immunity is one of your immune system's two arms. The other arm is

_____ immunity, which helps the body get rid of undesired cells like infected, cancerous, or transplanted cells. _____ consume antigens in this sort of immunity. If you split down macrophages, you can remember it easily. Big indicates macro- and phages means 'eaters.' So macrophages are voracious consumers of antigens. The macrophage then chews up the antigen and displays the fragments on its surface.

When helper T cells encounter macrophages, they give out _____ that activate other _____ blood _____, such as cytotoxic or killer T cells. These killer T cells multiply fast, forming an army ready to battle and eliminate the _____ cell that prompted the immune response.

Look It Up! Pop Quiz

Name: _____

Date: _____

Learn some basic vocabulary words that you will come across again and again in the course of your studies in algebra. By knowing the definitions of most algebra words, you will be able to construct and solve algebra problems much more easily.

Find the answer to the questions below by *looking up each word. (The wording can be tricky. Take your time.)*

1. improper fraction
   a. a fraction that the denominator is equal to the numerator
   b. a fraction in which the numerator is greater than the denominator, is always 1 or greater

2. equivalent fraction
   a. a fraction that has a DIFFERENT value as a given fraction
   b. a fraction that has the SAME value as a given fraction

3. simplest form of fraction
   a. an equivalent fraction for which the only common factor of the numerator and denominator is 1
   b. an equivalent fraction for which the only least factor of the denominator is -1

4. mixed number
   a. the sum of a whole number and a proper fraction
   b. the sum of a variable and a fraction

5. reciprocal
   a. a number that can be divided by another number to make 10
   b. a number that can be multiplied by another number to make 1

6. percent
   a. a percentage that compares a number to 0.1
   b. a ratio that compares a number to 100

7. sequence
   a. a set of addition numbers that follow a operation
   b. a set of numbers that follow a pattern

8. arithmetic sequence
   a. a sequence where EACH term is found by adding or subtracting the exact same number to the previous term
   b. a sequence where NO term is found by multiplying the exact same number to the previous term

9. geometric sequence
   a. a sequence where each term is found by multiplying or dividing by the exact same number to the previous term
   b. a sequence where each term is solved by adding or dividing by a different number to the previous term

10. order of operations
   a. the procedure to follow when simplifying a numerical expression
   b. the procedure to follow when adding any fraction by 100

11. variable expression
   a. a mathematical phrase that contains variables, numbers, and operation symbols
   b. a mathematical phrase that contains numbers and operation symbols

12. absolute value
   a. the distance a number is from zero on the number line
   b. the range a number is from one on the number line

13. integers
   a. a set of numbers that includes whole numbers and their opposites
   b. a set of numbers that includes equal numbers and their difference

14. x-axis
   a. the horizontal number line that, together with the y-axis, establishes the coordinate plane
   b. the vertical number line that, together with the y-axis, establishes the coordinate plane

15. y-axis

   a. the vertical number line that, together with the x-axis, establishes the coordinate plane

   b. the horizontal number line that, together with the x-axis, establishes the coordinate plane

16. coordinate plane

   a. plane formed by one number line (the horizontal y-axis and the vertical x-axis) intersecting at their -1 points

   b. plane formed by two number lines (the horizontal x-axis and the vertical y-axis) intersecting at their zero points

17. quadrant

   a. one of two sections on the four plane formed by the intersection of the x-axis

   b. one of four sections on the coordinate plane formed by the intersection of the x-axis and the y-axis

18. ordered pair

   a. a pair of numbers that gives the location of a point in the coordinate plane. Also known as the "coordinates" of a point.

   b. a pair of equal numbers that gives the range of a point in the axis plane. Also known as the "y-axis" of a point.

19. x-coordinate

   a. the number that indicates the position of a point to the left or right of the y-axis

   b. the number that indicates the range of a point to the left ONLY of the y-axis

20. y-coordinate

   a. the number that indicates the position of a point above or below the x-axis

   b. the number that indicates the value of a point only above the x-axis

21. inverse operations

   a. operations that equals to each other

   b. operations that undo each other

22. inequality

   a. a math sentence that uses a letter (x or y) to indicate that the left and right sides of the sentence hold values that are different

   b. a math sentence that uses a symbol ($<$, $>$, $\leq$, $\geq$, $\neq$) to indicate that the left and right sides of the sentence hold values that are different

23. perimeter

   a. the distance around the outside of a figure

   b. the distance around the inside of a figure

24. circumference

   a. the distance around a circle

   b. the range around a square

25. area

   a. the number of square units inside a 2-dimensional figure

   b. the number of circle units inside a 3-dimensional figure

26. volume

   a. the number of cubic units inside a 3-dimensional figure

   b. the number of cubic squared units inside a 2-dimensional figure

27. radius

   a. a line segment that runs from the middle of the circle to end of the circle

   b. a line segment that runs from the center of the circle to somewhere on the circle

28. chord

   a. a line segment that runs from somewhere on the circle to another place on the circle

   b. a circle distance that runs from somewhere on the far left to another place on the circle

29. diameter

   a. a chord that passes through the center of the circle

   b. a thin line that passes through the end of the circle

30. mean

   a. the sum of the data items added by the number of data items minus 2

   b. the sum of the data items divided by the number of data items

31. median

   a. the first data item found after sorting the data items in descending order

   b. the middle data item found after sorting the data items in ascending order

32. mode

   a. the data item that occurs most often

   b. the data item that occurs less than two times

33. range

    a. the difference between the highest and the lowest data item

    b. the difference between the middle number and the lowest number item

34. outlier

    a. a data item that is much higher or much lower than all the other data items

    b. a data item that is much lower or less than all the other data items

35. ratio

    a. a comparison of two quantities by multiplication

    b. a comparison of two quantities by division

36. rate

    a. a ratio that has equal quantities measured in the same units

    b. a ratio that compares quantities measured in different units

37. proportion

    a. a statement (ratio) showing five or more ratios to be equal

    b. a statement (equation) showing two ratios to be equal

38. outcomes

    a. possible results of action

    b. possible answer when two numbers are the same

39. probability

    a. a ratio that explains the likelihood of the distance and miles between to places

    b. a ratio that explains the likelihood of an event

40. theoretical probability

    a. the probability of the highest favorable number of possible outcomes (based on what is not expected to occur).

    b. the ratio of the number of favorable outcomes to the number of possible outcomes (based on what is expected to occur).

41. experimental probability

    a. the ratio of the number of times by 2 when an event occurs to the number of times times 2 an experiment is done (based on real experimental data).

    b. the ratio of the number of times an event occurs to the number of times an experiment is done (based on real experimental data).

42. distributive property

    a. a way to simplify an expression that contains a equal like term being added by a group of terms.

    b. a way to simplify an expression that contains a single term being multiplied by a group of terms.

43. term

    a. a number, a variable, or probability of an equal number and a variable(s)

    b. a number, a variable, or product of a number and a variable(s)

44. Constant

    a. a term with no variable part (i.e. a number)

    b. a term with no variable + y part (i.e. 4+y)

45. Coefficient

    a. a number that divides a variable

    b. a number that multiplies a variable

Match Politics Terms

Learn how to *look up* words in a *Spanish-English dictionary or online. Write the corresponding letter(s).*

1	Campaign		la diplomacia	A
2	Candidate		el político	B
3	Coalition		la libertad de expresión	C
4	Coup		el/la portavoz	D
5	Democracy		la oposición	E
6	Demonstration		la democracia	F
7	Demonstrator		electoral	G
8	Deputy, Representative		el golpe de Estado	H
9	Dictatorship		el diputado	I
10	Diplomacy		el presidente	J
11	Elections		el candidato	K
12	Electoral		el ministro	L
13	Foreign Policy		la campaña	M
14	Freedom Of Speech		el/la manifestante	N
15	Government		la minoría	O
16	Internal Affairs		las elecciones	P
17	Majority		la manifestación	Q
18	Minister		el voto	R

19	☐	Ministry	la coalición	S
20	☐	Minority	el primer ministro	T
21	☐	Movement	el gobierno	U
22	☐	Opposition	el partido	V
23	☐	Parliament	el ministerio	W
24	☐	Party	el estado	X
25	☐	Politician	la mayoría	Y
26	☐	President	la dictadura	Z
27	☐	Prime Minister	la política interior	AA
28	☐	Referendum	el parlamento	AB
29	☐	Spokesperson	el plebiscito/referendo	AC
30	☐	State	el movimiento	AD
31	☐	Vote	la política exterior	AE

Pick 7 politics Spanish words from above and work on arranging them in order alphabetically:

....

....

....

....

....

....

....

The History of the Calendar

Is there a calendar in your family's home? Every day, the majority of households use a calendar. Calendars help us stay organized. Using a calendar, you can keep track of the passing of time and plan ahead. The ancients based their calendars on the most apparent regular events they were aware of—the Sun, Moon, and stars changing positions. These calendars assisted them in determining when to plant and harvest their crops. Different groups of people developed other calendars over time based on their own needs and beliefs.

The Gregorian calendar is used by people all over the world. In 1752, the world switched to the Gregorian calendar. Otherwise, different calendars were used by people all over the world.

Julius Caesar first introduced the 12 months of the calendar as we know them today on January 1st, 45 BC.

The previous Roman calendar had the year begin in March and end in December. Romulus, Rome's legendary first king, had used it since 753 BC. Because it only accounted for 304 days in a year, this calendar was later modified.

To account for the missing days, Rome's second king, Numa Pompilius, added two months at the end of the calendar, Januarius and Februarius. He also put in place an intercalary month that fell after Februarius in some years. These years were nicknamed "leap years." In addition, he deleted one day from each month with 30 days, making them 29 days instead.

This resulted in 355 days in a regular year and 377 days in a leap year. The leap years were declared at the king's discretion. Despite its instability, the calendar was in use for 700 years.

However, it became highly perplexing because the seasons and calendars did not correspond. It wreaked havoc on the farmers.

So, in 45 BC, Julius Caesar, with the help of his astronomers, decided to change the calendar and make it more stable. The seasons finally had a chance to catch up.

Since 1752, when the Gregorian calendar was adopted worldwide to synchronize it with the English and American colonies, the same calendar had been in use. Since Caesar's time, the world and its boundaries have expanded dramatically! The Gregorian calendar corrected the Julian calendar error of calculating one revolution of the earth around the sun to account for 365.2422 days.

That's all there is to it! Julius Caesar was the first to institute the 12-month calendar we have today!

Unscramble the calendar words.

Tuesday	Saturday	November	February	Monday	March
Friday	weekend	May	Wednesday	Sunday	January
weekday	October	June	September	December	August
April	Thursday	July			

1. rauanjy   _ a _ _ _ _ y

2. uraeybfr   _ e _ _ u _ _ _

3. macrh   _ _ _ _ h

4. iralp   _ p _ _ _

5. yma   _ a _

6. nuej   J _ _ _

7. luyj   J _ _ _

8. suagut   A _ _ u _ _

9. ebpmeetrs   _ e _ _ _ m _ _ _

10. btcreoo   _ c _ _ _ e _

11. vmbeneor   _ o _ _ _ b _ _

12. eedcrmbe   D e _ _ _ _ _ _

13. dmnyoa   _ o _ _ a _

14. saetudy   _ _ _ _ d a _

15. deeawysnd   W _ d _ _ _ _ _ _

16. shtayudr   _ h _ r _ _ _ _

17. rdayfi   _ _ _ _ a y

18. yuartdas   _ _ _ _ _ d _ y

19. ydsaun   S _ _ _ a _

20. eenekwd   _ _ _ _ e n _

21. kaewedy   _ _ _ _ d a _

This, That, These, and Those

This, that, these and those are demonstratives. We use this, that, these, and those to point to people and things. This and that are singular. These and those are plural.

1. _____ orange I'm eating is delicious.
   a. This
   b. These
   c. Those
   d. That

2. It is better than _____ apples from last week.
   a. that
   b. those
   c. these
   d. this

3. Let's exchange _____ bread for these crackers.
   a. those
   b. this
   c. these
   d. that

4. Let's try some of _____ freeze-dried steak.
   a. this
   b. this here
   c. them
   d. those there

5. Is _____ water boiling yet?
   a. these here
   b. that
   c. that there
   d. this here

6. _____ granola bars are tasty too.
   a. These
   b. This here
   c. Them
   d. These here

7. _____ mountains don't look that far away.
   a. This
   b. Those
   c. These
   d. That

8. I like _____ pictures better than those.
   a. this
   b. that
   c. those
   d. these

9. _____ car at the far end of the lot is mine.
   a. That
   b. This
   c. These
   d. Those

10. I like the feel of _____ fabric.
   a. those
   b. this here
   c. that there
   d. this

11. In _____ early days, space travel was a dream.
   a. that
   b. them
   c. those
   d. this

12. _____ days, we believe humans will go to Mars.
   a. These
   b. This
   c. Those
   d. That

Airbags

First, read the entire passage. After that, go back and fill in the blanks. You can skip the blanks you're unsure about and finish them later.

original	abdomen	dispersed	threshold	milliseconds
trigger	inflate	dashboard	model	mandated
sensors	rigid	algorithm	discharge	shattering

In a collision, airbags _____ to cushion passengers from hitting the vehicle's interior or external objects (such as other cars or trees).

Instantaneously upon collision, sensors begin measuring the severity of the hit. If the crash is hard enough, the _____ tell the inflators to fill the bags with gas in a fraction of a second.

In most cases, airbags don't need to be serviced unless deployed during a collision. In this scenario, they must be replaced at a repair shop that utilizes _____ equipment manufacturer (OEM) replacement parts to verify that the replacement airbag is not counterfeit. During deployment, counterfeit airbags may fail to deploy or _____ metal shrapnel.

Airbags in the front

The federal government has _____ the installation of driver and passenger airbags for frontal collision protection in all vehicles, light trucks, and vans from the 1999 model year.

During moderate to severe frontal collisions, front airbags inflate so that people's heads and torsos do not touch the vehicle's _____ structures.

They provide the maximum protection when riders wear safety belts and sit properly in the seat, but they are designed to protect all occupants.

Newer airbags incorporate a safety belt sensor and a decision-making _____ to select whether or not to inflate the bag while passengers are wearing their seat belts.

For unbelted occupants, a front airbag will typically deploy when the crash is the equivalent of a 10–12 mph impact with a solid wall. Belted people, on the other hand, usually have a lower _____ for airbag deployment-around 16 mph-because the belts themselves are expected to provide adequate protection up to these modest speeds.

Front airbags can help protect passengers from side collisions if the vehicle moves forward enough during the crash.

The steering wheel contains the driver's airbag. The _____ houses the passenger airbag.

Knee airbags positioned lower are an option from some manufacturers. Using knee airbags is a good idea if you're concerned about preventing leg injuries due to collisions. It is possible that they may also help lessen the stress on an occupant's chest and _____ by limiting movement of the lower body.

Airbags on each side

Side airbags are designed to inflate in side accidents to protect people's heads and chests from the vehicle's side structure, a striking car, or a tree or pole. With side airbags, the power of an accident is _____ evenly across the body, reducing the chance of a direct hit to any one portion.

Due to the possibility of window glass _____ in an accident, a side airbag that protects the occupant's head is very crucial.

Side airbags must deploy within the first 10 to 20 _____ of a side impact to protect the people in the car. For narrow object collisions (e.g., trees and poles), deployment thresholds can be as low as 8 mph and 18 mph for the more widely spread side impacts (vehicle-to-vehicle crashes). Some frontal accidents _____ side airbags.

A federal rule about side-impact protection says that all occupants must have a specific head and torso protection level. While it does not technically require side airbags, they are commonly used to provide the necessary protection. A large majority of new passenger cars sold after the 2014 _____ year are also required to meet this standard. Because of this, side airbags are a standard feature in almost all passenger cars.

Organ Donations

A common question on driver's license applications and renewals is whether or not you'd like to be an organ donor. To make it easier to communicate your desires in the event of an untimely death, many states have joined with donor programs.

Being an organ donor is a big deal. It's possible that when you're asked this question while getting your driver's license, you won't know whether to select "yes" or "no" on the checkbox. Before you make a decision, consider the following information.

Who is eligible to become a donor?

People of all ages and medical backgrounds are welcome to sign up, regardless of prior medical history or current well-being. Through your state DMV, you can easily register to donate organs. However, you must be at least 18 years old to join on your own. Those under the age of 18 may be able to donate their organs if they have the approval of their parents. There are no restrictions on who can donate outside their age; persons of any color, ethnicity, or religion can do so if they are comfortable doing so.

What can you donate in terms of organs and tissues, and what can you do with them?

The heart, lungs, liver, pancreas, kidneys, and small intestines are all organs that can be donated. Organ donation can save lives by transplanting healthy organs into patients with sick organs.   Skin, bone, corneas, heart valves, and veins are examples of tissues that can be donated. Corneas can be transplanted to restore vision, and heart valves are frequently used in the valve replacement operation that is routinely performed on children. Patients who have suffered burns often require skin grafts. Using bone, tendons, and ligaments can be beneficial in reconstructive procedures.

If it is found that a particular organ or tissue cannot be used in a transplant, then it may be utilized for medical research and teaching, unless you have made other arrangements. You can designate which organs and tissues you are willing to donate and whether or not they should be disposed of properly.

What if I decide to go back on my decision?

If you already have the DONOR label on your driver's license or ID card and want it taken off, you must go to any DMV office and make the request. You will be sent a replacement license or ID that does not contain the indication you are a donor.

The decision to become an organ donor is an amazing way to bestow the gift of life on another person.

If you have questions about your state's donor program or any other driving-related questions, you can look in the driver's handbook for your state.

1. **You can quickly register to donate organs through the _____ in your state.**
    a. Department of Organ Donations
    b. Department of Motor Vehicles

2. **Donated organs can be _____ into another _____.**
    a. transplanted, person
    b. translational, facility

3. To remove the DONOR label from your driver's license or ID card, visit any ____ office.

    a. DVM
    b. DMV

4. There are many different types of _____ that can be donated, including skin, bone, corneas, heart valves, and _____.

    a. organism, plasma
    b. tissues, veins

5. Those under the age of _____ may be able to donate their organs if they have the _____ of their parents.

    a. 18, approval
    b. 17, agreement

6. If an organ or tissue _____ be transplanted, it may be used for medical research and _____, unless you make other arrangements.

    a. can, placement
    b. cannot, teaching

Lumberjack Paul Bunyan

First, read the entire passage. After that, go back and fill in the blanks. You can skip the blanks you're unsure about and finish them later.

chunks	household	journalist	national	carved
hands	complicated	Blue	nicknamed	Bangor

According to legend, it took five massive storks to deliver the infant (already enormous) Paul Bunyan to his parents in _____, Maine. As he grew older, a single drag of the mighty lumberjack's massive ax _____ out the Grand Canyon, while the giant footprints of his trusty companion, Babe the _____ Ox, filled with water and became Minnesota's 10,000 lakes. There is no way to know for sure, but was Paul Bunyan really a real person? As it turns out, there's more to this iconic figure's past than meets the eye.

Scholars believe that Bunyan was based on a real lumberjack: Fabian Fournier, a French-Canadian who moved south after the Civil War and became the foreman of a logging crew in Michigan after the war. Fournier was _____ "Saginaw Joe" because he was six feet tall (at a time when the ordinary person was barely five feet) and had huge _____. This man was known to have two full sets of teeth and was known to chew off _____ of rail in his spare time while also indulging in a bit of drinking and a little brawling. Fournier was killed on a November night in 1875 in the notoriously rowdy lumber town of Bay City, Michigan. People told stories about Saginaw Joe's _____ life in logging camps in Michigan, Minnesota, Wisconsin, and other places after his death and the dramatic trial of his alleged killer (who was acquitted).

"Round River," the first Paul Bunyan story, was published in 1906 by _____ James MacGillivray for a local newspaper in Oscoda, Michigan. MacGillivray and a poet collaborated on a Bunyan-themed poem for American Lumberman magazine in 1912, giving Paul Bunyan his first _____ exposure. Two years later, the first illustrations of the larger-than-life lumberjack appeared in an ad campaign for Minnesota's Red River Lumber Company. His prominent appearance as Red River's mascot and pamphlets rolling tales of his adventures would help turn Paul Bunyan into a _____ name and an enduring American icon.

Spelling: How Do You Spell It?
Part II

Score: _____

Date: _____

Write and circle the correct spelling for each word.

		A	B	C	D
1.	_____	compllain	complian	complain	compllian
2.	_____	negattyve	negatyve	negative	negattive
3.	_____	importance	importence	imporrtance	imporrtence
4.	_____	encourragement	encouragement	encourragenment	encouragenment
5.	_____	shallves	shelves	shellves	shalves
6.	_____	mixture	mixttore	mixtore	mixtture
7.	_____	honorrable	honorable	honorible	honorrible
8.	_____	lagall	legall	lagal	legal
9.	_____	manar	mannar	manner	maner
10.	_____	encycllopedia	encyclopedia	encycllopedai	encyclopedai
11.	_____	repllacement	replacenment	repllacenment	replacement
12.	_____	medycie	medycine	medicine	medicie
13.	_____	experriance	experience	experiance	experrience
14.	_____	hunger	hunjer	hungerr	hunjerr
15.	_____	sallote	sallute	salote	salute
16.	_____	horrizon	hurizon	hurrizon	horizon
17.	_____	sestion	session	setion	sesion
18.	_____	shorrten	shurten	shorten	shurrten
19.	_____	fuacett	faucett	fuacet	faucet
20.	_____	haadache	haadace	haedache	headache
21.	_____	further	furrther	forrther	forther
22.	_____	injurry	injory	injury	injorry
23.	_____	disstance	distence	distance	disstence
24.	_____	rattio	ratio	rattoi	ratoi
25.	_____	independense	independence	independance	independanse

Spelling: How Do You Spell It?
Part I

Score: _____

Date: _____

Write and circle the correct spelling for each word.

	A	B	C	D
1. _____	grade	grrada	grrade	grada
2. _____	elementary	elenmentary	ellenmentary	ellementary
3. _____	marks	marrcks	marrks	marcks
4. _____	repurt	reporrt	report	repurrt
5. _____	schedolle	schedule	schedole	schedulle
6. _____	timetible	timetable	timettable	timettible
7. _____	highlight	highllight	hyghllight	hyghlight
8. _____	foell	foel	fuell	fuel
9. _____	instrucsion	insstruction	instruction	insstrucsion
10. _____	senttence	sentance	senttance	sentence
11. _____	vaccination	vacination	vaccinasion	vacinasion
12. _____	proof	prwf	prouf	proph
13. _____	mandatury	mandattury	mandatory	mandattory
14. _____	final	fynall	finall	fynal
15. _____	envellope	envelope	envellupe	envelupe
16. _____	equattor	eqauttor	eqautor	equator
17. _____	bllanks	blanks	blancks	bllancks
18. _____	honorible	honorrable	honorable	honorrible
19. _____	scaince	sceince	science	sciance
20. _____	mussic	mosic	muscic	music
21. _____	history	hisstory	hisctory	histury
22. _____	lissten	liscten	lysten	listen
23. _____	entrence	enttrance	enttrence	entrance
24. _____	especialy	especailly	especaily	especially
25. _____	mariage	maraige	marraige	marriage

Spelling: How Do You Spell It?
Part III

Score: _____

Date: _____

Write and circle the correct spelling for each word.

		A	B	C	D
1.	_____	invitation	invittasion	invitasion	invittation
2.	_____	denuminator	denominator	denuminattor	denominattor
3.	_____	personal	perrsonal	perrsunal	persunal
4.	_____	rapkd	rapid	rahid	rapyd
5.	_____	oryginal	original	orryginal	orriginal
6.	_____	liquvd	liqiod	liqoid	liquid
7.	_____	desscendant	descendant	dessendant	desssendant
8.	_____	dissastrous	disastrous	dissastroos	disastroos
9.	_____	cooperasion	cooperation	coperation	coperasion
10.	_____	routine	roottine	routtine	rootine
11.	_____	earleist	earrleist	earrliest	earliest
12.	_____	acidentally	accidentally	acidentalli	accidentalli
13.	_____	rehaerrse	rehearrse	rehaerse	rehearse
14.	_____	quotte	qoote	quote	qootte
15.	_____	capablla	capablle	capable	capible
16.	_____	apointment	appointnment	apointnment	appointment
17.	_____	mussician	mussicain	musicain	musician
18.	_____	nomerrator	numerrator	numerator	nomerator
19.	_____	inquire	inqoire	inquirre	inqoirre
20.	_____	remote	remute	remutte	remotte
21.	_____	pryncipal	prrincipal	prryncipal	principal
22.	_____	sylent	sillent	syllent	silent
23.	_____	locatsion	locasion	location	locattion
24.	_____	edision	edition	editsion	edittion

Grammar: Singular and Plural

Score: _____

Date:_____

Nouns can take many different forms. Singular and plural are two of these forms. A singular noun refers to a single person, place, thing, or idea. A plural noun is one that refers to two or more people, places, things, or ideas. How do you pluralize a singular noun? Making a singular noun plural is usually as simple as adding a **s** to the end of the word.
Example: Singular toy | Plural toys

Some nouns, however, do not follow this rule and are referred to as irregular nouns. How do I pluralize a singular irregular noun?

We'll start with **singular nouns** that end in s, ss, ch, sh, x, or z. If a singular noun **ends in s, ss, ch, sh, x, or z**, add **es** at the end.
Example: beach--->beaches

If the singular noun **ends in a vowel**, the letters a, e, I o, and u are usually suffixed with an **s**.
Example: video--->videos

If a singular noun **ends with a consonant + o**, it is common to add an **es** at the end. Except for a, e, I o, and u, consonants are all the letters of the alphabet.
Example: potato--->potatoes

Simply add a **s** to the end of the word if the singular noun **ends in a vowel + y** pattern.
Example: day--->days

Now we'll look at singular nouns that **end in f or fe**. If the singular noun ends in a f or fe, **change it to a v and then add es**.
Example: life--->lives

Consonant + y is another unusual noun. If the singular noun **ends with a consonant + y** pattern, **change the y to I before adding es**.
Example: bunny---> bunnies

Some nouns are spelled the same way in both the singular and plural forms.

It's now time to make some spelling changes. When you switch from the singular to plural form of a noun, the spelling changes. The following are some examples of common words that change spelling when formed into plurals:
Example: child--->childrens

Select the best answer for each question.

1. **Which word is NOT a plural noun?**
   a. books
   b. hat
   c. toys

2. **Which word is a singular noun?**
   a. bikes
   b. cars
   c. pencil

3. **Which word can be both singular and plural?**
   a. deer
   b. bears
   c. mice

4. **Tommy _____ badminton at the court.**
   a. playing
   b. plays
   c. play's

5. **They _____ to eat at fast food restaurants once in a while.**
   a. likes
   b. like
   c. likies

6. **Everybody _____ Janet Jackson.**
   a. know
   b. known
   c. knows

7. He ___ very fast. You have to listen carefully.

    a. spoken

    b. speak

    c. speaks

8. Which one is the singular form of women?

    a. womans

    b. woman

    c. women

9. The plural form of tooth is

    a. tooths

    b. toothes

    c. teeth

10. The singular form of mice is _____.

    a. mouse

    b. mices

    c. mouses

11. The plural form of glass is _____.

    a. glassies

    b. glasses

    c. glassy

12. The plural form of dress is _____.

    a. dressing

    b. dresses

    c. dressy

13. Plural means many.

    a. True

    b. False

14. Singular means 1.

    a. True

    b. False

15. Is this word singular or plural? monsters

    a. plural

    b. singular

16. Find the plural noun in the sentence. They gave her a nice vase full of flowers.

    a. they

    b. flowers

    c. vase

17. Find the plural noun in the sentence. Her baby brother grabbed the crayons out of the box and drew on the wall.

    a. crayons

    b. box

    c. brothers

18. Find the plural noun in the sentence. My friend, Lois, picked enough red strawberries for the whole class.

    a. strawberries

    b. friends

    c. classes

19. What is the correct plural form of the noun wish?

    a. wishes

    b. wishs

    c. wishy

20. What is the correct plural form of the noun flurry?

    a. flurrys

    b. flurryies

    c. flurries

21. What is the correct plural form of the noun box?

    a. boxs

    b. boxses

    c. boxes

22. What is the correct plural form of the noun bee?

    a. beess

    b. beeses

    c. bees

23. What is the correct plural form of the noun candy?

    a. candys

    b. candyies

    c. candies

24. Find the singular noun in the sentence. The boys and girls drew pictures on the sidewalk.

    a. boys

    b. drew

    c. sidewalk

Reading a Timeline   DATE: _____   SCORE: _____

Use the timeline to answer the questions.

Lewis and Clark's Expedition

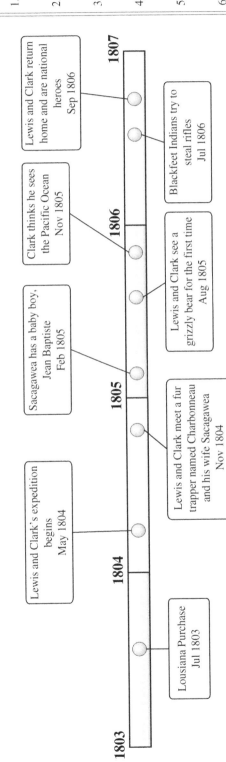

| 1803 | 1804 | 1805 | 1806 | 1807 |

Lousiana Purchase
Jul 1803

Lewis and Clark's expedition begins
May 1804

Lewis and Clark meet a fur trapper named Charbonneau and his wife Sacagawea
Nov 1804

Sacagawea has a baby boy, Jean Baptiste
Feb 1805

Lewis and Clark see a grizzly bear for the first time
Aug 1805

Clark thinks he sees the Pacific Ocean
Nov 1805

Blackfeet Indians try to steal rifles
Jul 1806

Lewis and Clark return home and are national heroes
Sep 1806

1) How many years did Lewis and Clark's expedition take? _____

2) Which happened earlier? A. Indians try to steal rifles or B. Lewis and Clark see a grizzly bear _____

3) What year was the Louisiana Purchase? _____

4) What year did Sacagawea have her child? _____

5) What is the span (number of years shown) of this timeline? _____

6) What year did Lewis and Clark meet Charbonneau? _____

7) What year did Lewis and Clark return home? _____

8) In September of 1804 Lewis and Clark saw a prairie dog. Could you put this event on the timeline above? (Yes / No)

9) What event happened in Nov 1805? _____

10) What is this timeline about?

Answers

1. _____

2. _____

3. _____

4. _____

5. _____

6. _____

7. _____

8. _____

9. Use Line

10. Use Line

Reading a Timeline

Use the timeline to answer the questions.

Lewis and Clark's Expedition

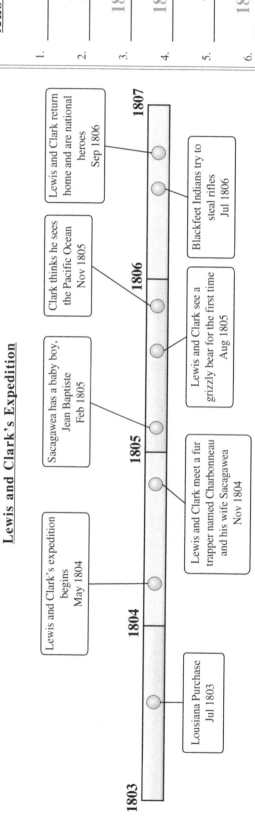

1803

1804

1805

1806

1807

Lousiana Purchase
Jul 1803

Lewis and Clark's expedition
begins
May 1804

Lewis and Clark meet a fur
trapper named Charbonneau
and his wife Sacagawea
Nov 1804

Sacagawea has a baby boy,
Jean Baptiste
Feb 1805

Lewis and Clark see a
grizzly bear for the first time
Aug 1805

Clark thinks he sees
the Pacific Ocean
Nov 1805

Blackfeet Indians try to
steal rifles
Jul 1806

Lewis and Clark return
home and are national
heroes
Sep 1806

1) How many years did Lewis and Clark's expedition take? ___2___

2) Which happened earlier? A. Indians try to steal rifles or B. Lewis and Clark see a grizzly bear ___B___

3) What year was the Louisiana Purchase? ___1803___

4) What year did Sacagawea have her child? ___1805___

5) What is the span (number of years shown) of this timeline? ___4___

6) What year did Lewis and Clark meet Charbonneau? ___1804___

7) What year did Lewis and Clark return home? ___1806___

8) In September of 1804 Lewis and Clark saw a prairie dog. Could you put this event on the timeline above? (Yes / No)

9) What event happened in Nov 1805? ___Clark thinks he sees the Pacific Ocean___

10) What is this timeline about? ___Lewis and Clark's Expedition___

Different Types of Dangerous Weather

Thunderstorms can form when moist warm air rises quickly. Thunderstorms bring strong winds, heavy rain, lightning, and occasionally hail. Every day, thunderstorms appear all over our planet. They can form at any time of year, but they are most common in the afternoon and evening during the warm seasons.

Thunderstorms are extremely dangerous. Every year, lightning from thunderstorms kills more people than tornadoes.

Lighting is a powerful electrical blast that can form in thunderstorms and strike the earth with great force. Before lightning can strike, high winds within a thunderstorm cause ice and water particles to cross paths at high speeds. This causes a charge to generate. The top of the thunderstorm is positively charged, but the bottom accumulates a negative charge. When the negative charge reaches a certain threshold, it will all discharge at once in the form of a lightning bolt. Because objects on the ground are also positively charged, lighting can frequently strike them.

Lighting will frequently strike the highest point on the land surface when it comes to landing. It is also drawn to metal. If there is a lightning storm, go inside. Don't stand under a tree or carry anything metal, such as a metal umbrella or a golf club. Also, get out of the water as soon as possible. Swimming in a pool during a thunderstorm is not recommended.

Huge and powerful storms that form over the ocean are known as hurricanes. They can stretch for up to 600 miles in width! **Hurricanes** bring high winds, heavy rain, flooding, and an ocean storm surge that can wreak havoc.

In summer and fall, when the ocean water is warm, hurricanes form. Hurricanes are powered by warm ocean water that must be at least 80 degrees Fahrenheit. Hurricanes get their high winds from spinning around the hurricane's center, known as the eye. They spin as a result of the planet's Coriolis force. The wind is usually calm in the center, but steady winds of 80 to 150 miles per hour can be found just outside the center.

Hurricanes can be found in some parts of the world. They form near the Caribbean Sea in the Atlantic Ocean, off the coast of Africa, and in the Gulf of Mexico. They also form in the Indian Ocean and are known as Cyclones. Typhoons are hurricanes that can threaten much of Southeast Asia in the Pacific Ocean.

Tornadoes are extremely fast-spinning columns of wind. They can have winds of up to 300 miles per hour and extend from the bottom of thunderstorms to the ground. Tornadoes are smaller than hurricanes and develop on land rather than at sea. Large thunderstorms provide them with energy. Waterspouts are tornadoes that form over water. A funnel cloud is what happens before a tornado hits the ground.

1. _____ are extremely fast-spinning columns of wind.
   a. Tornadoes
   b. Hurricanes

2. _____ can form when moist warm air rises quickly.
   a. Thunderstorms
   b. Lighting

3. Huge and powerful storms that form over the ocean are known as _____.
   a. hurricanes
   b. tornadoes

4. Lighting will frequently strike the _____ point on the land surface when it comes to landing.
   a. lowest
   b. highest

5. The top of the thunderstorm is _____ charged, but the bottom accumulates a negative charge.
   a. positively
   b. steadily

6. _____ is a powerful electrical blast that can form in thunderstorms and strike the earth with great force.
   a. Lighting
   b. High winds

Science Multiple Choice Quiz: Tyrannosaurus Rex

Score: _____

Date:_____

Select the best answer for each question.

1. The T-rex usually measures up to _____ and weighs as much as _____.
   a. 43 feet, 2 tons
   b. 43 feet, 7.5 tons
   c. 40 feet, 6 tons

2. The Tyrannosaurus rex was a _____ dinosaur.
   a. quadrupedal
   b. bipedal
   c. tripedal

3. The T-rex is a member of the dinosaur subgroup _____, which includes all the flesh-eating dinosaurs.
   a. Theropoda
   b. Sauropodomorpha
   c. Thyreophora

4. The Tyrannosaurus rex lived in North America between 65 and 98 million years ago, during the late _____ period.
   a. Cretaceous
   b. Triassic
   c. Jurassic

5. Where could we find the only documented track of a Tyrannosaurus Rex?
   a. at the Black Hills Museum of Natural History Exhibit in Hill City, South Dakota
   b. at Philmont Scout Ranch in New Mexico
   c. at the Field Museum of Natural History in Chicago

6. Which of the following is the largest and most complete T-rex specimen that can be found on display at the Field Museum of Natural History in Chicago?
   a. Sue
   b. Stan
   c. Susan

7. The Tyrannosaurus had a life span of around _____.
   a. 30 years
   b. 40 years
   c. 50 years

8. It is one of the most ferocious predators to ever walk the Earth.
   a. Giganotosaurus
   b. Spinosaurus
   c. Tyrannosaurus rex

9. Tyrannosaurus rex was also adept at finding its prey through its keen sense of _____.
   a. hearing
   b. smell
   c. sight

10. The famous Tyrannosaurus Sue fossil was purchased by the Chicago Museum for _____.
    a. $9 million
    b. $10 million
    c. $8 million

11. Given their ability to inflict deep wounds with four-inch claws, the T-rex's arms may have been adapted for _____ at close quarters.
    a. "harmful biting"
    b. "powerful smashing"
    c. "vicious slashing"

12. The word Tyrannosaurus is from the Greek word meaning _____.
    a. "Tyrant Flycatcher"
    b. "Tyrant Lizard"
    c. "Tyrant Dinosaur"

Science Multiple Choice
Quiz: Endangered Animals

Score: _____

Date:_____

Select the best answer for each question.

1. In 1973, an international treaty known as _____ was adopted as a far-reaching wildlife conservation measure.
   a. International Union for Conservation of Nature (IUCN)
   b. Wildlife (Protection) Act
   c. Convention on International Trade in Endangered Species of Wild Fauna and Flora (CITES)

2. _____ programs can help protect endangered species.
   a. Conservation
   b. Restoration
   c. Preservation

3. The Endangered Species Act was signed into law by _____ in 1973.
   a. Richard Pallardy
   b. John Dingell (D-Mich.)
   c. Richard Nixon

4. What percent of threatened species are at risk because of human activities alone?
   a. Roughly 99 %
   b. Below 50 %
   c. Almost 50 %

5. These animals are listed as critically endangered because they are primarily threatened by hunters who kill them for their horns.
   a. Black rhinoceros
   b. Antelope
   c. Oryx

6. Who wrote the Endangered Species Act and argued that "only natural extinction is part of natural order?"
   a. Richard Nixon
   b. John Dingell (D-Mich.)
   c. Julian Huxley

7. Species that only exist in captivity (for example in a zoo), are called _____.
   a. extinct species
   b. extinct in the wild
   c. critically endangered species

8. It is defined as any species that is at risk of extinction because of a sudden, rapid decrease in its population or a loss of its critical habitat.
   a. Distinct Species
   b. Endangered Animals
   c. Exotic Species

9. It is a law that protects endangered animals by taking into account any destruction to a species' habitat, whether it has been over-consumed, any disease or predation that threatens it, and whether any other man-made factors put it in danger.
   a. The United States' Endangered Species Act of 1973
   b. The Republic Act of 1947
   c. The Wildlife (Protection) Act of 1972

10. 10. By the early 21st century, it could be said that _____ are the greatest threat to biodiversity.
    a. human beings (Homo sapiens)
    b. exotic plants
    c. wild animals

11. Choose the correct order of the level of risk, starting with the most threatened animal and working your way down to the least threatened.
    a. Critically endangered, Endangered, Vulnerable
    b. a.Critically endangered, Vulnerable, Endangered
    c. b.Endangered, Critically Endangered, Vulnerable

12. The most pervasive threat to species in the wild is:
    a. Disease
    b. Unsustainable hunting
    c. Habitat loss and habitat degradation

Multiple Choice Quiz: Lebanon

Select the best answer for each question.

1. Lebanon is a country in the _____, on the Mediterranean Sea.
   a. Middle East
   b. Western Europe
   c. Africa

2. Lebanon has _____ rivers all of which are non-navigable.
   a. 17
   b. 18
   c. 16

3. What is the capital city of Lebanon?
   a. Tyre
   b. Sidon
   c. Beirut

4. Lebanon has a moderate _____.
   a. Continental climate
   b. Mediterranean climate
   c. Temperate climate

5. When the Ottoman Empire collapsed after World War I, which country took control of Lebanon?
   a. Russia
   b. France
   c. Britain

6. When did Lebanon become a sovereign under the authority of the Free French government?
   a. November 26, 1943
   b. September 1, 1926
   c. May 25, 1926

7. What is the national symbol in Lebanon?
   a. Cedar tree
   b. Maple tree
   c. Pine tree

8. Lebanon is bordered by _____ to the north and east, _____ to the south, and the Mediterranean Sea to the west.
   a. Syria, Israel
   b. Israel, France
   c. Japan, Korea

9. Lebanon is divided into how many governorates?
   a. 6
   b. 8
   c. 7

10. The Cedar Revolution occurred in 2005, following the assassination of Lebanese Prime Minister _____ in a car bomb explosion.
    a. Jabal Amel
    b. Rafik Hariri
    c. Fakhr-al-Din II

11. The city of _____ is one of the oldest continuously inhabited cities in the world.
    a. Beirut
    b. Byblos
    c. Baalbek

12. Lebanon is divided into how many districts?
    a. 24
    b. 22
    c. 25

Biography Multiple Choice
Quiz: Calvin Coolidge

Score: _____

Date: _____

Select the best answer for each question.

1. Calvin Coolidge was the _____ of the United States.
  a. 31st President
  b. 30th President
  c. 29th President

2. Calvin Coolidge served as President from _____ to _____.
  a. 1923-1929
  b. 1913-1921
  c. 1929-1933

3. He is also famous for _____ earning him the nickname _____.
  a. bing excellent in academic, schoolmaster
  b. being a man of few words, Silent Cal
  c. breaking up large companies, The Trust Buster

4. Calvin grew up in the small town of _____.
  a. Plymouth, Vermont
  b. Staunton, Virginia
  c. New York, New York

5. Calvin Coolidge signed the _____, which gave full U.S. citizen rights to all Native Americans.
  a. The Dawes Act
  b. Indian Civil Rights Act
  c. Indian Citizenship Act

6. Who was the Vice President under Calvin Coolidge's administration?
  a. Charles Gates Dawes
  b. Charles Curtis
  c. Thomas Riley Sherman

7. Coolidge gained national recognition during the 1919 _____ when he served as governor.
  a. Boston Police Strike
  b. Baltimore Police Strike
  c. NYPD Police Strike

8. Calvin died of a sudden heart attack _____ years after leaving the presidency.
  a. five
  b. four
  c. three

9. Calvin Coolidge became President of the United States after his predecessor, _____ died in office.
  a. William Taft
  b. Warren Harding
  c. Herbert Hoover

10. The _____ is a nickname for the 1920s in the United States as it was a time of hope, prosperity, and cultural change during President Calvin Coolidge's presidential term.
  a. Reconstruction
  b. Roaring Twenties
  c. Gilded Age

11. Which of the following words best describes President Calvin Coolidge's personality?
  a. talkative
  b. adventurous
  c. quiet

12. What was Calvin Coolidge's campaign slogan when he ran for President of the United States?
  a. Keep Cool with Coolidge
  b. Coolidge, For the Future
  c. Peace, Prosperity, and Coolidge

Biography Multiple Choice Quiz: Charles Lindbergh

Score: _____

Date: _____

Select the best answer for each question.

1. Charles Lindbergh was born on _____ in _____.
- a. February 4, 1902, Detroit, Michigan
- b. January 7, 1900, Lindberg, Germany
- c. January 29, 1905, Minneapolis, Minnesota

2. Charles' mother was _____.
- a. an aviator
- b. a schoolteacher
- c. a doctor

3. On May 20, 1927, Charles took off from New York aboard his plane, the _____.
- a. Spirit of St. Joseph
- b. Spirit of St. Louis
- c. Spirit of St. Luke

4. _____ were pilots that traveled the country performing stunts and giving people rides at air shows.
- a. Recreational pilot
- b. Barnstormers
- c. Sports pilot

5. Charles died in _____ at _____.
- a. August 25 1975, Detroit Michigan
- b. August 24, 1976, Minneapolis, Minnesota
- c. August 26, 1974, Maui, Hawaii

6. In 1924, Charles joined the _____ where he received formal training as a pilot.
- a. Army Aviation Branch
- b. Army Signal Corps
- c. Army Air Service

7. Charles Lindbergh was named the first ever _____ by Time Magazine in 1927.
- a. "Man of the Half-Century"
- b. "Man of the Year"
- c. "Man of the Decade"

8. In ____, Charles became a Brigadier General in the U.S. Air Force.
- a. 1929
- b. 1974
- c. 1954

9. When World War II began, Lindbergh flew around ____ during the war and helped to test out new planes.
- a. 50 combat missions
- b. 40 combat missions
- c. 60 combat missions

10. Charles was awarded the _____ by President Calvin Coolidge and a huge parade was held for him in New York City.
- a. Distinguished Flying Cross
- b. Aerial Achievement Medal
- c. Air Force Achievement Medal

11. Charles contributed to the development of _____.
- a. a water pump
- b. an artificial heart pump
- c. an air pump

12. Charles was one of the best-known figures in aeronautical history, remembered for the first nonstop solo flight across the Atlantic Ocean, from New York City to _____, on May 20–21, 1927.
- a. Paris
- b. United Kingdom
- c. Italy

Proofreading
Interpersonal Skills: Peer Pressure

In this activity, you'll see lots of grammatical *errors*. Correct all the grammar mistakes you see.

There are **30** mistakes in this passage. 3 capitals missing. 5 unnecessary capitals. 3 unnecessary apostrophes. 6 punctuation marks missing or incorrect. 13 incorrectly spelled words.

Tony is mingling with a large group of what he considers to be the school's cool kids. Suddenly, someone in the group begins mocking Tony''s friend Rob, who walk's with a limp due to a physical disability.

They began to imitate Rob's limping and call him 'lame cripple' and other derogatory terms Although Tony disapproves of their behavior, he does not want to risk being excluded from the group, and thus joins them in mocking Rob.

Peer pressure is the influence exerted on us by members of our social group. It can manifest in a variety of Ways and can lead to us engaging in behaviors we would not normally consider such as Tony joining in and mocking his friend Rob.

However, peer pressure is not always detrimental. Positive peer pressure can motivate us to make better choices. such as studying harder, staying in school, or seeking a better jub. when others influence us to make poor choices, such as smoking, using illicit drugs, or bullying, we succumb to negative peer pressure. We all desire to belong to a group and fit in, so developing strategies for resasting peer pressure when necessary can be beneficial.

Tony and his friends are engaging in bullying by mocking Rob. Bullying is defined as persistent, unwanted, aggressive behavior directed toward another person. It is most prevalent in school-aged children but can also affect adults. bullying can take on a variety of forms including the following

· Verbal bullying is when someone is called names threatened, or taunted verbally.

· Bullying is physical in nature - hitting, spitting, tripping, or pushing someone.

· Social bullying is intentoinally excluding someone from activities, spreading rumors, or embarrassing someone.

· Cyberbullying is the act of verbally or socially bullying someone via the internet, such as through socail media sites.

Peer pressure exert's a significant influence on an individual's decision to engage in bullying behavior. In Tony's case, even though Rob is a friend and Tony Would never consider mocking his disability, his desire to belung to a group outweighs his willingness to defend His friend.

Peer pressure is a strong force thit is exerted on us by our social group mambers. Peer pressure is classified into two types: negative peer pressure, which results in poor decision-making, and positive peer pressure, which influences us to make the correct choices. Adolescents are particularly susceptible to peer pressure because of their desire to fit in.

Peer pressure can motivate someone to engage in bullying behaviors such as mocking someone, threatening to harm tham, taunting Them online, or excluding them from an activity. Each year, bullying affects an astounding 3.2 million school-aged chaldren. Several strategies for avoiding peer pressure bullying include the following:

- Consider your actions by surrounding yourself with good company.
- acquiring the ability to say no to someone you trust.

Speak up - bullying is never acceptable and is taken extremely seriously In schools and the workplace. If someone is attempting to convince you to bully another person, speaking with a trosted adolt such as a teacher, coach, coonselor, or coworker can frequently help put things into perspective and highlight the issue.

Health Reading
Comprehension: Food & Sports

First, read the entire passage. After that, go back and fill in the blanks. You can skip the blanks you're unsure about and finish them later.

dairy	muscles	cramping	sluggish	journal
nutrients	sports	fresh	faint	supplements
mitt	fortified	balance	shin	faster
protein	activity	energy	leafy	Cereals

You have to have equipment if you play sports, right? Would you be willing to play baseball without a _____?

Would you play soccer if you didn't have _____ guards? No, it does not. Would you consider participating in sports

if you didn't have the most important piece of equipment - a fully fueled and ready-to-go body? Unfortunately, many children do

exactly that. You must eat healthily and fuel up before your _____ by eating the right foods at the right times.

Everything revolves around timing. You can eat healthy, but if you overeat before exercising, you will feel _____

and may experience stomach upset or _____. On the other hand, if you don't eat anything before working out,

you may feel weak, _____, or tired. It is always a good idea to eat a healthy breakfast and best prepare for your

day. If you're going to eat a large healthy meal, make sure you eat it at least three to four hours before exercising. Eat a smaller,

more nutritious meal if you only have two hours before your game. It would help if you also ate after exercising to help your

_____ recover.

So, what are you going to eat? Carbohydrates are your body's primary source of _____, so eat foods high in

carbohydrates but low in fat. Carbohydrates will be converted into energy by your body. _____, breads,

vegetables, pasta, rice, and fruit are all good carbohydrate sources. Proteins and fats are best consumed after exercise to help

your muscles recover. Meat, _____ products, and nuts are examples of high _____ foods. Water

consumption is also essential. Unless you exercise vigorously for more than 60 minutes, water is preferable to

_____ drinks such as Gatorade.

The American College of Sports Medicine recommends drinking enough fluid to _____ your daily fluid losses

during exercise to stay healthy and hydrated. On days when the temperature and humidity are high, you'll probably need more.

Before your workout:

- Drink 2 to 3 cups (0.5 to 0.8 liters) of water.

- Drink approximately 2 to 3 cups (0.5 to 0.8 liters) of water after your workout for every pound (0.5 kilograms) of weight lost.

- During your workout, drink about 1 cup (0.25 liters) of water every 15 to 20 minutes.

The larger your body or, the warmer the weather, the more you may require.

Everyone is unique, and you should listen to your body when deciding which healthy foods to eat and when. Pay close attention to what feels suitable for you. Keep a food _____ for a few days to see how much you're eating and if you're getting all of the nutrients you need.

Calcium and iron are two essential _____ for children. Calcium aids in the formation of strong bones, while iron provides energy. Dairy products, such as milk, yogurt, and cheese, are high in calcium. Dark, green _____ vegetables and calcium-fortified products, such as orange juice, are also good sources.

Iron can be found in various foods, including meat, dried beans, and _____ cereals.

Remember that if you don't get enough iron, you'll get tired _____. Make sure that you are not on a diet. When you're a kid athlete, your body needs every opportunity to grow to its full potential. Talk to your parents or another trusted adult if anyone, such as a coach or teammate, suggests that you change your diet to gain or lose weight. Avoid any diet _____ or aids as well. These could be harmful to a developing body. Eating healthy is appropriate at any age. When you're a kid athlete, you're always on the go, and it can be challenging to find time to eat healthy. Keeping a cooler in the car with _____ fruit, water, and a sandwich on whole-grain bread is preferable to driving through a fast-food restaurant. Plan ahead of time, but it will be worthwhile.

Remember to look after your most important piece of equipment: your body. If you do, you will be able to perform at your best and, more importantly, feel at your best.

Geography: Himalayas

Jurassic	Mount	earthquake	tallest	mountains
grasslands	Sheep	Abominable	oxygen	surface

The Himalayas are an Asian mountain range. The Himalayan region includes Nepal, Tibet, Bhutan, India, Afghanistan, and Pakistan. The Himalayas are home to the majority of the world's _____ mountains.

I'm almost sure you've heard of _____ Everest, the world's tallest mountain. Climbers train for years to scale this massive chunk of rock and ice. Because Everest is so high, most climbers require _____, which is a pure component of the air we breathe, to reach the summit, and many climbers must abandon their efforts before reaching the summit.

Plate tectonics created the Himalayas, which may sound like a technical term, but it's quite simple. Large swaths of land make up the earth's _____. Plate tectonics is basically what happens when the pieces move slightly and collide with each other. When these plates collide, one piece of land is forced beneath the other, raising the piece on top and eventually forming _____. Everest grew to a height of 29,000 feet as a result of this process!

The shifting that formed the Himalayas began during the _____ period; I wonder what the dinosaurs thought of the earth moving beneath their feet? But, just like us, they probably couldn't feel anything because plate tectonics is invisible to anyone living on the earth's surface - that is, until an _____ occurs, which is an extreme example of how plate tectonics work.

The name Himalayas means "home of snow," but most of the Himalayas are lower than the parts always covered in snow. The Himalayas are home to forests and _____ as well as ice. As you descend the mountains, the temperatures rise, and the snow melts. The Himalayas are the source (beginning point) of many important rivers in Asia, including the Ganges and the Yangtze. Many different kinds of animals and plants live in the forests and grasslands.

It's challenging to get past the image of bare mountains, but some areas of the Himalayas have fertile soil. The majority of farmable land in Nepal is in the foothills or lower hilly parts of the mountains. The majority of Nepal's rice is grown there. Apple, cherry, and grape orchards can be found in the Vale of the Kashmir region. _____, goats, and yaks are also raised. When the weather is warm, the animals graze higher in the mountains, but they move to lower pastures like snowfalls.

Have you ever heard of a Yeti? The Yeti, also known as the _____ Snowman, is a mythical creature that roams the Himalayas and resembles a giant hairy man. It is said to have shaggy, white fur and sharp teeth ready to devour anyone who comes into contact with it! According to monks, there are the remains of a Yeti hand in a Buddhist monastery in Pangboche, Nepal. Scientists believe they have proof that the Yeti is a rare type of polar bear, but others are skeptical. What are your thoughts? Is the Yeti a bear or a previously unknown monster?

Music: History of the Violin

Score: _____

Date: _____

First, read the entire passage. After that, go back and fill in the blanks. You can skip the blanks you're unsure about and finish them later.

strings	France	soundhole	bowed	ages
introduced	Italy	Baroque	existence	existence

Stringed instruments that use a bow to produce sound, such as the violin, are referred to as _____ stringed instruments. The ancestors of the violin are said to be the Arabian rabab and the rebec, which came from the Orient in the middle _____ and were popular in Spain and _____ in the fifteenth century. A bowed stringed instrument known as a fiddle first appeared in Europe near the end of the Middle Ages.

In terms of completeness, the violin is in a class by itself when compared to its forefathers. Furthermore, it did not evolve gradually over time but instead appeared in its current form abruptly around 1550. However, none of these early violins are still in _____ today. The violin's history is inferred from paintings from this era that depicts violins.

The two earliest recorded violin makers are from northern _____: Andre Amati of Cremona and Gasparo di Bertolotti of Salone (Gasparo di Salon). The history of the violin emerges from the fog of legend to hard fact thanks to these two violin makers. These two's violins are still in use today. The oldest violin still in _____ today is one built around 1565 by Andre Amati.

Though the violin was _____ to the world in the middle of the sixteenth century, a similar-looking instrument called the viol was made around the fourteenth century.

The viol flourished in the sixteenth and seventeenth centuries, and the violin and viol coexisted during the _____ period.

The viol family's instruments did not have the f-shaped _____ of the violin, but rather a C-shaped soundhole or a more decorative shape. The viol differs from the violin in that it has six, seven, or more _____ tuned in fourths (as opposed to the violin's four strings tuned in fifths), a fretted fingerboard, and a relatively thick body due to the sloping shoulder shape at the neck-body joint. There are several sizes, but the Viola da Gamba, which has a lower register similar to the cello, is the most well-known.

Art: Visual

First, read the entire passage. After that, go back and fill in the blanks. You can skip the blanks you're unsure about and finish them later.

splattering	Middle	ceramics	pencils	Greece
vases	inking	pharaohs'	oldest	three-dimensional

Visual arts are visible art forms such as drawing, painting, sculpture, printmaking, photography, and filmmaking. Design and textile work are also referred to as visual arts. The visual arts have evolved over time. During the _____ Ages, artists became well-known for their paintings, sculptures, and prints. Today, visual arts encompasses a wide range of disciplines.

Drawing is the process of creating a picture with a variety of tools, most commonly _____, crayons, pens, or markers. Artists draw on a variety of surfaces, such as paper or canvas. The first drawings were discovered in caves around 30,000 years ago.

The ancient Egyptians drew on papyrus, while the Greeks and Romans drew on other objects such as _____. Drawings were sketches made on parchment in the Middle Ages. Drawing became an art form when paper became widely available during the Renaissance, and it was perfected by Michelangelo, Leonardo Da Vinci, and others.

Painting is frequently referred to as the most important form of visual art. It's all about _____ paint on a canvas or a wall. Painters use a variety of colors and brush strokes to convey their ideas.

Painting is one of the _____ forms of visual art as well. Prehistoric people painted hunting scenes on the walls of old caves. Paintings became popular in ancient Egypt, where _____ tombs were adorned with scenes from everyday Egyptian life.

Printmaking is a type of art that is created by _____ a plate and pressing it against the surface of another object. Prints are now mostly made on paper, but they were originally pressed onto cloth or other objects. Plates are frequently made of wood or metal.

Sculptures are _____ works of art created by shaping various materials. Stone, steel, plastic, _____, and wood are among the most popular. Sculpture is frequently referred to as the plastic arts.
Sculpture can be traced back to ancient _____. Over many centuries, it has played an essential role in various religions around the world. During the Renaissance, Michelangelo was regarded as one of the masters of the art. David, a marble statue of a naked man, was his most famous work.

Art: Mary Cassatt

First, read the entire passage. After that, go back and fill in the blanks. You can skip the blanks you're unsure about and finish them later.

influenced	private	Fine	museums	techniques
pastels	Pittsburgh	Japanese	childhood	enrolled

Mary Cassatt was born on May 22, 1844, into a prosperous family near _____, Pennsylvania. She spent a significant

portion of her _____ in France and Germany, where she learned French and German. She developed an interest in art

while in Europe and decided that she wanted to be a professional artist early on.

Despite her parents' reservations about Mary pursuing a career as an artist, she _____ in the Pennsylvania Academy of

_____ Arts in 1860. Mary studied art at the academy for several years but became dissatisfied with the instruction and

limitations on female students. Mary moved to Paris in 1866 and began taking _____ lessons from art instructor Jean-Leon

Gerome. She also studied paintings in museums such as the Louvre on her own. One of her paintings (A Mandolin Player) was

accepted for exhibition at the prestigious Paris Salon in 1868. Cassatt continued to paint with some success over the next few years.

By 1877, Mary Cassatt had grown dissatisfied with Paris's traditional art scene. Fortunately, Mary became close friends with

Impressionist painter Edgar Degas around this time. She began to experiment with new painting _____ and discovered a

whole new world of art in Impressionism. She began to exhibit her paintings alongside the Impressionists and gained further acclaim in

the art world.

Early on, Cassatt's artistic style was _____ by European masters, and later, by the Impressionist art movement (especially

Edgar Degas). Mary also studied _____ art, which is evident in many of her paintings. Mary wanted to use her art to

express light and color. She frequently used _____. The majority of her paintings depict people. She primarily painted her

family for many years. Later, scenes depicting a mother and child together became a major theme in her paintings.

Mary Cassatt is widely regarded as one of America's greatest artists. She rose to prominence in the art world at a time when it was

extremely difficult for women to do so. Many of her paintings are currently on display at _____ such as the National

Gallery of Art, The Metropolitan Museum of Art, and the National Portrait Gallery.

English: Apostrophe

An apostrophe is a punctuation mark used to indicate where something has been removed. It can be used in contractions, to show possession, to replace a phrase, for the plural form of family names, for irregular plural possessives, and, on rare occasions, to provide clarity for a non-possessive plural. Avoid common apostrophe mistakes, such as using 'it's' for the possessive 'its,' which should be 'its.' Omitting the apostrophe, putting it in the wrong place for a possessive plural, and using 'of' when you mean to contract a word with 'have' are other common errors.

Apostrophes, like any other aspect of language, are prone to errors. The omission of the apostrophe is one of the most common.

Here are some examples:

'Let's go to McDonalds.' Correct: 'McDonald's'
'Whos responsible for the bill?' Correct: 'Who's'
'Its about five o'clock.' Correct: 'It's.' We are saying 'it is' here, so we need the apostrophe.

1. Where should the apostrophe go in didnt?
   a. didn't
   b. did'nt

2. How do you make the contraction for was not?
   a. was'nt
   b. wasn't

3. How do you make Jimmy possessive?
   a. Jimmy's
   b. Jimmys

4. Where should the apostrophe go in shouldnt?
   a. should'nt
   b. shouldn't

5. How do you make the contraction for she would?
   a. she'd
   b. sh'ed

6. What is the correct use of the apostrophe?
   a. brother's toys
   b. brother'is toys

7. Which of the following is the correct way to show possession with a plural noun ending in 's'?
   a. Add an apostrophe at the end.
   b. No apostrophe is required.

8. How would you express the plural possessive of the word 'child'?
   a. Child's
   b. Children's

9. What is the proper way to contract the possessive form of 'it'?
   a. Its
   b. It's

10. The _____ awfully good today.
    a. weather
    b. weather's

11. Adam believes _____ going to snow later.
    a. it's
    b. its

12. The dog was wagging _____ tail excitedly.
    a. its
    b. it's

13. Where did you leave _____ book?
    a. your
    b. you're

14. _____ going to Ms. Katy's room.
    a. Wer'e
    b. We're

15. Bobby always kicks _____ dolls around.
    a. Kim and Sandy's
    b. Jennifer and Katie

16. _____ not allowed to listen to music while they read.
    a. They're
    b. Their're

ELA: Informational Text

Score: _____

Date: _____

An informational text is a nonfiction piece of writing that aims to educate or inform the reader about a specific topic. An informational text, unlike fiction or some other types of nonfiction texts, does not contain any characters. It presents information in a way that allows the reader to learn more about something of interest to them.

Informational text is a type of nonfiction that is intended to convey factual information about a specific topic. The purpose of informational text is to deliver information about a topic, and it is distinguished by its formatting, which includes organization, written cues (visual variations in text), and visuals/graphics.

Literary nonfiction, expository writing, persuasive/argumentative writing, and procedural writing are the four basic types of informational text. Examples of informational text can be found in a variety of formats both online and in print.

Select the best answer for each question.

1. Identify the main idea: "You wouldn't use a nail file to peel carrots. You can't tune an engine with a cheese grater, either. So why would you buy a wrench to do the job of a screwdriver?"

    a. Always use the right tool.

    b. Wrench and screwdrivers are basically the same.

    c. Use nail file for your fingernails.

2. Autobiographies are written in which point of view?

    a. second

    b. third

    c. first

3. Differentiate between a plot and a theme.

    a. A plot is the ending in a story, a theme conveys the message in first person

    b. A theme is a collection of the main idea, while a plot conveys the point of the ending

    c. A plot is more of what happens in a story, whereas a theme conveys the message of the story

4. Which is not an article in a reference book?

    a. thesaurus entry for the word army

    b. encyclopedia article on World War II

    c. a review of a novel

5. When creating summaries, it's important to _____.

    a. tell the ending of the story

    b. Write down the main points in your own words

    c. Use the first person exact words

6. Which type of literary nonfiction is not meant to be published or shared?

    a. biography

    b. diary

    c. memoir

7. Which of the following should you do as you read an informational text?

    a. Take notes

    b. find clue words and text

    c. read as quickly as possible

8. What makes a speech different from an article?

    a. speeches are meant to be spoken aloud to an audience

    b. speeches do not inform about a topic

    c. articles can persuade a reader

9. Which type of literary nonfiction is a short piece on a single topic?

    a. essay

    b. letter

    c. memoir

10. Procedural writing example:

    a. letter to the editor, blog entry

    b. textbook, travel brochure

    c. cookbooks, how-to articles, instruction manuals

Science: Temperate Forest

First, read the entire passage. After that, go back and fill in the blanks.

Taiga	spring	strong	survive	Rainforests
Temperate	wildflowers	evergreen	Fahrenheit	mountain

There are many trees in all forests, but there are different types of forests. They are frequently referred to as different biomes. One of the most noticeable differences is where they are in relation to the equator and the poles.

Forest biomes are classified into three types: rainforest, temperate forest, and taiga. _____ are found near the equator in the tropics. _____ forests are found in the far north. _____ rainforests are found in the middle.

Temperate means "in moderation" or "not to extremes." Temperate refers to the temperature in this context. The temperate forest never gets extremely hot (as in the rainforest) or extremely cold (as in the Taiga). The temperature ranges between -20 and 90 degrees _____.

Four distinct seasons - Winter, _____, summer, and fall are the four distinct seasons. Each season lasts roughly the same amount of time. Plants have a long growing season with only a three-month winter.

Lots of rain - Throughout the year, there is a lot of rain, usually between 30 and 60 inches. Fertile soil - Rotted leaves and other decaying matter create a rich, deep soil that allows trees to grow _____ roots.

The plants in the forests grow in layers. The canopy is the top layer, which is made up of fully grown trees. Throughout the year, these trees form an umbrella, providing shade for the layers below. The understory refers to the middle layer. Smaller trees, saplings, and shrubs make up the understory. The forest floor, which is made up of _____, herbs, ferns, mushrooms, and mosses, is the lowest layer.

The plants that grow here share some characteristics.

They shed their leaves - Many of the trees that grow here are deciduous, which means they shed their leaves in the winter. There are a few _____ trees that keep their leaves throughout the winter.

Sap - sap is used by many trees to help them _____ the winter. It keeps their roots from freezing and is then used as energy to start growing again in the spring.

Animals that live here include black bears, _____ lions, deer, fox, squirrels, skunks, rabbits, porcupines, timber wolves, and a variety of birds. Mountain lions and hawks, for example, are predators. Many animals, such as squirrels and turkeys, rely on the nuts from the many trees to survive.

Science: Coral Reefs

Score: _____

Date: _____

First, read the entire passage. After that, go back and fill in the blanks. You can skip the blanks you're unsure about and finish them later.

biomes	rocks	Photosynthesis	Barrier	25%
living	harden	shallow	habitation	atoll
Fringe	survive	Australia	Great	algae

One of the most important marine _____ is the coral reef. Coral reefs are home to approximately _____ of all known marine species, despite being a relatively small biome.

Coral reefs may appear to be made of _____ at first glance, but they are actually _____ organisms. These organisms are polyps, which are tiny little animals. Polyps live on the reef's periphery. When polyps die, they _____ and new polyps grow on top of them, causing the reef to expand.

Because polyps must eat to _____, you can think of the coral reef as eating as well. They eat plankton and _____, which are small animals. _____ is how algae get their food from the sun. This is why coral reefs form near the water's surface and in clear water where the algae can be fed by the sun.

To form, coral reefs require warm, _____ water. They form near the equator, near coastlines, and around islands all over the world. Southeast Asia and the region around _____ are home to a sizable portion of the world's coral reefs. The Great Barrier Reef, located off the coast of Queensland, Australia, is the world's largest coral reef. The _____ Barrier Reef is 2,600 miles long.

Coral reefs are classified into three types:

_____ reefs are reefs that grow close to the shore. It may be attached to the shore, or there may be a narrow swath of water known as a lagoon or channel between the land and the coral reef.

_____ reef - Barrier reefs grow away from the shoreline, sometimes for several miles.

An _____ is a coral ring that surrounds a lagoon of water. It begins as a fringe reef surrounding a volcanic island. As the coral grows, the island sinks into the ocean, leaving only the coral ring. Some atolls are large enough to support human _____. The Maldives is an example of this.

11th Grade Biography: Helen Keller

1. Was Helen born a healthy baby?

   a. ☐ Yes, she was happy and healthy.

   b. Yes. But had some health issues.

2. Helen Keller was born in _____.

   a. Tallahassee, Alabama

   b. ☐ Tuscumbia, Alabama

3. Helen dad worked for a _____.

   a. bank

   b. ☐ newspaper

4. Helen became very ill when she was about _____.

   a. 2-3 years old

   b. ☐ 1-2 years old

5. Who was Annie?

   a. Helen's mom

   b. ☐ Helen's helper and companion

6. When did Helen parent's realize she lost her sight and hearing?

   a. ☐ After she became ill with a high fever and headache.

   b. They received a call from Helen's doctor.

7. Helen could read entire books in _____.

   a. ☐ Braille

   b. Spanish

8. When did Helen's parents realized that she needed some special help?

   a. ☐ After Helen was unable to communicate with people and became frustrated.

   b. After the teacher sent a note home about Helen's bad grades.

9. Who was Sarah?

   a. ☐ Sarah was a teacher for the deaf.

   b. Sarah was Helen's nurse.

10. At 16 years old Helen attended _____ in Massachusetts.

   a. High School

   b. ☐ Radcliffe College

11. A number of Helen's articles were published for a magazine called the _____.

   a. ☐ Ladies' Home Journal

   b. Deaf Ladies of Today

12. Helen died on _____ in _____.

   a. July 1, 1968, in Easton, Cincinnati

   b. ☐ June 1, 1968, in Easton, Connecticut

11th Grade English Refresher: 4 Types of Sentences

Declarative, imperative, interrogative, and exclamatory sentences are all types of sentences. Identifying and classifying sentences is easy once you know why each sort of sentence exists, how many there are, and how they are constructed. Each of these phrases' aims contributes to the uniqueness of the English language. The structure of conversation and written communication would be drastically different if these phrases were not used.

As the name implies, declarative phrases make statements. In most cases, they are expressed in a non-emotional, neutral manner. These sentences are used to state facts, describe things, and explain things.

Imperative sentences are used to express a command or a demand. Rather than being stated directly, the subjects of these sentences are frequently implied to be the listener.

Exclamatory sentences get their name from the fact that they exclaim something. Although exclamatory phrases can be classified in different ways, they are easily distinguished by the presence of intense emotions. An exclamation point marks the end of the sentence.

Interrogative sentences ask questions and are always followed by a question mark. Interrogative sentences frequently begin with "question words" such as who, what, where, when, how, or why. That is not always the case, however.

1. Which type of sentence might have an implied subject?
- a. interrogative
- b. declarative
- c. imperative

2. What end mark is used for interrogative sentences?
- a. period
- b. question mark
- c. exclamation mark

3. Which is an imperative sentence?
- a. What movie do you want to go see?
- b. Can you wash the car today?
- c. Please wash my car.

4. Which type of sentence shows strong emotion?
- a. interrogative
- b. declarative
- c. exclamatory

5. The sunset is beautiful tonight. This is what type of sentence?
- a. declarative
- b. imperative
- c. interrogative

6. Do not touch the stove! This is what type of sentence?
- a. exclamatory
- b. declarative
- c. imperative

7. Do you feel okay? This is what type of sentence?
- a. declarative
- b. Interrogative
- c. exclamatory

8. Declarative sentences make statements and end in _____.
- a. periods
- b. question mark
- c. exclamation mark

9. Imperative sentences make _____ or _____.
- a. commands or demand
- b. commands or thoughts
- c. commands or question

10. Interrogative sentences ask _____ and end in _____.
- a. commands and requests
- b. demand and exclamation mark
- c. questions and question marks

11th Grade English Refresher:
Simple, Compound & Complex

A **clause** is a collection of related words that includes a subject and a verb. Clauses are classified into two types: **independent clauses** and **dependent clauses**. **Independent clauses** constitute a complete thought and can function independently. **Dependent clauses** contain a subject and a verb but do not function as a complete thought. Clauses are important to understand because they are the foundation of all sentence types. Now we'll look at the three different types of sentences.

Simple sentences are made up of a single independent clause. That's how easy they are! It has a subject and a verb. It completes the thought.

Compound sentences contain at least two independent clauses and no dependent clauses. To put it another way, a compound sentence is formed by combining at least two simple sentences.

Complex sentences have at least one independent clause and one dependent clause.

Clauses, which are written expressions that contain a subject and a verb, are the building blocks of all sentences. Dependent clauses cannot stand on their own, whereas independent clauses can. Sentences are classified into three types: simple, compound, and complex. Simple sentences are made up of a single independent clause. Compound sentences are also made up of two or more independent clauses. Complex sentences contain an independent clause as well as one or more dependent clauses.

1. 'Darkness cannot drive out darkness; only light can do that.' - Martin Luther King Jr.
   a. [Compound sentence]
   b. Complex sentence
   c. Dependent clause

2. 'Beauty is in the heart of the beholder.' - H.G. Wells
   a. Dependent clause
   b. Independent clause
   c. [Simple sentence]

3. Their robot can follow a simple path through a maze.
   a. compound sentence
   b. [simple sentence]
   c. complex sentence

4. Kristina was late because she the traffic was terrible.
   a. compound sentence
   b. [complex sentence]
   c. simple sentence

5. He won the prize, but he was not happy.
   a. complex sentence
   b. [compound sentence]
   c. simple sentence

6. 'Silence is golden when you can't think of a good answer.' - Muhammad Ali
   a. Complex sentence
   b. [Dependent clause]
   c. Independent clause

7. Although it was cold, we played the match.
   a. [Complex sentence]
   b. Independent clause
   c. Dependent clause

8. 'People won't have time for you if you are always angry or complaining.' - Stephen Hawking
   a. Simple sentence
   b. Independent clause
   c. [Complex sentence]

11th Grade History: Age of Discovery

Tip: After you've answered the easy ones, go back and work on the harder ones.

valuable	Navigator	Middle	Discovery	Columbus
voyage	Africa	tobacco	sugar	sailed

Early in the 14th century, the Age of __Discovery__ (also known as the Age of Exploration) began. It lasted until the mid-1600s. European nations began to explore the globe during this time period. A large part of the Far East and the Americas were found as well as new routes to India and the __Middle__ East. The Renaissance occurred at the same time as the Age of Exploration.

The process of preparing for an expedition can be costly and time-consuming. Many ships __sailed__ away and never came back. So what was it about exploration that piqued the interest of Europeans? Answering this question is as easy as saying "money." Despite the fact that some explorers went on expeditions to acquire notoriety or to have an exciting experience, the primary goal of an organization was to make money.

New trade routes discovered by expeditions brought quite a lot of money for their countries. Many traditional routes to India and China were closed after the Ottoman Empire took Constantinople in 1453. Spices and silk were brought in via these trading routes, making them extremely __valuable__. New explorers were seeking oceangoing routes to India and the Far East. Gold and silver were discovered by some journeys, including the Spanish ones to the Americas, which made them wealthy. They also found fresh territory to create colonies and cultivate crops like __sugar__, cotton, and __tobacco__.

Henry the __Navigator__, a Portuguese explorer, kicked off the Age of Exploration in the country. Henry dispatched a fleet of ships to map and investigate the continent's western coast. They explored a large portion of west __Africa__ for the Portuguese after traveling further south than any previous European expedition had. Portuguese explorer Bartolomeu Dias discovered the southern tip of Africa and into the Indian Ocean in 1488

The Spanish urgently needed a trade route to Asia. The famed European explorer, Christopher __Columbus__, believed he might reach China by sailing west over the Atlantic Ocean. He turned to the Spanish for funding after failing to secure it from the Portuguese. Isabella and Ferdinand, the monarchs of Spain, agreed to foot the bill for Columbus' __voyage__. Columbus made his voyage to the New World in 1492 and discovered the Americas.

11th Grade Financial: Checking Accounts

Financial literacy is the integration of financial, credit, and debt management knowledge required to make financially responsible decisions—choices that are essential in our daily lives. Understanding how a checking account works, what using a credit card really means, and how to avoid debt are all examples of financial literacy. To summarize, financial literacy has a tangible impact on families as they attempt to balance their budgets, purchase a home, fund their children's education, and save for retirement.

A checking account is a type of financial account that allows you to easily access and secure your money for daily transactions. It will enable you to deposit your paychecks and withdraw funds for vacations, dining out, or whatever else you want to spend your money on. To use a debit card or withdraw cash from an ATM, you must first open a checking account with a financial institution. These accounts, which usually have a low or no fee, are essential for most people's financial lives.

Checking accounts come in a variety of options or packages to help meet the needs of different people. To make the best decision, it's critical to understand the various types of checking accounts and some of their unique features.

Some checking accounts are completely free.

This is a popular type of checking account for obvious reasons. There are no monthly service fees or additional fees with free checking accounts, regardless of balance, the number of checks written, or other activity. You can use these accounts to make direct deposits, pay bills online, and write checks, just like a regular checking account. However, when compared to other accounts, these accounts usually pay the least amount of interest.

Basic Checking

These accounts, as the name suggests, provide the fundamentals. If you want to use a debit card, get cash from an ATM once in a while, and write a few checks, this is the account for you. These accounts will most likely have a small monthly or yearly fee that can be waived if you maintain a minimum balance or direct deposit your check every month. These types of accounts typically pay little to no interest.

Summary

A checking account is a financial account that allows you to easily access your money for daily transactions. Basic, free, interest-bearing, or money market, student, and joint accounts are among the most common types of checking accounts. Checking accounts have several advantages over other types of accounts or simply carrying cash. They support direct deposit, which expedites the receipt of your paycheck, and they are a more secure way to store your money. They can also make bill paying more accessible and less expensive, save you money on check-cashing fees, and simplify tracking monthly expenses. They can also help you avoid carrying cash by allowing you to use a debit card, and they're highly liquid, so you can get your money the same day you need it.

1. These types of accounts will most likely have a small monthly or yearly fee.
   a. Basic Checking
   b. Free Checking

2. You must first open a checking account with a _____ to withdraw cash from an ATM.
   a. financial institution
   b. employer

3. There are no monthly service fees or additional fees with ____ checking accounts.
   a. Basic
   b. Free

4. ____ enables you to deposit your paychecks and withdraw funds for vacations.
   a. A checking account
   b. Stocks and bonds

5. Financial literacy has a tangible impact on_____.
   a. the bank
   b. families

6. Financial literacy is the integration of financial, credit, and ____.
   a. debt management
   b. checking accounts

11th Grade Math: Pre-Calculus Functions

We call something a "function" of another if it is dependent on another, such as the area of a circle is dependent on the radius. When the radius changes, the area changes. The radius affects the circle's area and vice versa.

If a rule that connects two variables, commonly x and y, assigns only one value of y to each of the x values, then the rule is termed a function.

When this is true, we say that *y* is a <u>function</u> of *x*.

Do you require any other assistance? Try looking for instructional videos on <u>Pre-Calculus Functions</u> on YouTube.

1. Given f(x) = x - 7, what will f(12) be equal to?

   a. 21

   b. 7

   c. 5

2. If h(x) = x +2, which of the following interpretation is incorrect?

   a. using the above relation, h(4) = 6

   b. h multiplied by g is equal to x+2

   c. h of x is equal to x+2

3. Given f(x) = (2,6), (-7,4), (9,2), (-5,1), and (7,2), the corresponding domain and range for f(x) are:

   a. Domain = {9, 4, 2, 1, 2} Range = {4, -7, 2, -5, 7}

   b. Domain = {6, 4, 2, 1, 2} Range = {2, -7, 9, -5, 7}

   c. Domain = {2 , -7, 9, -5, 7} Range = {6, 4, 2, 1, 2}

4. Identify which of the following statements about functions is incorrect.

   a. A function may have one input and generate multiple corresponding outputs.

   b. A function may never have multiple outputs for a single input.

   c. A function may have one input corresponding to one output.

5. Which of the following is the name given to the collection of all the outputs of a function?

   a. Inputs

   b. Range

   c. Domain

6. Which direction will the graph shift if the graph of f(x - 1) + 3 is changed to the graph of f(x + 1) + 3?

   a. 2 units to the right

   b. 2 units up

   c. 2 units to the left

7. Find the inverse of the following function: f(x) = 2x + 1

   a. 2x-1+f

   b. (x - 1)/2

   c. 2f-x

8. What is the symmetry line, or axis, of the following equation? y= (x+2)^2 + 10

   a. x=10

   b. x=-2

   c. x=2

9. If f(x) = 5 + 3x and g(x) = 5 - 9x, find f(g(2)).

   a. -44

   b. -13

   c. -34

10. Which type of transformation stretches or shrinks the function's graph?

   a. Translation

   b. Reflection

   c. Dilation

11th Grade Math: Inequalities

Mathematics isn't always about "equals"; sometimes all we know is that something is greater or less than another. An inequality is a mathematical equation that uses greater or less than symbols and is useful in situations where there are multiple solutions.

For example: Alexis and Billy compete in a race, and Billy wins!

What exactly do we know?

We don't know how fast they ran, but we do know Billy outpaced Alexis:

Billy was quicker than Alexis. That can be written down as follows: b > a

(Where "b" represents Billy's speed, ">" represents "greater than," and "a" represents Alex's speed.)

Do you require any other assistance? Try looking for instructional videos on Pre-Calculus Functions on YouTube.

1. A truck is driving across a bridge that has a weight limit of 50,000 pounds. The front of the truck weighs 19,800 pounds when empty, and the back of the truck weighs 12,500 pounds. How much cargo (C), in pounds, can the truck carry and still cross the bridge?

   a. C ≤ 10000

   b. C ≤ 17700

   c. C ≥ 2200

2. Monica wants to buy a phone, and the cheapest one she's found so far is $15. Monica has $4.25 set aside for a cell phone. How many hours (H) will Monica have to work to afford a mobile phone if she earns $2.15 per hour?

   a. H < 2.75

   b. H ≥ 5.50

   c. H ≥ 5

3. Solve the inequality 4x + 8 > 5x +9

   a. x > 8

   b. x > 2

   c. x < -1

4. Solve the following inequality - 4|2 - x| - 4 < -28

   a. x > 8 or x < -4

   b. x > 8 or x < 4

   c. x > 4 or x < 28

5. Which of the following best describes the appearance of these two inequalities when graphed together? 2y - 9 ≥ 4x and 4 < x + y

   a. both boundary lines will be solid or dotted

   b. both boundary lines will be dotted

   c. one boundary line will be solid and one will be dotted

6. Which compound inequality has the solution x < -8 ?

   a. x + 2 > 16 OR x - 6 < 8

   b. 6 - 2x > 22 OR 3x + 14 < -10

   c. 4x + 2 > 7 AND 2 - 6x > 1

7. If 2x - 8 ≥ 2, then

   a. x < 4

   b. x ≥ 5

   c. x ≤ 6

8. Which of the following is an example of an inequality?

   a. 70 - 2(10) = 12

   b. 60 + 2x < 120

   c. 20 + 3x = 80

11th Grade Math: Linear Equation

What exactly is a linear equation?

First, consider the word equation. An equation is a mathematical statement containing the equals sign. Of course, linear means "in a straight line."

A linear equation is an equation with degree 1 -, which means that the highest exponent on all variables in the equation is 1. It turns out that if you plot the solutions to a linear equation in a coordinate system, they form a straight line.

A linear equation resembles an equation (there must be an equals sign) with variables that all have an exponent of one (in other words, no variable is raised to a higher power, and no variable is under a square root sign).

These equations are linear: y=2x+9 or 5x=6+3y

1. Which of the following is a solution to both y - 3x = 6 and y - 6x = 3?
   a. (6,9)
   b. (3,6)
   c. (1,9)

2. Different plans are available from two cellphone carriers. AT&K charges a monthly flat rate of $100 plus $10 for each gigabyte of data used. Verikon Communications does not have a flat rate, but instead charges $40 for each gigabyte of data used. Let c represent your total cost and d represent the data used. What is the equation system that represents these two plans?
   a. V = 100 + 10d and A = 40d
   b. A = 100d and V = 40d
   c. c = 100 + 10d and c = 40d

3. Solve the following system of equations 3x + y = 1 and -x + 2y = 2
   a. (2, 1)
   b. (3, 1)
   c. (0, 1)

4. What is the slope of a line with a graph that moves one place to the right by going up three places on a coordinate plane?
   a. -3
   b. 3
   c. 2

5. Find the slope of the line 2x - y = 6.
   a. 6
   b. 2
   c. -2

6. Which of the following linear equations has a y-intercept of 3 and a graph that slopes upward from left to right?
   a. -4x + 2y - 6 = 0
   b. -4x + 2y + 6 = 0
   c. 4x + y + 3 = 0

7. What are the x and y-intercepts of 3x + 4y = 12?
   a. (0, 12) and (3, 0)
   b. (4, 0) and (0, 3)
   c. (12, 4) and (4, 3)

8. Which linear equation has the solutions (1, 3) and (3, 9)?
   a. x = 1y
   b. y = 9x + 2
   c. y = 3x

11th Grade Math: Geometry and Trigonometry

We all know that geometry is the study of various shapes, sizes, and positions of various shapes based on the number of sides, angles, etc. On the other hand, trigonometry is a subset of geometry that deals with the properties of one of geometry's shapes called "Triangle." Both trigonometry and geometry appear to be related, but they are not the same thing.

Trigonometry is primarily concerned with the study of various properties of triangles, lengths, and angles. It does, however, deal with waves and oscillations. We primarily study the relationships between the side lengths and angles of a right-angle triangle in trigonometry. Six trigonometric relationships exist. Secant, Cosecant, and Cotangent are subsets of the three fundamental ones, Sine, Cosine, and Tangent.

Geometry is defined as the study of various sizes, shapes, and properties of empty spaces with a given number of dimensions, such as 2D or 3D. Plane geometry involves two-dimensional geometric objects like points, lines, curves, and various plane figures like circles, triangles, and polygons. Solid geometry is the study of three-dimensional objects such as polyhedra, spheres, cubes, prisms, and pyramids. Spherical geometry is also concerned with three-dimensional objects such as spherical triangles and polygons.

Do you require any other assistance? Try looking for instructional videos on YouTube.

---

1. A right triangle's hypotenuse is 10 feet long. It has a 6-foot-long side. What is the value on the third side?

   a. 6 ft.
   b. 8 ft.
   c. 8.1 ft.

2. In order to form a right triangle, which of the following measurements must be taken?

   a. 6, 8, 10
   b. 3, 4, 5
   c. All of these will produce a right triangle.

3. There are six and eight-inch sides to an abc right triangle. Third side length is how many feet?

   a. 8.0 in.
   b. 10.0 in.
   c. 9.5 in.

4. A right triangle's two shorter sides are 12 feet and 14 feet long, respectively. What's the hypotenuse measured at?

   a. 10.85 ft.
   b. 18.43 ft.
   c. 20.24 ft.

5. What's the volume of a 5-inch cube with straight sides?

   a. 125 square inches
   b. 125 cubic inches
   c. 25 cubic inches

6. The height of a square pyramid is two feet. Calculate the pyramid's volume if the base has a 4 foot side.

   a. 5.6 cubic feet
   b. 6 cubic feet
   c. 10.7 cubic feet

Answers

Absolute Value of a Complex Number

Find the absolute value of each complex number.

1) $|\ 3 + 3i\ |$

$3\sqrt{2}$

2) $|\ 4 + 7i\ |$

$\sqrt{65}$

3) $|\ -1 + 6i\ |$

$\sqrt{37}$

4) $|\ 4 - 6i\ |$

$2\sqrt{13}$

5) $|\ 5 - i\ |$

$\sqrt{26}$

6) $|\ 6 - i\ |$

$\sqrt{37}$

7) $|\ -1 + i\ |$

$\sqrt{2}$

8) $|\ 8 - i\ |$

$\sqrt{65}$

9) $|\ -1 + i\ |$

$\sqrt{2}$

10) $|\ -7 - 5i\ |$

$\sqrt{74}$

Infinite Geometric Series

Determine whether each series converges or diverges.

1) 4.70 + 0.47 + 0.05 + 0.00...

Converges

2) $\sum_{n=1}^{\infty} -2.70 \cdot \left(2.1 \right)^{n-1}$

Diverges

3) $\sum_{n=1}^{\infty} 1.90 \cdot \left(0.3 \right)^{n-1}$

Converges

4) $\sum_{n=1}^{\infty} 6.80 \cdot \left(2.3 \right)^{n-1}$

Diverges

Evaluate each series.

5) $a_1 = -4.40$, $r = 0.5$

-8.80

6) 2.30 + 5.75 + 14.37 + 35.94...

No sum

7) $a_1 = -3.10$, $r = 0.7$

-10.33

8) -4.60 - 12.42 - 33.53 - 90.54...

No sum

Determine the common ratio of each series.

9) -4.30 - 12.04 - 33.71 - 94.39...

2.8

10) $a_1 = 2.10$, $S = 1.91$

-0.1

11) $a_1 = 5.00$, $S = 4.17$

-0.2

12) $\sum_{n=1}^{\infty} -5.70 \cdot \left(-0.3 \right)^{n-1}$

-0.3

11th Grade Math: Domain and Range

The collection of all input values on which a function is defined is known as the domain. If a value is entered into the function, the function will remain defined regardless of what value is entered. A function's range is defined as the set of all possible output values for the function. It can also be thought of as the collection of all possible values that the function will accept as input.

1. Which of the following describes a collection of a function's outputs?

   a. Domain

   b. Inputs

   c. Range

2. What is the range of the function: $g(x) = |x| + 1$

   a. $R = \{1 \geq x\}$

   b. $R = \{x \geq 1\}$

   c. $R = \{y \geq 1\}$

3. A set of ordered pairs is called what?

   a. the domain

   b. a function

   c. a relation

4. What is the domain of a relation?

   a. the set of all y-values

   b. the set of all y + x values

   c. the set of all x-values

5. Which is the set of all y-values or the outputs?

   a. Domain

   b. Function

   c. Range

6. For the function {(0,1), (1,-3), (2,-4), (-4,1)}, write the domain and range.

   a. D:{0, 1, 2, -4} R:{1, -3, -4}

   b. D: {1, -3, -4,} R: {0, 1, 2, -4}

   c. D:{0, 1, 2, 3, 4} R:{1, -3, -4}

7. Identify the range of the following function when given the domain { 2, 3, 10}: y = 4x - 12

   a. -10, 0, 28

   b. -4, 0, 28

   c. 4, 5, 20

8. Which set of ordered pairs is not a function?

   a. (-9, 4), (-6, 3), (-2, 8), (0, 21)

   b. (1, 2), (3, 5), (6, 9), (7, 11)

   c. (2, 3), (4, 9), (3, 8), (4, 15)

9. What variable does Domain represent?

   a. Range

   b. X

   c. output

10. Which is the set of all y-values or the outputs?

   a. Range

   b. Domain

   c. Relation

11th Grade Language: Spanish

Use Google to help translate.

1. You would answer: ¡Muy bien! to which of the following questions in Spanish?
   a. 'Cómo te llamas?
   b. 'De dónde eres?
   c. 'Cómo estás?

2. What does Soy de Virginia means?
   a. I am from Virginia
   b. My name is Virginia
   c. I am Virginia

3. Buenas tardes is a Spanish greeting for which time of the day?
   a. Good night
   b. Good morning
   c. Afternoon

4. You would answer: Me llamo Antonio to which of the following questions in Spanish?
   a. 'A quién llamas?
   b. 'Cómo te llamas?
   c. 'Cuando llamas?

5. You would answer: Soy de Carolina to which of the following questions in Spanish?
   a. 'De dónde eres?
   b. 'Dónde vas?
   c. 'Cómo te llamas?

6. How would you say 'Good morning' to a store clerk?
   a. Buenos días
   b. Hola
   c. My llamo

7. 'Soy de California.
   a. 'She from California
   b. 'I am from California.
   c. I live in California.

8. Which of the following persons would you address by using the pronoun 'Tú'?
   a. A teacher
   b. Your aunt
   c. Your sibling

9. What would be the best greeting for the nighttime?
   a. Buenas tardes
   b. Soy
   c. Buenas noches

10. Which of the following is NOT a way to tell someone your name?
    a. Soy de...
    b. Me llamo...
    c. Mi nombre es

11. Which two words mean 'you?'
    a. Tú and Usted
    b. Yo and Como
    c. Usted and Nonde

12. Buenos días, señor. ?
    a. Good night sir. ?
    b. Good morning sir. ?
    c. Good afternoon sir. ?

13. Cómo se llama ud.?'
    a. What's your name.?'
    b. What time is it.?
    c. Where are you?

14. Where it is?'
    a. Me dónde es?
    b. De dónde es?'
    c. Re dónde see?

11th Grade Biography: Daniel Boone

As a woodsman, his exploits were _legendary_ .

He was a highly skilled _hunter_ , marksman, and tracker. He was in charge of Kentucky's exploration and settling.

He had _eleven_ brothers and sisters, and his father was a farmer.

By the age of five, he was _chopping_ wood and caring for his father's cows, and by the age of ten, he was managing his father's _herd_ .

He would hunt small _wildlife_ and learn to find their trails in the woods while monitoring his father's cowherd. He also made acquaintances with the Delaware _Indians_ in the area.

Daniel bought his first _rifle_ when he was thirteen years old.

He'd go for _foxes_ , beavers, deer, and wild turkeys.

Daniel gathered enough animal hides to assist his family in purchasing 1300 _acres_ of property.

This was a conflict between the _British_ colonies and a French-Indian coalition.

Daniel joined the British army and served as a _blacksmith_ and a supply wagon driver. He was present at the Battle of Turtle _Creek_ , in which French-Indian forces easily _defeated_ British forces.

Daniel moved back to North Carolina, where he married _Rebecca_ .

Daniel encountered a man named John Findley, who told him about Kentucky west of the _Appalachian_ Mountains.

The Cumberland Gap, a tiny gap through the _Appalachian_ Mountains, was found by him.

The _Shawnee_ Indians, however, quickly grabbed them.

Daniel's _furs_ , firearms, and horses were taken from him, and he was instructed never to return.

He and a group of men assisted in the _construction_ of the Wilderness Trail, a road leading to Kentucky.

11th Grade Art: Pablo Picasso

His father was a _painter_ who also taught art. Pablo has always enjoyed drawing since he was a child.

According to legend, his first word was "piz," which is _Spanish_ for "pencil."

Pablo enrolled in a _prestigious_ art school in _Barcelona_ when he was fourteen years old. He transferred to another school in _Madrid_ a few years later.

Pablo's close friend _Carlos_ Casagemas committed _suicide_ in 1901. Pablo became _depressed_ .

He began painting in Paris around the same time. For the next four years, the color _blue_ dominated his paintings.

He depicted people with elongated _features_ and faces in his paintings.

Pablo eventually _recovered_ from his depression. He also had feelings for a _French_ model.

The Rose Period is a term used by art _historians_ to describe this period in Pablo's life.

He also started painting happier scenes like _circuses_ .

Picasso began experimenting with a new _painting_ style in 1907. He _collaborated_ with another artist, Georges Braque.

The sections are then reassembled and painted from various perspectives and _angles_ .

He would use _sand_ or plaster in his paint to give it texture in this area.

He would also add dimension to his paintings by using materials such as colored paper, _newspapers_ , and wallpaper.

Although Picasso continued to experiment with Cubism, he went through a period of painting more _classical-style_ paintings around 1921.

They frequently resemble something out of a nightmare or a _dream_ .

Guernica and The Red Armchair are two examples of surrealism's _influence_ on Picasso's art.

Many consider him to be one of the _greatest_ artists in all of history.

He painted several self-portraits near the end of his _life_ .

He _died_ a year later, on April 8, 1973, at the age of 91.

11th Grade Financial: Money, Stocks and Bonds

Three important __conditions__ must be met in order for something to qualify as a financial asset.

As a result, financial assets differ from physical assets such as land or __gold__.

You can touch and feel the actual physical asset with land and gold, but you can only touch and feel something (usually a __piece__ of paper) that represents the asset of value with financial assets.

Money is a government-defined official medium of __exchange__ that consists of cash and __coins__.

Money, __currency__, cash, and legal tender all refer to the same thing.

They are all __symbols__ of a central bank's commitment to keep money's value as stable as possible.

Money is obviously a __valuable__ financial asset. We would all have to __barter__ with one another without a common medium of exchange, trading whatever __goods__ and __services__ we have for something else we need, or trade what we have for something else we could then trade with someone else who has what we need.

Stock is another crucial financial asset in the US __economy__.

Stock, like money, is simply a piece of paper that represents something of value. The something of value' represented by stock is a __stake__ in a company.

Stock is also known as 'equity' because you have a stake in its __profits__ when you own stock in a company.

Jane, her parents, a friend, and her brother are now all __shareholders__ in her company.

The complexities arise when we attempt to assign a __monetary__ value to that stock. A variety of factors determines a stock's __value__.

These are the most basic and fundamental factors that can influence the value of a share of stock. Individual stock __prices__ are affected by macroeconomic trends as well.

Thousands of books have been written in an attempt to discover the __golden__ rule that determines the exact value of a share of stock.

The New York Stock Exchange and __NASDAQ__ were the world's two largest stock exchanges in 2014. (both located in the United States).

When an organization, such as a company, a city or state, or even the federal government, requires funds, bonds can be __issued__. Bonds come in various forms, but they are all debt instruments in which the bondholder is repaid their __principal__ investment, plus interest, at some future maturity date.

The only way a bondholder's money is lost is if the entity that issued the bond declares __bankruptcy__. Bonds are generally safer investments than stocks because they are a legal __obligation__ to repay debt, whereas stocks represent ownership, which can make or lose money.

11th Grade Financial: Vocabulary Crossword

Across

1. The profit or loss on an investment over a one-year period.
2. The cost of borrowing money on a yearly basis, expressed as a percentage rate.
5. Twice a month.
6. To receive something on loan with the understanding that you will return it.
8. The loss that comes from selling an investment for less than you paid for it.

Down

3. An item with economic value, such as stock or real estate.
4. Stands for "automated teller machine
7. The profit that comes from selling an investment for more than you paid for it.
9. An individual who signs a loan, credit account, or promissory note of another person
10. Borrowing money, or having the right to borrow money, to buy something.

ANNUAL RETURN
CAPITAL LOSS   ATM
CAPITAL GAIN   COSIGNER
BORROW   CREDIT
BIMONTHLY   ASSET   APR

11th Grade Science: Protists

First, read the entire passage. After that, go back and fill in the blanks. You can skip the blanks you're unsure about and finish them later.

Amoebas	scoot	oxygen	molds	reproduce
enormous	color	unclassifiable	energy	acellular
tiny	cell	consume	tail	cellular

Protists are organisms that are classified under the biological kingdom protista. These are neither plants, animals, bacteria, or fungi, but rather __unclassifiable__ organisms. Protists are a large group of organisms with a wide variety of characteristics. They are essentially all species that do not fit into any of the other categories.

Protists as a group share very few characteristics. They are eukaryotic microorganisms with eukaryote __cell__ structures that are pretty basic. Apart from that, they are defined as any organism that is not a plant, an animal, a bacteria, or a fungus.

Protists can be classified according to their mode of movement.

Cilia - Certain protists move with __tiny__ hair called cilia. These tiny hairs can flap in unison to assist the creature in moving through water or another liquid.

Other protists have a lengthy __tail__ known as flagella. This tail can move back and forth, aiding in the organism's propulsion.

Pseudopodia - When a protist extends a portion of its cell body in order to __scoot__ or ooze. Amoebas move in this manner.

Different protists collect __energy__ in a variety of methods. Certain individuals consume food and digest it internally. Others digest their food through the secretion of enzymes. Then they __consume__ the partially digested meal. Other protists, like plants, utilize photosynthesis. They absorb sunlight and convert it to glucose.

Algae is a main form of protist. Algae are photosynthesis-capable protists. Algae are closely related to plants. They contain chlorophyll and utilize __oxygen__ and solar energy to generate food. They are not called plants, however, because they lack specialized organs and tissues such as leaves, roots, and stems. Algae are frequently classified according on their __color__ , which ranges from red to brown to green.

Slime __molds__ are distinct from fungus molds. Slime molds are classified into two types: cellular and plasmodial. Slime molds of Plasmodium are formed from a single big cell. They are also referred to as __acellular__ . Even though these organisms are composed of only one cell, they can grow quite __enormous__ , up to several feet in width. Additionally, they can contain several nuclei inside a single cell. Cellular slime molds are little single-celled protists that can form a single organism when combined. When combined, various __cellular__ slime molds will perform specific activities.

__Amoebas__ are single-celled organisms that move with the assistance of pseudopods. Amoebas have no structure and consume their food by engulfing it with their bodies. Amoebas __reproduce__ by dividing in two during a process called mitosis.

11th Grade Science: Black Hole

Black holes are one of the universe's most mysterious and powerful forces. A black hole is a region of space where gravity has become so strong that nothing, not even light, can escape. A black hole's mass is so compact or dense that the force of gravity is so strong that even light cannot escape.

Black holes are entirely invisible. Because black holes do not reflect light, we cannot see them. Scientists can detect black holes by observing light and objects in their vicinity. Strange things happen in the vicinity of black holes due to quantum physics and space-time. Even though they are authentic, they are a popular subject for science fiction stories.

When giant stars explode at the end of their lives, black holes form, this type of explosion is known as a supernova. If a star has enough mass, it will collapse in on itself and shrink to a tiny size. Because of its small size and massive mass, the gravity will be so strong that it will absorb light and turn into a black hole. As they continue to absorb light and mass around them, black holes can grow enormously large. They can absorb other stars as well. Many scientists believe that supermassive black holes exist at the centers of galaxies.

An event horizon is a special boundary that exists around a black hole. At this point, everything, including light, must gravitate toward the black hole. Once you've crossed the event horizon, there's no turning back!

In the 18th century, two scientists, John Michell and Pierre-Simon Laplace, proposed the concept of a black hole. The term "black hole" was coined in 1967 by physicist John Archibald Wheeler.

1. Black holes are _____.
   a. can be seen with telescope
   b. invisible
   c. partial visible

2. Black holes are one of the most mysterious forces in the _____.
   a. near the moon
   b. under the stars
   c. universe

3. A black hole is where _____ has become so strong that nothing around it can escape.
   a. black dust
   b. gravity
   c. the sun

4. We can't actually see black holes because they don't _____.
   a. need sun
   b. reflect light
   c. have oxygen

5. Black holes are formed when _____ explode at the end of their lifecycle.
   a. giant stars
   b. planets
   c. Mars

6. Black holes can grow incredibly huge as they continue to absorb_____.
   a. stars
   b. other planets
   c. light

11th Grade Biology: Life on Earth

To learn how life came to be on Earth, many scientists have committed their careers to do so.

We'll look at a few significant tests to better understand how scientists have proposed how life began on Earth,

but first, let's go back in time, around four billion years.

The environment on primitive Earth was vastly different from what it is today. Numerous oceans and seas had

hot vents at their bottoms, and the land also had plenty of volcanic activity.

Unlike our current atmosphere, which is primarily composed of nitrogen and oxygen, the ancient atmosphere

was likely to contain water, methane, ammonia , and hydrogen.

Creating tiny organic compounds like amino acids for proteins and nucleotides for DNA is the first stage. Even

while these organic molecules are present in living things, they are not live creatures in and of themselves.

The next stage was the joining of these small organic molecules to produce larger ones.

The study of protozoa is critical for gaining a better understanding of the earliest stages of life. Protobionts are

microscopic droplets with membranes that can regulate their own internal environment. Cells can proliferate,

 metabolize , and even adjust to their environs as these microbes can. These pre-cell formations have

formed spontaneously, according to numerous studies.

The basic protobionts evolved a fourth step: the ability to transmit genetic information.

A cell's ability to reproduce and pass on genetic information from one generation to the next and digest matter

and energy sets it apart from other living things.

11th Grade Language: Technology

Match the English and German words. Use Google translate.

1	C	mouse	→	Maus
2	F	touch	→	berühren
3	H	screen	→	Bildschirm
4	L	Wi-Fi	→	WLAN
5	A	message	→	Nachricht
6	E	game	→	Spiel
7	O	website	→	Webseite
8	B	mobile	→	Handy
9	K	smart	→	klug, intelligent
10	G	computer	→	Rechner
11	I	desktop	→	Schreibtischplatte
12	D	lap	→	Schoß
13	M	net	→	Netz
14	N	app(lication)	→	App, Anwendung
15	J	keyboard	→	Tastatur

11th Grade Geography: Australia

Captain Arthur Phillip led a fleet of 11 British ships carrying convicts to the colony of New South Wales on January 26, 1788, effectively founding Australia. After overcoming a period of adversity, the fledgling colony began to commemorate this date with great fanfare, and it eventually became known as Australia Day. Australia Day has become increasingly contentious in recent years. It marks the beginning of the process by which the continent's Indigenous people were gradually evicted from their land as white colonization spread across the continent.

Australia, formerly known as New South Wales, was intended to be a penal colony. The British government appointed Arthur Phillip captain of the HMS Sirius in October 1786, and commissioned him to establish an agricultural work camp for British convicts there. Phillip had difficulty assembling the fleet that was to make the journey because he had no idea what to expect from the mysterious and distant land. His requests for more experienced farmers to help the penal colony were repeatedly denied, and he was both underfunded and underequipped. Nonetheless, Phillip led his 1,000-strong party, of which more than 700 were convicts, around Africa to the eastern side of Australia, accompanied by a small contingent of Marines and other officers. The voyage lasted eight months and claimed the lives of 30 men.

_____

Unscramble the words and then identify which capital city goes with each state/territory.

Victoria	Canberra	Western Australia	Adelaide	New South Wales	Perth
Australia Capital Territory	Hobart	Brisbane	South Australia	Sydney	Northern Territory
Tasmania	Darwin	Queensland	Melbourne		

1. rcotviia — Victoria
2. ldenneusaq — Queensland
3. amsatani — Tasmania
4. rnrotenh etityrror — Northern Territory
5. tohsu lairustaa — South Australia
6. rteewns tlraaisua — Western Australia
7. ratisaaul tcpiala oterytrri — Australia Capital Territory
8. wne ohtus lswea — New South Wales

9. racnaebr — Canberra
10. nyeyds — Sydney
11. banibesr — Brisbane
12. aaleeddi — Adelaide
13. htepr — Perth
14. bmlunroee — Melbourne
15. batrho — Hobart
16. randiw — Darwin

11th Grade Grammar: Preposition

Prepositional phrases are collections of words that contain prepositions. Remember that prepositions are words that indicate the relationships between different elements in a sentence, and you'll have no trouble identifying prepositional phrases.

Another way to look at it, a prepositional phrase is a group of words that function as a unified part of speech despite the absence of a verb or a subject. It is usually made up of a preposition and a noun or a preposition and a pronoun.

Under the rock is an example of a prepositional phrase. In this example, the preposition is "under," and the prepositional phrase is "under the rock."

Choose the correct preposition.

up	up	off	out	through
down	on	away	together	off
about	out	upon	off	across

1. He pulled _through_ his cancer treatment very well.

2. We must pull _together_ to make this work.

3. Why don't you put _on_ the yellow dress?

4. I have put _off_ my holidays until later this year.

5. I don't know how she puts _up_ with noisy children all day.

6. The CFS put _out_ six fires today.

7. I feel quite run _down_ since I got my cold.

8. I might go to Hobart to run _away_ from this heat.

9. Coles has run _out_ of bread today.

10. You need to set _about_ writing your resume.

11. You will never guess who I ran _across_ today!

12. I will go to the airport to see _off_ my best friend.

13. He set _off_ for Paris last Saturday.

14. The little dog was set _upon_ by a big dog.

15. Many students want to set _up_ their own business.

11th Grade Geography Multiple Choice: Passport

Select the best answer for each question.

1. When traveling abroad, the most important item to take along is the _____.
   - a. passport
   - b. ticket
   - c. ID

2. Passports usually expire after a period of _____ and thus need to be extended in time prior to your travels.
   - a. five years
   - b. six years
   - c. ten years

3. The most powerful passport in the world is from which country?
   - a. United Kingdom
   - b. United Arab Emirates
   - c. United States of America

4. In _____, _____ ordered the first US passports to be printed.
   - a. 1901, John Edward Briscoe
   - b. 15th century, King Henry V
   - c. 1783, Benjamin Franklin

5. Standard passports contain _____ in most countries.
   - a. 32 pages
   - b. 52 pages
   - c. 60 pages

6. The Emirati passport allows travel to _____ countries without visa.
   - a. 38
   - b. 157
   - c. 179

7. The most expensive passports are from _____ in 2019.
   - a. United States of America
   - b. Australia
   - c. United Arab Emirates

8. Citizens of the _____ state in Italy (the smallest country in the world!) carry passports, but there are no immigration control or border posts.
   - a. Bologna
   - b. Vatican
   - c. Rome

9. In the UK, one passport is printed every ___! This allows for 5 million passports to be printed each year in the UK.
   - a. 5 seconds
   - b. 2.5 seconds
   - c. 10 seconds

10. The _____ allows the visitor to remain in the foreign nation for a specific length of time.
    - a. passport
    - b. visas
    - c. re-entry permit

11. US passports are valid for _____ for adults, but only _____ for persons under 16 years of age.
    - a. 10 years ; 7 years
    - b. 5 years ; 3 years
    - c. 10 years ; 5 years

12. In what year did the United States also began producing a passport card, which, for less than the cost of a traditional passport book?
    - a. 2002
    - b. 1783
    - c. 2008

11th Grade Geography Multiple Choice Quiz: 7 Continents

Select the best answer for each question.

1. The continents are the huge landmasses that separated by the _____ of the oceans.
   a. waters
   b. glaciers
   c. Ten

2. 60% - 70% of the world's freshwater supply is stored in _____.
   a. Antarctica
   b. Europe
   c. Asia

3. It is the largest continent in size and has the biggest land area.
   a. Asia
   b. Europe
   c. Africa

4. The _____ continent has the most populous cities, where almost _____ people lived here.
   a. Europe ; 5.3 billion
   b. Asia ; 4.6 billion
   c. Africa ; 1.4 billion

5. What is the smallest continent on the planet?
   a. Antarctica
   b. Australia/Oceania
   c. Asia

6. This is the continent with the most countries which consists of 54 countries.
   a. North America
   b. Australia
   c. Africa

7. North America is a continent that is located entirely in the _____ and _____ hemispheres.
   a. southern and western
   b. northern and western
   c. northern and eastern

8. What continent is considered to be the wealthiest and richest continent?
   a. Africa
   b. Europe
   c. North America

9. _____ is a continent of many natural superlatives.
   a. Antarctica
   b. South America
   c. North America

10. What is the smallest continent by population numbers?
   a. Australia
   b. Africa
   c. Antarctica

11. This continent has the largest number of people who speak English either as their first language or as their second language fluently.
   a. North America
   b. South America
   c. Europe

12. _____ is the most active volcano in Antarctica.
   a. Mount Melbourne
   b. Deception Island
   c. Mount Erebus

11th Grade Geography Multiple Choice Quiz: Argentina

Select the best answer for each question.

1. Argentina is located on the _____ continent and borders Bolivia, Brazil, Chile, Paraguay, and Uruguay.
   - a. South American
   - b. North American
   - c. Central America

2. About _____ people live in Argentina.
   - a. 46 million
   - b. 460 million
   - c. 55 million

3. What type of government does Argentina have?
   - a. Oligarchy, Democracy
   - b. Democracy, Republic
   - c. Monarchy, Republic

4. Argentina gained independence from _____ in 1816.
   - a. France
   - b. Spain
   - c. Portugal

5. Argentina is the _____ country in South America after Brazil.
   - a. second largest
   - b. third largest
   - c. seventh largest

6. The original flag of Argentina was adopted in _____.
   - a. 1816
   - b. 1817
   - c. 1812

7. The name 'Argentina' comes from the _____ word 'argentum' which means silver.
   - a. British
   - b. Latin
   - c. Greek

8. _____ of the people live in urban centres, which means cities and towns.
   - a. 92%
   - b. 95%
   - c. 91%

9. This is the second largest city in Argentina and it is also one of the oldest cities in Argentina.
   - a. Rosario
   - b. Córdoba
   - c. Buenos Aires

10. The official language used in Argentina is _____.
    - a. Spanish
    - b. Italian
    - c. French

11. The _____, Argentina's longest river, forms a natural border between Paraguay and Argentina
    - a. Uruguay River
    - b. Negro River
    - c. Paraná River

12. The _____ is the second biggest wetland in the world after the Pantanal in Brazil.
    - a. Grand Affluents
    - b. Okavango Delta
    - c. Ibera Wetlands

11th Grade Geography Multiple Choice Quiz: Costa Rica

Select the best answer for each question.

1. **The population of Costa Rica is _____.**
   a. 3.2 million people
   b. 5.1 million people
   c. 5.5 million people

2. **_____ is the official language of Costa Rica.**
   a. French
   b. Spanish
   c. Italian

3. **Costa Rica is a country on the _____ continent and is one of the countries in the region called Central America.**
   a. South American
   b. North American
   c. Central America

4. **_____ was the first European to set foot in Costa Rica.**
   a. Miguel Mora Porras
   b. José María Castro Madriz
   c. Christopher Columbus

5. **Costa Rica remained a _____ colony for almost 300 years.**
   a. Spanish
   b. English
   c. French

6. **In year _____, Costa Rica became an independent country.**
   a. 1563
   b. 1821
   c. 1838

7. **The total population of Costa Rica in 2021 is _____.**
   a. 5,047,561
   b. 5,470,561
   c. 5,740,615

8. **The capital of Costa Rica is _____ with _____ people.**
   a. Heredia with 356,000
   b. Limon with 63,081
   c. San José with 1.4 million

9. **The name Costa Rica comes from the _____ for Rich Coast**
   a. Greek
   b. Spanish
   c. Latin

10. **The climate of Costa Rica from December to April is _____.**
    a. summer season
    b. dry season
    c. rainy season

11. **Costa Rica's natural resources comes from _____.**
    a. Biomass
    b. Coal and petroleum
    c. Hydropower

12. **What is the standard currency in Costa Rica?**
    a. Costa Rican Colon
    b. Costa Rican Dollar
    c. Costa Rican Peso

11th Grade Geography Multiple Choice Quiz: World Flags

Select the best answer for each question.

1. The first flags were flown in the _____ to tell others that we own a piece of land and that we rule over the people and land.
   a. 17th century
   b. 16th century
   c. 18th century

2. _____ was the first man to set foot on the moon, taking the first steps in 1969 and erecting an American flag.
   a. Wing Commander Rakesh Sharma AC
   b. Astronaut Buzz Aldrin
   c. Neil Armstrong

3. The _____ flag is one of the only two square flags in the world.
   a. Argentina
   b. Tunisia
   c. Swiss

4. In ancient times and in the 4th century, the _____ symbolized the different points of the compass and later as the symbol of faith.
   a. square
   b. cross
   c. sun

5. The flag of _____, is the only world flag that is not rectangular or square shaped.
   a. Vatican
   b. Nepal
   c. Switzerland

6. This country uses a maple leave in its flag which shows that the country is caring for its nature and environment.
   a. Belize
   b. Canada
   c. Cyprus

7. The first men to climb and reach the top of the world's highest mountain, Mount Everest, put up the _____ when they reached the summit of Mount Everest in May 1953.
   a. Swiss flag
   b. Five-starred Red Flag
   c. British 'Union Jack'

8. When was the first flag raised on the moon?
   a. June 20, 1699
   b. July 20, 1969
   c. August 20, 1969

9. In combination with a star, the _____ represents divinity and especially the Islam.
   a. moon
   b. triangle
   c. sun

10. The triangle in a flag often also symbolizes _____ and _____.
    a. energy and love
    b. strength and power
    c. unity and faith

11. The three points of a triangle in a flag represent the Trinity (Father, Son and Holy Spirit) in _____.
    a. Christianity
    b. Islam
    c. Judaism

12. The _____ color is a strong color in Islam, while in China, it is associated with good luck.
    a. green
    b. red
    c. blue

11th Grade Health Multiple Choice Quiz: Heart

Select the best answer for each question.

1. The human heart has _____ chambers or closed spaces.
- a. two
- b. three
- c. four

2. The heart of a grown-up person weighs about _____.
- a. 8 to 12 ounces
- b. 6 to 8 ounces
- c. 8 to 10 ounces

3. The heart is made up of _____ layers.
- a. five
- b. three
- c. four

4. The _____ is the inner layer of the heart. This is the smooth, thin lining of the heart chambers.
- a. pericardium
- b. endocardium
- c. myocardium

5. The _____ is the outer covering of the heart and is a strong sack that protects it.
- a. pericardium
- b. endocardium
- c. myocardium

6. _____ occurs when the heart muscle contracts (pushes in).
- a. Diastole
- b. Ventricular systole
- c. Systole

7. _____ is when the heart muscle relaxes (stops pushing in).
- a. Systole
- b. Diastole
- c. Ventricular systole

8. _____ refers to the heart muscle.
- a. Myocardium
- b. Endocardium
- c. Pericardium

9. The heart muscle beats at a rate of __ beats per minute on average.
- a. 80
- b. 70
- c. 60

10. The two bottom chambers of the heart are the _____ and the _____. These pump blood out of the heart to the body and lungs.
- a. right atrium, left atrium
- b. right ventricle, left ventricle
- c. pulmonary valve, aortic valve

11. The two top chambers are the _____ and the _____. They receive the blood entering the heart.
- a. superior vena cava, aorta
- b. right ventricle, left ventricle
- c. right atrium, left atrium

12. The main artery going out of the right ventricle is the _____.
- a. pulmonary artery
- b. aorta
- c. superior vena cava

11th Grade Science Multiple Choice Quiz: Noble Gases

Select the best answer for each question.

1. The noble gases are located to the far right of the periodic table and make up the _____.
   a. 16th column
   b. 18th column
   c. 17th column

2. Noble gases are _____, meaning each molecule is a single atom and almost never react with other elements.
   a. diatomic
   b. polyatomic
   c. monoatomic

3. The six noble gases are:
   a. Chlorine, bromine, iodine, astatine, tennessine
   b. Helium, hydrogen, radon, lithium, krypton, neon
   c. helium, neon, argon, krypton, xenon, and radon.

4. Helium is the second most abundant element in the universe after _____.
   a. radon
   b. hydrogen
   c. argon

5. Xenon gets its name from the _____ word "xenos" which means "stranger or foreigner."
   a. Greek
   b. Latin
   c. Spanish

6. _____ has the lowest melting and boiling points of any substance.
   a. Neon
   b. Radon
   c. Helium

7. All of the noble gases except for _____ have stable isotopes.
   a. radon
   b. argon
   c. neon

8. This element is non-flammable and it is much safer to use in balloons than hydrogen.
   a. Krypton
   b. Helium
   c. Xenon

9. Many of the noble gases were either discovered or isolated by _____ chemist _____.
   a. Scottish, Sir William Ramsay
   b. Russian, Dmitri Mendeleev
   c. German, Robert Bunsen

10. Krypton gets its name from the _____ word "kryptos" meaning "_____".
    a. Greek; "sweet"
    b. Greek; "the hidden one."
    c. Greek; "lazy"

11. _____, mixed with nitrogen, is used as a filler gas for incandescent light bulbs.
    a. Carbon monoxide
    b. Hydrogen
    c. Argon

12. _____, a highly radioactive element and is only available in minute amounts, is utilized in radiotherapy.
    a. Radon
    b. Carbon
    c. Uranium

11th Grade Science Multiple Choice Quiz: Alkali Metals

Select the best answer for each question.

1. The elements of the alkali metals include _____, _____, _____, _____, _____, and _____.
   a. magnesium, calcium, radium, beryllium, silicon, and lithium
   b. lithium, sodium, potassium, rubidium, cesium, and francium
   c. radium, beryllium, lithium, sodium, calcium, and francium

2. The alkali metals are all in the _____ of the periodic table except for hydrogen.
   a. 1st column
   b. 2nd column
   c. 16th column

3. Alkali Metals have a _____ when compared to other metals.
   a. high density
   b. low density
   c. light density

4. The word "alkali" comes from the _____ word meaning "ashes."
   a. German
   b. Arabic
   c. Greek

5. _____ is the most important alkali metal.
   a. lithium
   b. sodium
   c. potassium

6. Alkali metals are generally stored in _____.
   a. oil
   b. soil
   c. water

7. All alkali metals have _____ atomic numbers.
   a. even
   b. odd
   c. prime

8. Potassium's atomic number is ___ and its symbol is _____.
   a. 19 and P
   b. 19 and K
   c. 11 and Na

9. Alkali metals are the _____ in group one of the periodic systems.
   a. non metals
   b. chemical elements
   c. late transition metals

10. _____ is the lightest known metal.
    a. Sodium
    b. Lithium
    c. francium

11th Grade Organisms Multiple Choice Quiz: Domestic Pig

Select the best answer for each question.

1. Domestic pigs are often _____ but small pigs kept as pets (pot-bellied pigs) are often other colors.
   a. white
   b. black
   c. pink

2. The dental formula of adult pigs is 3.1.4.3/3.1.4.3, giving a total of _____ teeth.
   a. 36
   b. 44
   c. 50

3. Pigs are_____ in the genus Sus
   a. reptiles
   b. amphibians
   c. mammals

4. _____ of piglet fatalities are due to the mother attacking, or unintentionally crushing, the newborn pre-weaned animals.
   a. 60%
   b. 50%
   c. 30%

5. The ancestor of the domestic pig is the _____, which is one of the most numerous and widespread large mammals.
   a. wild boar
   b. babirusa
   c. warthog

6. Pigs are _____, which means that they consume both plants and animals.
   a. omnivores
   b. herbivores
   c. carnivores

7. Pigs need a _____, _____ under a roof to sleep, and they should not be crowded.
   a. warm, muddy area
   b. warm, clean area
   c. cold, clean area

8. Piglets weigh about _____ at birth, and usually double their weight in one week.
   a. 1.5 kilograms
   b. 2.2 kilograms
   c. 1.1 kilograms

9. Pigs often roll in _____ to protect themselves from sunlight.
   a. water
   b. mud
   c. grass

10. Pigs are among the smartest of all domesticated animals and are even smarter than _____.
    a. dogs
    b. cats
    c. birds

11th Grade History Multiple Choice Quiz: The Emancipation Proclamation

Select the best answer for each question.

1. The Emancipation Proclamation was an order given on _____ by 16th US president to free the slaves.
   a. January 1, 1863
   b. December 6, 1865
   c. September 22, 1862

2. Only about _____ of the 4 million slaves were immediately set free.
   a. 60,000
   b. 50,000
   c. 39,000

3. The proclamation gained the Union the support of international countries such as _____ and _____ where slavery had already been abolished.
   a. Great Britain and France
   b. Missouri and Kentucky
   c. Delaware, and Maryland

4. The Emancipation Proclamation was an edict issued by U.S. President _____ that freed the slaves of the Confederate states in rebellion against the Union.
   a. James Madison
   b. George Washington
   c. Abraham Lincoln

5. When was the Thirteenth Amendment adopted and became part of the United States Constitution?
   a. September 17, 1862
   b. December 6, 1865
   c. December 18, 1864

6. _____ arrived on Virginia's shores in 1619, only a dozen years after the first white settlers.
   a. African Americans
   b. Latino Americans
   c. European Americans

7. The Emancipation Proclamation was _____.
   a. a constitutional order
   b. a formal order
   c. an executive order

8. Emancipation Proclamation pave the way for the _____.
   a. 14th Amendment
   b. 12th Amendment
   c. 13th Amendment

9. Around _____ black soldiers fought on the side of the Union Army helping the North win the war.
   a. 100,000
   b. 150,000
   c. 200,000

10. Which states still had slavery after the Emancipation Proclamation?
    a. Virginia and Texas
    b. Delaware and Kentucky
    c. North Carolina and Ohio

11th Grade History Multiple Choice Quiz: The Battle of Fort Sumter

Select the best answer for each question.

1. The Battle of Fort Sumter was the _____ of the American Civil War and signaled the start of the war.
   - a. second battle
   - b. first battle
   - c. third battle

2. The Battle of Fort Sumter took place over two days from _____.
   - a. April 12–13, 1861.
   - b. February 8-9, 1861
   - c. August 28-29, 1861

3. Fort Sumter is an island in _____ not far from Charleston.
   - a. Virginia
   - b. California
   - c. South Carolina

4. The main commander from the North was Major _____.
   - a. Ulysses S. Grant
   - b. Harriet Tubman
   - c. Robert Anderson

5. He was a student of Major Anderson's at the army school of West Point and the leader of the Southern forces.
   - a. Jefferson Davis
   - b. General P. T. Beauregard
   - c. Major Robert Anderson

6. How many people died in the Battle of Fort Sumter?
   - a. 618,222
   - b. 0
   - c. 504

7. Who is the former U.S. senator who'd pledged to drink the blood of casualties?
   - a. Stephen A. Douglas
   - b. James Chesnut, Jr.,
   - c. Charles Sumner

8. 8. The Northern states fell in behind Lincoln, while _____, _____ and _____ duly tumbled into the Confederacy.
   - a. Texas, North Carolina, and Pennsylvania
   - b. Virginia, North Carolina, and Tennessee
   - c. Virginia, Tennessee, and Massachusetts

9. After many hours of bombardment, _____ realized that he had no chance to win the battle.
   - a. Harriet Tubman
   - b. Robert Anderson
   - c. General P. T. Beauregard

10. How many states were there in the Confederate States of America?
    - a. 9
    - b. 11
    - c. 5

11. Who was the president of the Confederate States of America during the American Civil War?
    - a. Andrew Johnson
    - b. Abraham Lincoln
    - c. Jefferson Davis

12. What was the site of the Confederacy's largest prison camp for captured Union soldiers?
    - a. Rock Island
    - b. Andersonville
    - c. Alton

11th Grade History Multiple Choice Quiz: Siege of Vicksburg

Select the best answer for each question.

1. **Which army surrounded the city of Vicksburg, Mississippi during the siege and eventually took control?**
   a. Union Army
   b. South Army
   c. North Army

2. **The siege began on _____.**
   a. May 18, 1863
   b. April 26, 1865
   c. July 4, 1863.

3. **Who was the overall commander of the Confederate Army during the siege?**
   a. John Clifford Pemberton
   b. Theodore R. Davis
   c. John McClernand

4. **Around _____ people live in the city of Vicksburg today.**
   a. 36,000
   b. 17,000
   c. 24,000

5. **Which state did the Siege of Vicksburg took place?**
   a. Texas
   b. Mississippi
   c. California

6. **Around how long did the Siege of Vicksburg last?**
   a. Over 1 month
   b. Over one week
   c. One year

7. **The people of Vicksburg were _____ by the time they surrendered.**
   a. starving
   b. dehydrated
   c. sick

8. **Which side won the Siege of Vicksburg?**
   a. Neither side won
   b. North
   c. South

9. **Vicksburg was an important port city in which major river?**
   a. Mississippi River
   b. Missouri River
   c. Ohio River

10. **What other major battle did the Union won around the same time as the Siege of Vicksburg?**
    a. Battle of Gettysburg
    b. Battle of Ford Sumter
    c. Battle of the Ironclads

11. **Who was the overall commander of the Union Army in the battle?**
    a. Ulysses S. Grant
    b. Theodore R. Davis
    c. John Pemberton

12. **On what day did Vicksburg finally surrender to the Union army?**
    a. July 4, 1863
    b. July 21, 1863
    c. April 26, 1865

11th Grade History Multiple Choice Quiz: Renaissance

Select the best answer for each question.

1. Renaissance began in the 1300s, during the late _____.
   a. Ancient History
   b. Middle Ages
   c. Modern Eras

2. _____ and others from Spain and Portugal discovered two continents that had been unknown to Europeans.
   a. Christopher Columbus
   b. John Cabot
   c. Amerigo Vespucci

3. Renaissance is a French word meaning _____.
   a. resurrection
   b. rebirth
   c. renacimiento

4. The Age of Exploration, also called the _____, began in the 1400s and continued through the 1600s.
   a. Age of Investigation
   b. Age of Discovery
   c. Age of Enlightenment

5. The Age of Exploration began in the nation of _____ under the leadership of _____.
   a. Spain ; Francisco Pizarro
   b. Portugal ; Henry the Navigator
   c. Mexico ; Vasco da Gama

6. The early leaders in the Age of Exploration are _____ and ___.
   a. Portugal and Spain
   b. Mexico and China
   c. Africa and India

7. The Age of Exploration was one of the most important times in the history of _____.
   a. Philology
   b. world geography
   c. world historiography

8. Which technique was used by Leonardo da Vinci to add additional perspective and dimension to paintings?
   a. Use of light and dark
   b. Sfumato
   c. Balance and proportion

9. The main religion of Renaissance Europe was _____ and the main church was the _____.
   a. Confucianism; Confucian church
   b. Buddhism; Buddhist monastery
   c. Christianity; Catholic Church

10. _____ and _____ were popular forms of entertainment and a big part of Renaissance daily life.
    a. Reading and drawing
    b. Music and dancing
    c. Dancing and reading

11. The renaissance architecture style was taken from _____ and _____ and then altered to fit their current lifestyle.
    a. Ancient Roman Architecture and Egypt
    b. Ancient Rome and Greece
    c. Germany and India

12. What year did Johannes Gutenberg, a German, invented the printing press?
    a. 1458
    b. 1450
    c. 1374

11th Grade History Multiple Choice Quiz: American Civil War Weapons

Select the best answer for each question.

1. At the start of the war, many soldiers used old-style guns called _____.
   a. rifle
   b. lorenz rifle
   c. muskets

2. The _____ was a type of bullet that was used throughout the Civil War.
   a. cannonballs
   b. Enfield bullet
   c. Minie ball

3. The Civil War, and the major events leading up to the war, lasted from _____ to _____.
   a. 1853 to 1860
   b. 1950 to 1869
   c. 1860 to 1865

4. The Civil War was the first major war that involved _____.
   a. ironclad ships
   b. cannons
   c. submarines

5. The Civil War was the deadliest war in American history. There were around _____ soldiers killed in action and _____ total dead.
   a. 201,000 ; 657,000
   b. 210,000 ; 625,000
   c. 2,100,000 ; 1,064,000

6. What does Virginia's State Motto "Sic semper tyrannis" means?
   a. Public sentiment is everything
   b. Prelude to war
   c. Thus always to tyrants

7. Who was the 16th US president at the time of the American civil war?
   a. Ulysses S. Grant
   b. Abraham Lincoln
   c. James Buchanan

8. Which form of communication was popular on the home front during the civil war that people used to find out news of loved ones who were in the army?
   a. newspapers
   b. radio
   c. tabloid

9. The war began in Charleston, S.C., when Confederate artillery fired on Fort Sumter on _____.
   a. April 12, 1861
   b. February 15, 1862
   c. July 12, 1861

10. _____ was a famous nurse to the Union Troops. She was called the "Angel of the Battlefields" and founded the American Red Cross.
    a. Bull Run
    b. Dorethea Dix
    c. Clara Barton

11. Which of the following is best at destroying enemy fortification?
    a. bayonets
    b. swords
    c. cannons

12. Future steel tycoon _____ was in charge of the U.S. Military Telegraph Corps during the war.
    a. Andrew Carnegie
    b. Robert E. Lee
    c. Ulysses S. Grant

11th Grade Health Multiple Choice: Small Intestine

Select the best answer for each question.

1. The small intestine is between the _____ and the ____.
   - a. stomach, large intestine
   - b. gallbladder, pancreas
   - c. liver, stomach

2. What are the three regions of small Intestine?
   - a. cecum, colon, and the rectum
   - b. duodenum, jejunum, and ileum
   - c. ileum, colon, cecum

3. The ____ is the small intestine's final section. It is around 3m long and has villi comparable to the jejunum.
   - a. cecum
   - b. duodenum
   - c. ileum

4. The _____ receives bile and juice from the pancreas and it is where most digestion takes place.
   - a. ileum
   - b. jejunum
   - c. duodenum

5. The ____ is where digested products (sugars, amino acids, and fatty acids) are absorbed into the bloodstream.
   - a. jejunum
   - b. duodenum
   - c. ileum

6. A small intestine can be ___ to ___ meters long in adults over the age of five.
   - a. four to five meters
   - b. five to six meters
   - c. three to four meters

7. Food enters the small intestine after it leaves the ____.
   - a. large intestine
   - b. bile
   - c. stomach

8. The ileum absorbs _____, bile salts, and any digestive products that were not absorbed by the jejunum.
   - a. vitamin B12
   - b. Iron
   - c. vitamin B6

9. The small intestine is ____ to ____ long and coils like a maze.
   - a. 35 to 37 feet
   - b. 22 to 25 feet
   - c. 18 to 20 feet

10. The_____ break down proteins and bile emulsifies fats into micelles.
   - a. gastric juice
   - b. digestive enzymes
   - c. saliva

Reading Comprehension: Law Enforcement Dogs

Police dogs are dogs that assist cops in solving crimes. In recent years, they have grown to be an essential part of law enforcement. With their unique abilities and bravery, police dogs have saved many lives. They are often regarded as an important and irreplaceable part of many police departments because they are loyal, watchful, and protective of their police officer counterparts.

Today, police dogs are trained in specific areas. They could be considered experts in their field. Some of the particular police dog roles are as follows:

Tracking: Tracking police dogs use their keen sense of smell to locate criminal suspects or missing people. Tracking dogs are trained for years and can track down even the most elusive criminal. Without police tracking dogs, many suspects would be able to elude capture.

Substance Detectors: Like tracking dogs, these police dogs use their sense of smell to assist officers. Substance dogs are trained to detect a specific substance. Some dogs are trained to detect bombs or explosives. These brave dogs are trained not only to detect explosives but also to respond (very carefully!) and safely alert their officer partner to the explosive location. Other dogs may be drawn to illegal drugs. By quickly determining whether an illegal substance is nearby, these dogs save officers from searching through luggage, a car, or other areas by hand.

Public Order - These police dogs assist officers in keeping the peace. They may pursue a criminal suspect and hold them until an officer arrives, or they may guard an area (such as a jail or prison) to prevent suspects from fleeing.

Cadaver Dogs: Although it may sound disgusting, these police dogs are trained to locate dead bodies. This is a critical function in a police department, and these dogs perform admirably.

A police dog is not just any dog. Police dogs require very special and specialized training. There are numerous breeds of dogs that have been trained for police work. What breed they are often determined by the type of work they will do. German Shepherds and Belgian Malinois are two of the most popular breeds today, but other dogs such as Bloodhounds (good for tracking) and Beagles (good for drug detection) are also used. Police dogs, regardless of breed, are typically trained to do their job from the time they are puppies.

Typically, police dogs are regarded as heroes. They frequently go to live with their human partner police officer. They've known this person for years and have grown to consider them family, which works out well for both the officer and the dog.

1. Tracking police dogs use their _____ to locate criminal suspects or missing people.
   a. keen sense of training
   b. keen sense of taste
   c. keen sense of smell

2. Some substance dogs are trained to detect _____.
   a. runaway children
   b. bombs or explosives
   c. metal and iron

3. Police dogs are trained in ___ areas.
   a. many
   b. a few
   c. specific

4. Police dogs are dogs that assist cops in solving _____.
   a. littering
   b. homelessness
   c. crimes

5. Substance dogs are trained to detect a specific _____.
   a. substance
   b. person
   c. other police dogs

6. What type of police dog is trained pursue a criminal suspect and hold them until an officer arrives?
   a. Crime Fighting dog
   b. Tracking dog
   c. Public Order dog

7. These police dogs are trained to locate dead bodies
   a. Law and Order dogs
   b. Cadaver dogs
   c. Deadly Substance dogs

8. What are the two most popular police dogs used today?
   a. German Shepherds and Belgian Malinois
   b. Bloodhounds and German Shepherds
   c. Belgian Malinois and Rottweiler

English: Tenses

Verbs are classified into three tenses: past, present, and future. The term "past" refers to events that have already occurred (e.g., earlier in the day, yesterday, last week, three years ago). The present tense is used to describe what is happening right now or what is ongoing. The future tense refers to events that have yet to occur (e.g., later, tomorrow, next week, next year, three years from now).

borrowed	went	eat	play	go	giving
read	give	gave	will eat	yelled	seeing
will have	had	reading	will go	do	will borrow
playing	doing	yelling	did	will yell	will do
will give	fight	borrow	yell	will fight	will play
borrowing	played	fighting	read	have	will see
going	see	will read	fought	eating	ate
saw	having				

Simple Present (11)	Present Progressive (IS/ARE +) (11)	Past (11)	Future (11)
play	playing	played	will play
go	going	went	will go
read	reading	read	will read
borrow	borrowing	borrowed	will borrow
eat	eating	ate	will eat
have	having	had	will have
see	seeing	saw	will see
fight	fighting	fought	will fight
do	doing	did	will do
give	giving	gave	will give
yell	yelling	yelled	will yell

Music: Jimi Hendrix

First, read the entire passage. After that, go back and fill in the blanks. You can skip the blanks you're unsure about and finish them later.

guitar	odd	acoustic	mother	Animals
guitarist	stage	Seattle	rock	childhood

Jimi Hendrix, a __guitarist__ , singer, and songwriter, wowed audiences in the 1960s with his outrageous electric guitar skills and experimental sound.

Jimi Hendrix began playing guitar as a teenager and grew up to become a __rock__ legend known for his innovative electric guitar playing in the 1960s. His performance of "The Star-Spangled Banner" at Woodstock in 1969 was one of his most memorable. Hendrix died of drug-related complications in 1970, leaving his imprint on the world of rock music and remaining popular to this day.

On November 27, 1942, in __Seattle__ , Washington, Hendrix was born Johnny Allen Hendrix (later changed by his father to James Marshall). He had a difficult __childhood__ , living in the care of relatives or acquaintances at times.

When Hendrix was born, his __mother__ , Lucille, was only 17 years old. She had a rocky relationship with his father, Al, and eventually left the family after the couple had two more sons, Leon and Joseph. Hendrix only saw his mother on rare occasions before her death in 1958.

Music became a haven for Hendrix in many ways. He was a fan of blues and rock and roll and taught himself to play the __guitar__ with the help of his father.

When Hendrix was 16, his father bought him his first __acoustic__ guitar, and the following year, his first electric guitar - a right-handed Supro Ozark that he had to play upside down because he was naturally left-handed. Soon after, he started performing with his band, the Rocking Kings. In 1959, he dropped out of high school and worked __odd__ jobs while pursuing his musical dreams.

In mid-1966, Hendrix met Chas Chandler, bassist for the British rock band the __Animals__ , who agreed to become Hendrix's manager. Chandler persuaded Hendrix to travel to London, where he formed the Jimi Hendrix Experience with bassist Noel Redding and drummer Mitch Mitchell.

While performing in England, Hendrix amassed a cult following among the country's rock royalty, with the Beatles, Rolling Stones, Who, and Eric Clapton all praising his work. According to one critic for the British music magazine Melody Maker, he "had great __stage__ presence" and appeared to be playing "with no hands at all" at times.

According to one journalist in the Berkeley Tribe, "Nobody could get more out of an electric guitar than Jimi Hendrix. He was the ultimate guitarist."

History: The Mayflower

First, read the entire passage. After that, go back and fill in the blanks. You can skip the blanks you're unsure about and finish them later.

ship	sail	voyage	assist	settlers
passengers	illness	load	leaking	Cape

In 1620, a __ship__ called the Mayflower transported a group of English colonists to North America. These people established New England's first permanent European colony in what is now Plymouth, Massachusetts. Later, they were named the Pilgrims.

The Mayflower was approximately 106 feet long, 25 feet wide, and had a tonnage of 180. The deck of the Mayflower was about 80 feet long, roughly the length of a basketball court. The ship had three masts for holding sails:

The fore-mast (in front)

The main-mast (in the middle)

The mizzen mast (in the back) (back)

On August 4, 1620, the Mayflower and the Speedwell set sail from Southampton, England. They had to come to a halt in Dartmouth, however, because the Speedwell was leaking. They left Dartmouth on August 21, but the Speedwell began __leaking__ again, and they came to a halt in Plymouth, England. They decided to abandon the Speedwell at Plymouth and __load__ as many passengers as possible onto the Mayflower. On September 6, 1620, they set sail from Plymouth.

The Mayflower set __sail__ from Plymouth, England, west across the Atlantic Ocean. The ship's original destination was Virginia, but storms forced it to change course. On November 9, 1620, more than two months after leaving Plymouth, the Mayflower sighted __Cape__ Cod. The Pilgrims decided to stay even though they were north of where they had planned to settle.

It is estimated that around 30 children were on board the Mayflower during the epic __voyage__ to America, but little is known about many of them.

They were children of passengers, some traveled with other adults, and some were servants - but having young people among the __settlers__ was critical to the Plymouth Colony's survival.

It is believed that when the colonists faced their first harsh winter of __illness__ and death in a new land, the children would __assist__ the adults by tending to the sick, assisting in the preparation of food, and fetching firewood and water.

While nearly half of the ship's __passengers__ died during the winter of 1620/1621, it is believed that there were fewer deaths among the children, implying that the struggling colony had a better chance of thriving.

Health: The Food Groups

Eating healthy foods is especially important for children because they are still developing. Children's bodies require nutrition to develop strong, healthy _bones_ and muscles. You will not grow as tall or as strong as you could if you do not get all the _vitamins_ and minerals you require while growing.

Healthy food includes a wide variety of fresh foods from the five healthy food groups:

Dairy: Milk, cheese, and _yogurt_ are the most critical dairy foods, which are necessary for strong and healthy bones. There aren't many other foods in our diet that have as much calcium as these.

Fruit: Fruit contains vitamins, minerals, dietary fiber, and various phytonutrients (nutrients found naturally in plants) that help your body stay healthy. Fruits and vegetables provide you with energy, vitamins, antioxidants, fiber, and _water_ . These nutrients help protect you against diseases later in life, such as heart disease, stroke, and some cancers.

Vegetables and legumes/beans: Vegetables should account for a large _portion_ of your daily food intake and should be encouraged at all meals (including snack times). To keep your body healthy, they supply vitamins, minerals, dietary fiber, and phytonutrients (nutrients found naturally in plants).

Grain (cereal) foods: choose wholegrain and/or high _fiber_ bread, cereals, rice, pasta, noodles, and so on. These foods provide you with the energy you require to grow, develop, and learn. Refined grain products (such as cakes and biscuits) can contain added sugar, fat, and sodium.

Protein from lean meats and poultry, fish, eggs, tofu, nuts and seeds, and legumes/beans is used by our bodies to _produce_ specialized chemicals such as hemoglobin and adrenalin. Protein also helps to build, maintain, and _repair_ tissues in our bodies. Protein is the primary component of muscles and organs (such as your heart).

Calories are a unit of measurement for the amount of energy in food. We gain calories when we eat, which gives us the energy to run around and do things. If we _consume_ more calories than we expend while moving, our bodies will store the excess calories as fat. If we burn more calories than we consume, our bodies will begin to burn the previously _stored_ fat.

Art: J. M. W. Turner

Joseph Mallord William Turner, also known as William Turner, was an English Romantic painter, printmaker, and watercolorist. He is well-known for his expressive colorizations, imaginative landscapes, and turbulent, often violent sea paintings.

On April 23, 1775, J. M. W. Turner was born above his father's barbershop in London, England. When Joseph was a child, he began to draw pictures. He enjoyed drawing outside scenes, particularly buildings. His father's shop sold some of his drawings.

He began attending the Royal Academy of Art in London when he was fourteen years old. He kept sketching and painting with watercolors. Many of his sketches were published in magazines. While he mostly drew buildings and architecture, he also began to draw some seascapes.

In 1796, Turner completed his first oil painting. Fishermen at Sea was the title. Turner gained a national reputation as a talented artist as a result of the painting's critical acclaim. Many people compared his work to that of other well-known painters.

Turner was captivated by the power of God in natural scenes, particularly the ocean and the sun. He would make numerous sketches in numbered notebooks, which he would then reference when painting in his studio. He frequently included people in his paintings, but they were small and insignificant compared to the power of nature around them.

Turner's work evolved, with less emphasis on detail and more emphasis on the energy of the natural phenomenon he was painting, such as the sea, a storm, a fire, or the sun. The paintings' objects became less recognizable.

The painting Rain, Steam, and Speed is an example of this. Light and mist are used to power the train engine as it moves down the track in this landscape of a locomotive crossing a bridge. The focus is on the color and changing light as the train passes through the landscape.

Many of Turner's later works are reminiscent of the Impressionist style of painting that would emerge in France in the coming years. Turner's work undoubtedly influenced artists like Monet, Degas, and Renoir.

Many art historians regard J. M. W. Turner as the most incredible landscape painter of all time. His artwork had a significant influence on many artists who came after him, including many impressionists.

1. Turner's later works are reminiscent of the _____ style of painting.
   a. [Impressionist]
   b. Watercolor

2. In 1796, Turner completed his first _____ painting.
   a. colored
   b. [oil]

3. Turner began attending the _____ of Art in London.
   a. Royal State University
   b. [Royal Academy]

4. Turner was born above his father's _____.
   a. mechanic shop
   b. [barbershop]

5. J. M. W. Turner was an English Romantic painter, _____, and watercolorist.
   a. teacher
   b. [printmaker]

6. Turner frequently included _____ in his painting.
   a. animals
   b. [people]

Weather and Climate

The difference between weather and climate is simply a matter of time. Weather refers to the conditions of the atmosphere over a short period of time, whereas climate refers to how the atmosphere "behaves" over a longer period of time.

When we discuss climate change, we are referring to changes in long-term averages of daily weather. Today's children are constantly told by their parents and grandparents about how the snow was always piled up to their waists as they trudged off to school. Most children today have not experienced those kinds of dreadful snow-packed winters. The recent changes in winter snowfall indicate that the climate has changed since their parents were children.

Weather is essentially the atmosphere's behavior, particularly in terms of its effects on life and human activities. The distinction between weather and climate is that weather refers to short-term (minutes to months) changes in the atmosphere, whereas climate refers to long-term changes. Most people associate weather with temperature, humidity, precipitation, cloudiness, brightness, visibility, wind, and atmospheric pressure, as in high and low pressure.

Weather can change from minute to minute, hour to hour, day to day, and season to season in most places. However, the climate is the average of weather over time and space. A simple way to remember the distinction is that climate is what you expect, such as a very hot summer, whereas weather is what you get, such as a hot day with pop-up thunderstorms.

Use the word bank to unscramble the words!

Pressure	Density	Cloudy	Latitude	Elevation	Weather
Absorb	Humid	Precipitation	Windy	Forecast	Climate
Sunshine	Temperature				

1. IUMHD — Humid

2. UDLOYC — Cloudy

3. FSEATOCR — Forecast

4. UDLTITAE — Latitude

5. IEOCAIIPPTRNT — Precipitation

6. TEEERPAURMT — Temperature

7. RSEREUPS — Pressure

8. LEICATM — Climate

9. SNNIEHUS — Sunshine

10. OBBASR — Absorb

11. VETIEOANL — Elevation

12. EATWRHE — Weather

13. NDWIY — Windy

14. TYNEIDS — Density

Science: Vertebrates

To begin, all animals are classified as either vertebrates or invertebrates. Invertebrates lack a backbone, whereas vertebrates do. Scientists can't stop there, because each group contains thousands of different animals! As a result, scientists divide vertebrates and invertebrates into increasingly smaller groups. Let's talk about vertebrates and some of their classifications.

Vertebrates range in size from a frog to a blue whale. Because there are at least 59,000 different types of vertebrates on the planet, they are further classified into five major groups: mammals, birds, fish, amphibians, and reptiles. Remember that animals are classified into these groups based on what they have in common. Why is an elephant classified as a mammal while a crocodile is classified as a reptile? Let's go over some of the characteristics of each vertebrate group.

Warm-blooded animals are mammals. This means that their bodies maintain their temperature, which is usually higher than the temperature of the surrounding air. They also have hair or fur; they have lungs to breathe air; that they feed milk to their babies; and that most give birth to live young, rather than laying eggs, as a dog does.

- Birds have feathers, two wings (though not all birds, such as the ostrich and penguin, can fly), are warm-blooded, and lay eggs.
- Fish have fins or scales, live in water, and breathe oxygen through gills.
- Like salamanders and frogs, Amphibians have smooth, moist skin (amphibians must keep their skin wet); lay eggs in water; most breathe through their skin and lungs.
- Reptiles have scales (imagine a scaly lizard), are cold-blooded (their body temperature changes as the temperature around them changes), breathe air. Most reptiles, including the crocodile and snake, lay hard-shelled eggs on land.

Vertebrates play several vital roles in an ecosystem. Many predator species are large vertebrates in ecosystems. Lions, eagles, and sharks are examples of predatory vertebrates. Many prey species in ecosystems are also vertebrates. Mice, rabbits, and frogs are examples of these animals. Many vertebrates serve as scavengers in ecosystems. They are significant because they remove dead animals from the environment. Turkey vultures and hyenas, for example, are both vertebrate scavengers. Furthermore, many vertebrates serve as pollinators in ecosystems. Bats and monkeys, for example, may aid in pollen spread by visiting various trees and plants.

Humans value vertebrates for a variety of reasons. Vertebrates are domesticated animals used by humans. These animals are capable of producing milk, food, and clothing. They can also help with work. Agricultural animals are usually vertebrates. Humans also hunt a variety of wild vertebrate animals for food.

1. Vertebrates range in _____ from a frog to a blue whale.
   - a. age
   - b. [size]

2. Fish have fins or scales, live in water, and breathe ___ through gills.
   - a. [oxygen]
   - b. water

3. Invertebrates lack a _____, whereas vertebrates _____.
   - a. skin, whereas vertebrates do
   - b. [backbone, whereas vertebrates do]

4. Warm-blooded animals are _____.
   - a. [mammals]
   - b. producers

5. Some vertebrates serve as _____, they remove dead animals from the environment.
   - a. [scavengers]
   - b. invertebrates

6. Lions, eagles, and sharks are examples of _____ vertebrates.
   - a. ecofriendly
   - b. [predatory]

7. _____ animals are capable of producing milk, food, and clothing.
   - a. Non produced
   - b. [Domesticated]

8. Many vertebrates serve as _____ in ecosystems, they may aid in pollen spread by visiting various trees and plants.
   - a. water lilies
   - b. [pollinators]

Science: Organelles

Do you and your dog have a similar appearance? We are all aware that people and dogs appear to be very different on the outside. However, there are some similarities on the inside. Cells make up all animals, including humans and dogs.

All animal cells appear to be the same. They have a cell membrane that contains cytoplasm, which is a gooey fluid. Organelles float in the cytoplasm. Organelles function as tiny machines that meet the needs of the cell. The term organelle refers to a "miniature organ." This lesson will teach you about the various organelles found in animal cells and what they do.

The nucleus of the cell is the cell's brain. It is in charge of many of the cell's functions. The nucleus is where DNA, the genetic instructions for building your body, is stored. DNA contains vital information! Your nucleus has its membrane to protect this essential information, similar to the membrane that surrounds the entire cell.

Your cells require energy. Energy is produced by mitochondria, which are oval-shaped organelles. Mitochondria convert the nutrients that enter the cell into ATP. Your cells use ATP for energy. Because they are the cell's powerhouses, you might think of these organelles as the mighty mitochondria.

The nutrients must be digested before they can be converted into energy by the mitochondria. Digestion is carried out by a group of organelles known as lysosomes. Digestive enzymes are found in lysosomes. Enzymes can sometimes be released into the cell. Because the enzymes kill the cell, lysosomes are known as "suicide bags."

Use Google or your preferred source to help match each term with a definition.

1	L	nucleus	→	where DNA is stored
2	B	lysosomes	→	degradation of proteins and cellular waste
3	J	Golgi Apparatus	→	modification of proteins; "post-office" of the cell
4	I	Mitochondria	→	powerhouse of the cell
5	D	SER	→	lipid synthesis
6	K	RER	→	protein synthesis + modifications
7	A	Microtubules	→	responsible for chromosome segregation
8	C	ribosomes	→	protein synthesis
9	H	peroxysomes	→	degradation of H2O2
10	G	cell wall	→	prevents excessive uptake of water, protects the cell (in plants)
11	E	chloroplast	→	site of photosynthesis
12	F	central vacuole	→	stores water in plant cells

Science:
Invertebrates

Invertebrates can be found almost anywhere. Invertebrates account for at least 95% of all animals on the planet! Do you know what one thing they all have in common? Invertebrates lack a backbone.

Your body is supported by a backbone, which protects your organs and connects your other bones. As a result, you are a vertebrate. On the other hand, invertebrates lack the support of bones, so their bodies are often simpler, softer, and smaller. They are also cold-blooded, which means their body temperature fluctuates in response to changes in the air or water around them.

Invertebrates can be found flying, swimming, crawling, or floating and provide essential services to the environment and humans. Nobody knows how many different types of invertebrates there are, but there are millions!

Just because an invertebrate lacks a spinal column does not mean it does not need to eat. Invertebrates, like all other forms of animal life, must obtain nutrients from their surroundings. Invertebrates have evolved two types of digestion to accomplish this. The use of intracellular digestion is common in the most simple organisms. The food is absorbed into the cell and broken down in the cytoplasm at this point. Extracellular digestion, in which cells break down food through the secretion of enzymes and other techniques, is used by more advanced invertebrates. All vertebrates use extracellular digestion.

Still, all animals, invertebrates or not, need a way to get rid of waste. Most invertebrates, especially the simplest ones, use the process of diffusion to eliminate waste. This is merely the opposite of intracellular digestion. However, more advanced invertebrates have more advanced waste disposal mechanisms. Similar to our kidneys, specialized glands in these animals filter and excrete waste. But there is a happy medium. Even though some invertebrates do not have complete digestive tracts like vertebrates, they do not simply flush out waste through diffusion. Instead, the mouth doubles as an exit.

Scientists have classified invertebrates into numerous groups based on what the animals have in common. Arthropods have segmented bodies, which means that they are divided into sections. Consider an ant!

Arthropods are the most numerous group of invertebrates. They can live on land, as spiders and insects do, or in water, as crayfish and crabs do. Because insects are the most numerous group of arthropods, many of them fly, including mosquitoes, bees, locusts, and ladybugs.

They also have jointed legs or limbs to help them walk, similar to how you have knees for your legs and elbows for your arms. The majority of arthropods have an exoskeleton, tough outer skin, or shell that protects their body. Have you ever wondered why when you squish a bug, it makes that crunching sound? That's right; it's the exoskeleton!

Mollusks are the second most numerous group of invertebrates. They have soft bodies and can be found on land or in water. Shells protect the soft bodies of many mollusks, including snails, oysters, clams, and scallops. However, not all, such as octopus, squid, and cuttlefish, have a shell.

1. Invertebrates lack a _____.
   a. backbone
   b. tailbone

2. Invertebrates are also _____.
   a. cold-blooded
   b. warm-blooded

3. _____ can live on land, as spiders and insects do, or in water, as crayfish and crabs do.
   a. Vertebrates
   b. Arthropods

4. All animals, invertebrates or not, need a way to get rid of _____.
   a. their skin
   b. waste

5. _____ have soft bodies and can be found on land or in water.
   a. Arthropods
   b. Mollusks

6. Just because an invertebrate lacks a _____ column does not mean it does not need to eat.
   a. spinal
   b. insects

7. Your body is supported by a backbone, which protects your ____ and connects your other bones.
   a. organs
   b. muscles

8. Invertebrates lack the support of bones, so their bodies are often simpler, ___, and smaller.
   a. softer and bigger
   b. softer and smaller

Music: Musical Terms

Complete the crossword by filling in a word that fits each clue. Fill in the correct answers, one letter per square, both across and down, from the given clues. There will be a gray space between multi-word answers.

Tip: Solve the easy clues first, and then go back and answer the more difficult ones.

Across

2. the highest adult male singing voice; singing falsetto
4. the part of a song that transitions between two main parts
5. a combination of three or more tones sounded simultaneously
8. making up the song or melody as you play
11. a song written for one or more instruments playing solo
12. the highest of the singing voices
13. is a poem set to music with a recurring pattern of both rhyme and meter
14. timing or speed of the music

Down

1. singing without any instruments
3. low, the lowest of the voices and the lowest part of the harmony
6. to play a piece of music sweetly, tender, adoring manner
7. the sound of two or more notes heard simultaneously
9. is a musical interval; the distance between one note
10. played by a single musical instrument or voice
15. a range of voice that is between the bass and the alto
16. the repeating changing of the pitch of a note

CHORD   BRIDGE   ALTO
HARMONY   SOPRANO
IMPROVISATION   DOLCE
OCTAVE   VIBRATO   STANZA
SONATA   A CAPPELLA   TEMPO
BASS   SOLO   TENOR

History: The Vikings

During the Middle Ages, the Vikings lived in Northern Europe. They first settled in the Scandinavian lands that are now Denmark, Sweden, and Norway. During the Middle Ages, the Vikings played a significant role in Northern Europe, particularly during the Viking Age, which lasted from 800 CE to 1066 CE.

In Old Norse, the word Viking means "to raid." The Vikings would board their longships and sail across the seas to raid villages on Europe's northern coast, including islands like Great Britain. In 787 CE, they first appeared in England to raid villages. When the Vikings raided , they were known to attack defenseless monasteries. This earned them a bad reputation as barbarians, but monasteries were wealthy and undefended Viking targets.

The Vikings eventually began to settle in areas other than Scandinavia. They colonized parts of Great Britain, Germany, and Iceland in the ninth century. They spread into northeastern Europe, including Russia, in the 10th century. They also established Normandy, which means "Northmen," along the coast of northern France.

By the beginning of the 11th century, the Vikings had reached the pinnacle of their power. Leif Eriksson, son of Erik the Red, was one Vikings who made it to North America. He established a brief settlement in modern-day Canada. This was thousands of years before Columbus.

The English and King Harold Godwinson defeated the Vikings, led by King Harald Hardrada of Norway, in 1066. The defeat in this battle is sometimes interpreted as the end of the Viking Age. The Vikings stopped expanding their territory at this point, and raids became less frequent.

The arrival of Christianity was a major factor at the end of the Viking age. The Vikings became more and more a part of mainland Europe as Scandinavia was converted to Christianity and became a part of Christian Europe. Sweden's, Denmark's, and Norway's identities and borders began to emerge as well.

The Vikings were perhaps best known for their ships. The Vikings built longships for exploration and raiding. Longships were long, narrow vessels built for speed. Oars primarily propelled them but later added a sail to help in windy conditions. Longships had a shallow draft, which allowed them to float in shallow water and land on beaches.

The Vikings also built cargo ships known as Knarr for trading. The Knarr was wider and deeper than the longship, allowing it to transport more cargo.

Five recovered Viking ships can be seen at the Viking Ship Museum in Roskilde, Denmark . It's also possible to see how the Vikings built their ships. The Vikings used a shipbuilding technique known as clinker building. They used long wood planks that overlapped along the edges.

Geography: Canada

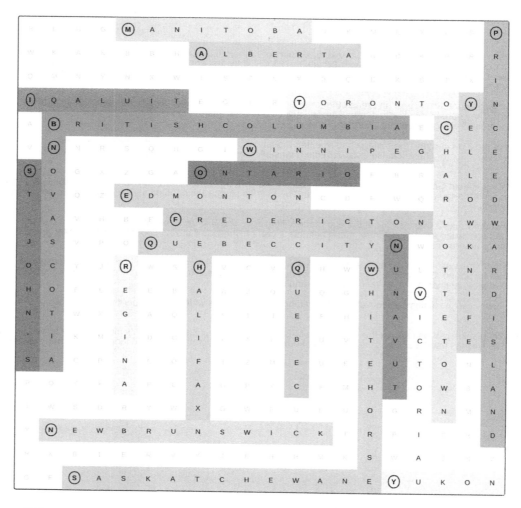

Yukon →   Nunavut ↓   Nova Scotia ↓   Prince Edward Island ↓   New Brunswick →   Quebec ↓   Ontario →   Manitoba →

Saskatchewan →   Alberta →   British Columbia →   Victoria ↓   Edmonton →   Regina ↓   Winnipeg →   Toronto →

Quebec City →   Fredericton →   Charlottetown ↓   Halifax ↓   St. John's ↓   Iqaluit →   Yellowknife ↓   Whitehorse ↓

24 words in Wordsearch: 11 vertical, 13 horizontal, 0 diagonal. (0 reversed.)

Environmental Health: Water Pollution

First, read the entire passage. After that, go back and fill in the blanks. You can skip the blanks you're unsure about and finish them later.

naturally	spills	toxic	crops	causes
streams	Gulf	wastewater	Acid	ill

Water pollution occurs when waste, chemicals, or other particles cause a body of water (e.g., rivers, oceans, lakes) to become __toxic__ to the fish and animals that rely on it for survival. Water pollution can also disrupt and hurt nature's water cycle.

Water pollution can occur __naturally__ due to volcanoes, algae blooms, animal waste, and silt from storms and floods.

Human activity contributes significantly to water pollution. Sewage, pesticides, fertilizers from farms, wastewater and chemicals from factories, silt from construction sites, and trash from people littering are some human __causes__ .

Oil __spills__ have been some of the most well-known examples of water pollution. The Exxon Valdez oil spill occurred when an oil tanker collided with a reef off the coast of Alaska, causing over 11 million gallons of oil to spill into the ocean. Another major oil spill was the Deepwater Horizon oil spill, which occurred when an oil well exploded, causing over 200 million gallons of oil to spill into the __Gulf__ of Mexico.

Water pollution can be caused directly by air pollution. When sulfur dioxide particles reach high altitudes in the atmosphere, they can combine with rain to form acid rain. __Acid__ rain can cause lakes to become acidic, killing fish and other animals.

The main issue caused by water pollution is the impact on aquatic life. Dead fish, birds, dolphins, and various other animals frequently wash up on beaches, killed by pollutants in their environment. Pollution also has an impact on the natural food chain. Small animals consume contaminants like lead and cadmium.

Clean water is one of the most valuable and essential commodities for life on Earth. Clean water is nearly impossible to obtain for over 1 billion people on the planet. They can become __ill__ from dirty, polluted water, which is especially difficult for young children. Some bacteria and pathogens in water can make people sick to the point of death.

Water pollution comes from a variety of sources. Here are a few of the main reasons:

Sewage: In many parts of the world, sewage is still flushed directly into __streams__ and rivers. Sewage can introduce dangerous bacteria that can make humans and animals very sick.

Farm animal waste: Runoff from large herds of farm animals such as pigs and cows can enter the water supply due to rain and large storms.

Pesticides: Pesticides and herbicides are frequently sprayed on __crops__ to kill bugs, while herbicides are sprayed to kill weeds. These potent chemicals can enter the water through rainstorm runoff. They can also contaminate rivers and lakes due to unintentional spills.

Construction, floods, and storms: Silt from construction, earthquakes, and storms can reduce water oxygen levels and suffocate fish. Factories - Water is frequently used in factories to process chemicals, keep engines cool, and wash things away. Sometimes used __wastewater__ is dumped into rivers or the ocean. It may contain pollutants.

Health Spelling Words: Healthy Routines

Write the correct word for each sentence.

Reading	overeat	Eating	read	fat
fresh	fruit	health	glass	chair
floss	Breakfast	Staying	daily	Sleep
fiber	enough	burn	Walking	body

1. Creating a healthy _daily_ routine is simple.

2. _Staying_ hydrated is vital for our health.

3. Exercise has tremendous _health_ benefits.

4. Exposure to the sun enables the _body_ to produce vitamin D.

5. _Walking_ is one of the most underrated healthy habits you can do.

6. Vegetables are low in calories, yet high in vitamins, minerals, and _fiber_.

7. _Reading_ has benefits to both your physical and mental health.

8. _Sleep_ is the only time during the day where our bodies are able to relax, unwind and recover.

9. _Eating_ a variety of good foods.

10. _Breakfast_ is the most important meal of the day.

11. Drink a _glass_ of water.

12. Sitting in your _chair_ all day long isn't good for you.

13. Excess body _fat_ comes from eating more than we need.

14. Cooking the right amount makes it easier to not _overeat_.

15. Physical activity helps us _burn_ off the extra calories.

16. Eat _fruit_ instead of eating a candy bar.

17. Make time to _read_ every day.

18. Don't forget to _floss_.

19. Swap sugary desserts for _fresh_ fruit.

20. Get _enough_ sleep.

Science: Titanium (Ti) Element

Titanium is the first element in the periodic table's fourth column. It is a transition metal. Titanium atoms contain 22 protons and 22 electrons.

Titanium is a complex, light, silvery metal under normal conditions. It can be brittle at room temperature, but it becomes more bendable and pliable as the temperature rises.

Titanium's high strength-to-weight ratio is one of its most desirable properties. This means it is both extremely strong and lightweight. Titanium is double the strength of aluminum but only 60% heavier. It is also as strong as steel but weighs a fraction of the weight.

Compared to other metals, titanium is relatively non-reactive and highly resistant to corrosion caused by different metals and chemicals such as acids and oxygen. As a result, it has relatively low thermal and electrical conductivity.

Titanium is not found in nature as a pure element but rather as a compound found in the Earth's crust as a component of many minerals. According to the International Atomic Energy Agency, it is the ninth most prevalent element in the Earth's crust. Rutile and ilmenite are the two most essential minerals for titanium mining. Australia, South Africa, and Canada are the top producers of these ores.

Titanium is mostly used in the form of titanium dioxide (TiO2). Tio2 is a white powder used in various industrial applications such as white paint, white paper, white polymers, and white cement.

Metals like iron, aluminum, and manganese are combined with titanium to create strong and lightweight alloys that can be utilized in spacecraft, naval vessels, missiles, and armor plating. Due to its corrosion resistance, it is particularly well-suited for seawater applications.

The biocompatibility of titanium is another valuable property of the metal. This indicates that the human body will not reject it. Together with its strength, durability, and lightweight, titanium is a good material for medical applications. It is utilized in various applications, including hip and dental implants. Titanium is also utilized in the manufacture of jewelry, such as rings and watches.

Reverend William Gregor recognized titanium as a new element for the first time in 1791. As a hobby, the English clergyman was fascinated by minerals. He coined the term menachanite for the element. M.H. Kalproth, a German chemist, eventually altered the name to titanium. M. A. Hunter, an American scientist, was the first to create pure titanium in 1910.

Titanium is named after the Greek gods Titans.

Titanium has five stable isotopes: titanium-46, titanium-47, titanium-48, titanium-49, and titanium-50. The isotope titanium-48 accounts for the vast bulk of titanium found in nature.

1. Titanium has five stable _____.
   a. isotopes

2. Titanium is the first element in the periodic table's _____ column.
   a. third
   b. fourth

3. Titanium is a transition _____.
   a. metal

4. Titanium is mostly used in the form of _____ (TiO2).
   a. titanium dioxide
   b. dioxide oxygen

VOLUNTEER

Proofreading Skills:
Volunteering

There are **10** mistakes in this passage. 3 capitals missing. 4 unnecessary capitals. 3 incorrect homophones.

Your own life can be changed and the lives of others, through volunteer work. ~~to~~ To cope with the news that there has been a disaster, you can volunteer to help those in need. Even if you can't contribute financially, you can donate ~~you're~~ your time instead.

Volunteering is such an integral part of the American culture that many high schools require their students to participate in community service to graduate.

When you volunteer, you have the freedom to choose what you'd like to do and who or what you think is most deserving of your time. Start with these ideas if you need a little inspiration. We've got just a few examples here.

Encourage the growth and development of young people. Volunteer as a ~~Camp~~ camp counselor, a Big Brother or Big Sister, or an after-school sports program. Special Olympics games and events are excellent opportunities to know children with special needs.

Spend the holidays doing good deeds for others. Volunteer at a food bank or distribute toys to children in need on Thanksgiving Day, and you'll be doing your part to help those in need. ~~your~~ Your church, temple, mosque, or another place of worship may also require your assistance.

You can visit an animal shelter and play with the ~~Animals.~~ animals. Volunteers are critical to the well-being of shelter animals. (You also get a good workout when you walk rescued dogs.)

Become a member of a political campaign. ~~Its~~ It's a great way to learn more about the inner workings of politics if ~~your~~ you're curious about it. If you are not able ~~To~~ to cast a ballot, you can still help elect your preferred candidate.

Help save the planet. Join a river preservation group and lend a hand. Participate in a park cleanup day in your community. Not everyone is cut out for the great outdoors; if you can't see yourself hauling trees up a hill, consider working in the park's office or education center instead.

Take an active role in promoting health-related causes. Many of us know someone afflicted with a medical condition (like cancer, HIV, or diabetes, for example). ~~a~~ A charity that helps people with a disease, such as delivering meals, raising money, or providing other assistance, can make you ~~Feel~~ feel good about yourself.

Find a way to combine your favorite things if you have more than one. For example, if you're a fan of kids and have a talent for arts and crafts, consider volunteering at a children's hospital.

Jackie Robinson: The First African-American Player In MLB

On January 31, 1919, in Cairo, Georgia, Jack Roosevelt Robinson was born. There were five children in the family, and the youngest one was him. After Jackie was born, Jackie's father left the family, and he never returned. His mother, Millie, took care of him and his three brothers and one sister when they were young.

The family moved to Pasadena , California, about a year after Jackie was born. Jackie was awed by his older brothers' prowess in sports as a child. Meanwhile, his brother Mack rose to prominence as a track star and Olympic silver medalist in the 200-meter dash.

Jackie was an avid sports enthusiast . Like his older brother, he competed in track and field and other sports like football, baseball, and tennis. Football and baseball were two of his favorite sports to play. Throughout high school, Jackie was subjected to racism daily. Even though white teammates surrounded him, he felt like a second-class citizen off the field.

After high school, Jackie went to UCLA, where he excelled in track, baseball, football , and basketball. To his credit, he was the first player at UCLA to receive all four varsity letters in the same season. The long jump was another event where he excelled at the NCAA level.

With the outbreak of World War II, Robinson's football career was over before it began. He was called up for military service. Jackie made friends with the legendary boxing champion Joe Lewis at basic training. Robinson was accepted into officer training school thanks to Joe's assistance.

After completing his officer training, Jackie was assigned to the 761st Tank Battalion at Fort Hood, Texas . Only black soldiers were assigned to this battalion because they could not serve alongside white soldiers. When Jackie refused to move to the back of an army bus one day, he got into trouble. In 1944, he was discharged with an honorable discharge after nearly being expelled from the military.

Robinson began his professional baseball career with the Kansas City Monarchs soon after he was discharged from the military. The Negro Baseball League was home to the Monarchs. Black players were still not allowed to play in Major League Baseball at this time. Jackie performed well on the field. He was an outstanding shortstop, hitting .387 on average.

While playing for the Monarchs, Branch Rickey, the Dodgers' general manager, approached Jackie. Branch hoped that the Dodgers could win the pennant by signing an African-American player. Branch warned Robinson that he would encounter racial prejudice when he first joined the Dodgers. Branch was looking for a person who could take insults without reacting. This famous exchange between Jackie and Branch occurred during their first conversation:

Jackie: "Are you looking for a Negro who is afraid to fight back, Mr. Rickey?"
Jackie: "Are you looking for a Negro who is afraid to fight back, Mr. Rickey?" Robinson, I'm looking for a baseball player who has the guts not to fight back."

For the Montreal Royals, Jackie first played in the minor leagues. He was constantly confronted with racism. Because of Jackie, the opposing team would occasionally fail to show up for games. Then there were the times when people would verbally abuse or throw objects at him. In the midst of all this, Jackie remained calm and focused on the game. He had a .349 batting average and was named the league's most valuable player.

Robinson was called up to play for the Brooklyn Dodgers at the start of the 1947 baseball season, and he did. On April 15, 1947, he became the first African-American to play in the sport's major leagues. Racially charged taunts were once again directed at Jackie from both fans and fellow players alike. Death threats were made against him. But Jackie had the courage not to fight back. He kept his word to Branch Rickey and dedicated himself solely to the game of baseball. The Dodgers won the pennant that year, and Jackie was named the team's Rookie of the Year for his achievements.

Jackie Robinson was one of the best major league baseball players for the next ten years. During his lengthy career, his batting average stood at.311, and he hit 137 home runs while also stealing 197 bases. Six times he was selected to the All-Star team, and in 1949 he was named the National League MVP.

Because of Jackie Robinson's groundbreaking work, other African-American players could play in the major leagues. He also paved the way for racial integration in different facets of American life. He was inducted into the Baseball Hall of Fame in 1962. On October 24, 1972, Robinson suffered a heart attack and died.

Flamingos Bird Facts

Flamingos are the show stoppers of the avian world. Their long legs, bending beaks, and _vivid_ orange hue make them a sight to behold. They're a popular attraction at zoos and nature preserves because they are fascinating to see up close.

Phoenicopterus ruber is the scientific name for the American Flamingo. They reach a height of 3 to 5 feet and a weight of 5 to 6 pounds at maturity. Males tend to be larger than _females_ in general. Feathers of the common flamingo are typically pinkish red. Additionally, their pink feet and pink and white bill, which has a black tip, distinguish them.

Central and South America and the Caribbean are home to the American Flamingo. It can also be found in the Bahamas and Cuba, and the Yucatan Peninsula of Mexico's Caribbean coast. As far as Brazil, there are some that can be found on the northern _coast_. In addition, the Galapagos Islands have a population.

Lagoons and low-lying _mudflats_ or lakes are the preferred environments for the Flamingos. They like seeking food by wading across the water. They form enormous flocks, sometimes numbering in the tens of thousands.

Flamingos come in a variety of colors, including pink and orange. Carotenoids are responsible for the orange hue of several foods, such as carrots. Carrots would turn your skin and eyes orange if you just ate them. Flamingoes appear pink or orange because they eat _algae_ and small shellfish rich in carotenoids. They would lose their vibrant hue if they switched to a different _diet_.

Is it possible for flamingoes to fly? Yes. Flamingos can fly, even though we usually associate them with _wading_ in the water. Before they can take off, they have to run to build up their speed. They often fly in big groups.

Scientists don't know why Flamingos stand on one leg, but they have a few ideas. There is a rumor that it is to keep one leg warm. Because it's cold outside, they can keep one leg near their body to keep it warm. Another _theory_ is that they are drying out one leg at a time. A third idea argues that it aids them in deceiving their _prey_, as one leg resembles a plant more than two.

It doesn't matter the reason; these _top-heavy_ birds can stand on one leg for long periods. They even sleep with one leg balanced on the ground!

Boston Tea Party

Was it a big, boisterous tea party? Not at all. There was tea in the mix, but no one was drinking it. It was a protest by the American Colonists against the British government that resulted in the Boston Tea Party. They boarded three trade ships in Boston Harbor and threw the ships' cargo of tea into the ocean to show their anger at the government. Into the water, they threw 342 chests of tea. Some of the colonists dressed up as Mohawk Indians , but they fooled no one. The British knew who had thrown away the tea.

First, it might seem like a silly idea to throw tea into the ocean dressed as Mohawks. But the people who lived in colonial America knew why they did this. Among the British, tea was a favorite drink. People who worked for the East India Trading company made a lot of money from it. They were told they could only buy tea from this one company in the colonies. This was a British company. They were also informed that the tea would be taxed at a hefty rate. The Tea Act was the name given to the tax that was levied on the sale of tea.

People in the colonies didn't think this was fair because they weren't represented in British Parliament and didn't say how taxes were done. They asked that the tea be returned to Great Britain since they refused to pay taxes on it. As a result, they decided to toss the tea into the ocean as a form of protest against Britain's excessive taxes.

Historians wouldn't know for sure if the protest was planned or not. People in the town had met earlier that day to talk about the tea taxes and fight them. Samuel Adams was in charge of the meeting, which was significant. Samuel Adams was a key revolutionary leader in Boston. Many people liked him because he could use public displeasure with Parliament's power to tax the colonies to do good things for the country. The tea was destroyed, but no one is sure if Samuel Adams planned to do this. Instead, a group of people did it on their own because they were angry. In the future, Samuel Adams said that it was people defending their rights, not a group of people who were mad at each other. Although Adams did not participate in the Boston Tea Party, he was undoubtedly one of its planners.

It was, in fact, a lot of tea. The 342 containers had 90,000 pounds of tea in them! In today's money, that would be equivalent to around one million dollars in tea.

Littering

The annual cost of cleaning up litter in the nation's __streets__ , parks, and coastal areas is estimated to be in the millions of dollars. The cleanup of trash has a direct expense, but it also has a __negative__ impact on the surrounding environment, the value of property, and other economic activity. Food packaging, bottles, cans, plastic bags, and paper are the most common sources of litter. Did you know cigarette __butts__ remain the most littered item in the U.S. and across the globe? One of the many strategies that states can use to reduce the amount of litter in their communities is to enact and strictly adhere to laws that carry criminal penalties for the behavior. The penalties for littering vary significantly from state to state, depending on the __amount__ , nature, and location of the litter. The seriousness of the offense is determined by the weight or volume of litter in 10 states, for example. For instance, several states penalize people for disposing of large goods like furniture or major appliances in public places. Legislation addressing trash on public roadways, along the beaches, and in __recreational__ areas has been passed in several states due to these concerns.

In situations that are considered to be relatively small, the courts will typically impose a fine. They may also compel the defendant to perform __community__ service, such as picking up garbage. In Massachusetts, for instance, the minimum __fine__ is $25, whereas, in the state of Maryland, the maximum penalty is $30,000. When a crime is more serious, the offender may be sentenced to up to six years in __jail__ , depending on the state. In addition, the laws in the states of Maryland, Massachusetts, and Louisiana all include provisions that allow the __suspension__ of a driver's license for those who violate the laws. In almost every state, a person's sentence worsens with each subsequent conviction.

It doesn't matter if someone throws trash out on purpose or accidentally; either way, they're contributing to pollution by doing so. Our city's parks, sidewalks, roads, and private property and parks are all impacted by litter. Research has shown that litter leads to the accumulation of even more garbage. A clean __neighborhood__ , on the other hand, lowers the incidence of littering and enhances both the local living standards and the quality of life.

STATE BIKE LAWS

1. State laws and local ordinances often include measures requiring cyclists to wear _____.

   a. headlights

   b. [helmets]

2. A bicycle violation will not affect your automobile insurance.

   a. [True]

   b. False

3. Bicyclists are expected to use the appropriate _____ while turning, changing lanes, or stopping, even though some bicycles come equipped with turn signals.

   a. motion sensors

   b. [hand signals]

4. Rules pertaining to the use of bicycles are enforced at the _____ levels, just like other traffic laws.

   a. [state and local]

   b. state and countrywide

5. Bicyclists are prohibited from proceeding through a _____ or _____ without first coming to a complete stop, just like vehicles are.

   a. [stop sign, stoplight]

   b. yield sign, yellow light

6. _____ on back and _____ lights on the front are required in nearly every state, as well as white and red reflectors on the front and back.

   a. [Red lights, white]

   b. White lights, flashing

Identification (ID Only) License

In this activity, you'll see lots of grammatical *errors*. Correct all the grammar mistakes you see.

There are **8** mistakes in this passage. 2 capitals missing. 2 unnecessary capitals. 4 incorrectly spelled words.

For the sole purpose of proving your identity, you can get one of two types of ~~identificatoin~~ identification licenses. No testing is needed. All candidates, however, ~~Must~~ must meet the same ~~conditoins~~ conditions for verification of identification, legal presence, and residency as any other license. IDs are not valid for driving a car. A parent or legal guardian must sign a portion of the Minor/Teen-age Affidavit and Cancellation form at the time of application if the applicant is under the age of 18.

One ID-only license is called an "Expiring Identification License," and it can be provided to anyone who does not currently have a valid driver's license and can show that ~~They~~ they meet all of the other requirements for obtaining one.

The second form is a "permanent identification license" that anyone with intellectual or physical disabilities can ~~obtian.~~ obtain. ~~a~~ A positive proof of identity is required, and in addition to that, a certified declaration from a licensed physician declaring that the individual is unable to operate a vehicle must also be submitted. Those who meet the eligibility requirements can get this ~~iD~~ ID for free. The ID licenses ~~iscued~~ issued in this manner do not expire.

History of the Driving Age Part 2

As the driver's license became highly common, many were compelled to ask: who may apply for a license? It was not a simple question. For some families, especially those in rural areas, having younger teens who could drive was essential to daily living. Others questioned whether or not youngsters were capable of handling the responsibility of driving. In 1909, Pennsylvania was the first state to impose a strict driving age limit of 18 years. The age ranged from 14 in California to 15, 16, 17, or even 18 in other states. It wasn't until 1921 that Connecticut issued the first graduated licenses, allowing sixteen-year-olds to drive in the company of an adult driver who was also licensed, while the first learner's permit was issued in New York in 1925.

More Americans were able to purchase automobiles, and more permits were awarded throughout the 1920s. This sparked discussions regarding the necessity for a national driving age standard. This resulted in the First National Conference on Street Highway Safety in 1924. Two years later, in 1926, the second national conference established the Uniform Vehicle Code , which mandated that the minimum driving age be 16. This was merely a model law that states were encouraged to adopt. By the decade's conclusion, most states in the United States had adopted a minimum driving age of 16 in their state legislation .

After World War II, the argument over the driving age resumed. The growing middle class in the United States in the postwar years of the 1950s made automobile ownership even more feasible for the typical American. It wasn't until the 1950s and 1960s that the average American teenager could anticipate having access to a car and a license. With more young drivers on the road, more teen accidents and fatalities led to new policies' emergence.

History of the Driving Age Part 1

In this activity, you'll see lots of grammatical *errors*. Correct all the grammar mistakes you see.

There are **20** mistakes in this passage. 4 capitals missing. 3 unnecessary capitals. 2 unnecessary apostrophes. 3 punctuation marks missing or incorrect. 8 incorrectly spelled words.

In the United States, reaching the age of sixteen is a significant milestone. You are not a legal adult, but you have taken the first critical step toward freedom because you are now of driving age. ~~it~~ It is a crucial moment for many teens. In the United States, the minimum driving age is 16. Still, there is also a graduated licensing program in which teens learn to drive with a learner's permit, then advance to a full license with restrictions such as the number of ~~passengers~~ passengers. After a ~~period~~ period, those restrictions are lifted. ~~the~~ The fact that the United ~~State's~~ States and many other countries have only lately embraced this practice illustrates that the ~~Argument~~ argument over the appropriate age to ~~began~~ begin driving is far from being settled. Cars weren't a concern for the country's founding fathers in 1776; ~~therefore~~ therefore, this is a problem unique to the 20th century that has never been faced before. How did America handle this debate? Let's embark on a journey through history to find ~~oot.~~ out.

Starting at the turn of the century is an excellent place to begin our adventure. In the late 19th century, automobiles were only beginning to enter society. It's vital to remember that Henry ~~ford's~~ Ford's assembly line production, which made cars affordable and accessible, didn't start ~~untal~~ until 1913; ~~therephore,~~ therefore, automobiles were relatively uncommon before this time. Local governments at the time began to consider requiring drivers to ~~regaster~~ register to generate revenue for the ~~stite~~ state government and hold drivers accountable ~~For~~ for vehicle-related damages. According to most ~~exparts,~~ experts, the first driver's license was awarded to a man in Chicago in 1899. The license wasn't actually for a car, but for some kind of "steam-powered vehicle."

As the United ~~State's~~ States entered the 20th century, registration of ~~Both~~ both automobiles and drivers became the norm. In 1903, New York was the first ~~stite~~ state to require auto registration, followed by Massachusetts and ~~missouri.~~ Missouri. The method quickly gained popularity and spread throughout the United States.

Teen Drinking and Driving

1. Even just a few beers can put your life and the lives of others in jeopardy if you get behind the wheel of a vehicle while _____.

   a. intoxicated

   b. incinerated

   c. indecencies

2. Teenagers, because of their lack of driving experience, are less skilled at recognizing and reacting to driving _____.

   a. legislation

   b. hazards

   c. stressors

3. BAC stands for _____.

   a. blood alcohol content

   b. blood alcohology confinement

   c. blood alcoholic nonattainment

4. Under the _____ law, which applies to drivers younger than 21, it is against the law to get behind the wheel with any amount of alcohol in your system, even traces of it.

   a. zero-tolerance

   b. zero-non-impaired

   c. zero-alcohol and beverages

5. (BAC) of _____ per deciliter (g/dL) or higher is considered to be alcohol-impaired.

   a. .02 grams

   b. .08 grams

   c. .3% grams

6. When a police officer has _____, a student's privilege to drive a vehicle can be instantly withdrawn and suspended.

   a. parent's permission

   b. a court order

   c. sufficient evidence

7. If a student is found guilty of driving under the influence of alcohol or another controlled substance, the student faces the possibility of being _____ from school.

   a. given a warning

   b. enrolled

   c. expelled

8. Driving under the influence of alcohol or drugs is referred to as driving _____.

   a. DIU

   b. DWI

   c. DUI

9. Signs of legal impairment

   a. Nausea, Diarrhea, Coughing

   b. Nausea, Slur speech, Impaired vision

   c. Slur speech, Workaholic, Laughing a lot

10. Always fasten your _____, no matter how _____ the drive may be.

   a. seat belt, short

   b. belt buckle, fast

   c. seat belt, long

A Community Garden Letter
Questions

1. Who sent this letter?

    a. Andrew Fitzgerald

    b. Jill Kindle

    c. Dawn Clover

2. Who is the letter for?

    a. Jill Kindle

    b. Dawn Clover

    c. Andrew Fitzgerald

3. How much is the 10 x 12 plot per year?

    a. $90.00

    b. $45.00

    c. $55.00

4. What is Dawn Clover's phone number?

    a. 693-555-9006

    b. 963-555-9669

    c. 693-555-9009

5. What job does Jill Kindle have?

    a. Community Garden Person

    b. Director of Community Gardens

    c. Garden Coordinator

6. What town or city is this community garden in?

    a. Gibbons

    b. Billings

    c. Riverstide

7. Where is the Greendale Community Garden?

    a. 678 Warren Drive

    b. 780 Billings St.

    c. 789 Gibbons St.

8. How many plots are available?

    a. 2

    b. 10

    c. 12

9. The water costs extra.

    a. True

    b. False

10. When was this letter written?

    a. June 5, 2018

    b. June 5, 2019

    c. June 9, 2015

GEORGE WASHINGTON

1. George Washington was born on _____.
   a. 02-22-1732
   b. February 24, 1732

2. The United States Constitution is the law of the ____.
   a. land
   b. world

3. George's _____ had deteriorated.
   a. teeth
   b. feet

4. George Washington can be seen on a _____.
   a. one-dollar bill
   b. five-dollar bill

5. George's father died when he was 20 years old.
   a. True
   b. False

6. George was a plantation owner.
   a. True
   b. False

7. George married the widow _____.
   a. Martha Custis
   b. Mary Curtis

8. In his will, Washington freed his _____.
   a. children
   b. slaves

9. George served in the _____ legislature.
   a. Virginia
   b. Maryland

10. George Washington was elected as the _____ President of the USA.
    a. forth
    b. first

11. A widow is someone whose husband has died.
    a. True
    b. False

12. George died on December 14, 1699.
    a. True
    b. False

13. George grew up in _____.
    a. Washington DC
    b. Colonial Virginia

14. The capital of the United States is named after George.
    a. True
    b. False

15. A plantation is a town that is tended by a large number of officials.
    a. True
    b. False

16. Washington caught a ____ just a few years after leaving the presidency.
    a. cold
    b. flight

Health: Immune System

white	defends	cell-mediated	cells	Immune
external	Macrophages	signals	foreign	invading

Your immune system __defends__ you against harmful intruders. __Immune__ responses occur when your body's immune system detects threats. Learn about antibody-mediated and cell-mediated immunity.

Your immune system, which detects and eliminates __foreign__ invaders, provides this tremendous service. An immunological reaction occurs when your body's immune system detects __external__ intruders. Your immune system is a great asset that selflessly protects you from antigens, or foreign intruders.

Immunity by Cells

Antibody-mediated immunity is one of your immune system's two arms. The other arm is __cell-mediated__ immunity, which helps the body get rid of undesired cells like infected, cancerous, or transplanted cells. __Macrophages__ consume antigens in this sort of immunity. If you split down macrophages, you can remember it easily. Big indicates macro- and phages means 'eaters.' So macrophages are voracious consumers of antigens. The macrophage then chews up the antigen and displays the fragments on its surface.

When helper T cells encounter macrophages, they give out __signals__ that activate other __white__ blood __cells__, such as cytotoxic or killer T cells. These killer T cells multiply fast, forming an army ready to battle and eliminate the __invading__ cell that prompted the immune response.

Look It Up! Pop Quiz

Learn some basic vocabulary words that you will come across again and again in the course of your studies in algebra. By knowing the definitions of most algebra words, you will be able to construct and solve algebra problems much more easily.

Find the answer to the questions below by *looking up each word. (The wording can be tricky. Take your time.)*

1. improper fraction

a. a fraction that the denominator is equal to the numerator

b. a fraction in which the numerator is greater than the denominator, is always 1 or greater

2. equivalent fraction

a. a fraction that has a DIFFERENT value as a given fraction

b. a fraction that has the SAME value as a given fraction

3. simplest form of fraction

a. an equivalent fraction for which the only common factor of the numerator and denominator is 1

b. an equivalent fraction for which the only least factor of the denominator is -1

4. mixed number

a. the sum of a whole number and a proper fraction

b. the sum of a variable and a fraction

5. reciprocal

a. a number that can be divided by another number to make 10

b. a number that can be multiplied by another number to make 1

6. percent

a. a percentage that compares a number to a 1

b. a ratio that compares a number to 100

7. sequence

a. a set of addition numbers that follow a operation

b. a set of numbers that follow a pattern

8. arithmetic sequence

a. a sequence where EACH term is found by adding or subtracting the exact same number to the previous term

b. a sequence where NO term is found by multiplying the exact same number to the previous term

9. geometric sequence

a. a sequence where each term is found by multiplying or dividing by the exact same number to the previous term

b. a sequence where each term is solved by adding or dividing by a different number to the previous term

10. order of operations

a. the procedure to follow when simplifying a numerical expression

b. the procedure to follow when adding any fraction by 100

11. variable expression

a. a mathematical phrase that contains variables, numbers, and operation symbols

b. a mathematical phrase that contains numbers and operation symbols

12. absolute value

a. the distance a number is from zero on the number line

b. the range a number is from one on the number line

13. integers

a. a set of numbers that includes whole numbers and their opposites

b. a set of numbers that includes whole numbers and their difference

14. x-axis

a. the horizontal number line that, together with the y-axis, establishes the coordinate plane

b. the vertical number line that, together with the y-axis, establishes the coordinate plane

15. y-axis

   a. the vertical number line that, together with the x-axis, establishes the coordinate plane

   b. the horizontal number line that, together with the x-axis, establishes the coordinate plane

16. coordinate plane

   a. plane formed by one number line (the horizontal y-axis and the vertical x-axis) intersecting at their -1 points

   b. plane formed by two number lines (the horizontal x-axis and the vertical y-axis) intersecting at their zero points

17. quadrant

   a. one of two sections on the four plane formed by the intersection of the x-axis

   b. one of four sections on the coordinate plane formed by the intersection of the x-axis and the y-axis

18. ordered pair

   a. a pair of numbers that gives the location of a point in the coordinate plane. Also known as the "coordinates" of a point.

   b. a pair of equal numbers that gives the range of a point in the axis plane. Also known as the "y-axis" of a point.

19. x-coordinate

   a. the number that indicates the position of a point to the left or right of the y-axis

   b. the number that indicates the range of a point to the left ONLY of the y-axis

20. y-coordinate

   a. the number that indicates the position of a point above or below the x-axis

   b. the number that indicates the value of a point only above the x-axis

21. inverse operations

   a. operations that equals to each other

   b. operations that undo each other

22. inequality

   a. a math sentence that uses a letter (x or y) to indicate that the left and right sides of the sentence hold values that are different

   b. a math sentence that uses a symbol ($<, >, \leq, \geq, \neq$) to indicate that the left and right sides of the sentence hold values that are different

23. perimeter

   a. the distance around the outside of a figure

   b. the distance around the inside of a figure

24. circumference

   a. the distance around a circle

   b. the range around a square

25. area

   a. the number of square units inside a 2-dimensional figure

   b. the number of circle units inside a 3-dimensional figure

26. volume

   a. the number of cubic units inside a 3-dimensional figure

   b. the number of cubic squared units inside a 2-dimensional figure

27. radius

   a. a line segment that runs from the middle of the circle to end of the circle

   b. a line segment that runs from the center of the circle to somewhere on the circle

28. chord

   a. a line segment that runs from somewhere on the circle to another place on the circle

   b. a circle distance that runs from somewhere on the far left to another place on the circle

29. diameter

   a. a chord that passes through the center of the circle

   b. a thin line that passes through the end of the circle

30. mean

   a. the sum of the data items added by the number of data items minus 2

   b. the sum of the data items divided by the number of data items

31. median

   a. the first data item found after sorting the data items in descending order

   b. the middle data item found after sorting the data items in ascending order

32. mode

   a. the data item that occurs most often

   b. the data item that occurs less than two times

33. range

    a. the difference between the highest and the lowest data item

    b. the difference between the middle number and the lowest number item

34. outlier

    a. a data item that is much higher or much lower than all the other data items

    b. a data item that is much lower or less than all the other data items

35. ratio

    a. a comparison of two quantities by multiplication

    b. a comparison of two quantities by division

36. rate

    a. a ratio that has equal quantities measured in the same units

    b. a ratio that compares quantities measured in different units

37. proportion

    a. a statement (ratio) showing five or more ratios to be equal

    b. a statement (equation) showing two ratios to be equal

38. outcomes

    a. possible results of action

    b. possible answer when two numbers are the same

39. probability

    a. a ratio that explains the likelihood of the distance and miles between to places

    b. a ratio that explains the likelihood of an event

40. theoretical probability

    a. the probability of the highest favorable number of possible outcomes (based on what is not expected to occur)

    b. the ratio of the number of favorable outcomes to the number of possible outcomes (based on what is expected to occur).

41. experimental probability

    a. the ratio of the number of times by 2 when an event occurs to the number of times times 2 an experiment is done (based on real experimental data).

    b. the ratio of the number of times an event occurs to the number of times an experiment is done (based on real experimental data).

42. distributive property

    a. a way to simplify an expression that contains a equal like term being added by a group of terms.

    b. a way to simplify an expression that contains a single term being multiplied by a group of terms.

43. term

    a. a number, a variable, or probability of an equal number and a variable(s)

    b. a number, a variable, or product of a number and a variable(s)

44. Constant

    a. a term with no variable part (i.e. a number)

    b. a term with no variable + y part (i.e. 4+y)

45. Coefficient

    a. a number that divides a variable

    b. a number that multiplies a variable

Match Politics Terms

Learn how to *look up* words in a *Spanish-English dictionary or online. Write the corresponding letter(s).*

1	M	Campaign	→	la campaña
2	K	Candidate	→	el candidato
3	S	Coalition	→	la coalición
4	H	Coup	→	el golpe de Estado
5	F	Democracy	→	la democracia
6	Q	Demonstration	→	la manifestación
7	N	Demonstrator	→	el/la manifestante
8	I	Deputy, Representative	→	el diputado
9	Z	Dictatorship	→	la dictadura
10	A	Diplomacy	→	la diplomacia
11	P	Elections	→	las elecciones
12	G	Electoral	→	electoral
13	AE	Foreign Policy	→	la política exterior
14	C	Freedom Of Speech	→	la libertad de expresión
15	U	Government	→	el gobierno
16	AA	Internal Affairs	→	la política interior
17	Y	Majority	→	la mayoría
18	L	Minister	→	el ministro

19	W	Ministry	⇢	el ministerio
20	O	Minority	⇢	la minoría
21	AD	Movement	⇢	el movimiento
22	E	Opposition	⇢	la oposición
23	AB	Parliament	⇢	el parlamento
24	V	Party	⇢	el partido
25	B	Politician	⇢	el político
26	J	President	⇢	el presidente
27	T	Prime Minister	⇢	el primer ministro
28	AC	Referendum	⇢	el plebiscito/referendo
29	D	Spokesperson	⇢	el/la portavoz
30	X	State	⇢	el estado
31	R	Vote	⇢	el voto

Pick 7 politics Spanish words from above and work on arranging them in order alphabetically:

[Student worksheet has a 7 line writing exercise here.]

The History of the Calendar

Tuesday	Saturday	November	February	Monday	March
Friday	weekend	May	Wednesday	Sunday	January
weekday	October	June	September	December	August
April	Thursday	July			

1. rauanjy — January

2. uraeybfr — February

3. macrh — March

4. iralp — April

5. yma — May

6. nuej — June

7. luyj — July

8. suagut — August

9. ebpmeetrs — September

10. btcreoo — October

11. vmbeneor — November

12. eedcrmbe — December

13. dmnyoa — Monday

14. saetudy — Tuesday

15. deeawysnd — Wednesday

16. shtayudr — Thursday

17. rdayfi — Friday

18. yuartdas — Saturday

19. ydsaun — Sunday

20. eenekwd — weekend

21. kaewedy — weekday

This, That, These, and Those

This, that, these and those are demonstratives. We use this, that, these, and those to point to people and things. This and that are singular. These and those are plural.

1. _____ orange I'm eating is delicious.
- a. This
- b. These
- c. Those
- d. That

2. It is better than _____ apples from last week.
- a. that
- b. those
- c. these
- d. this

3. Let's exchange _____ bread for these crackers.
- a. those
- b. this
- c. these
- d. that

4. Let's try some of _____ freeze-dried steak.
- a. this
- b. this here
- c. them
- d. those there

5. Is _____ water boiling yet?
- a. those here
- b. that
- c. that there
- d. this here

6. _____ granola bars are tasty too.
- a. These
- b. This here
- c. Them
- d. Those here

7. _____ mountains don't look that far away.
- a. This
- b. Those
- c. These
- d. That

8. I like _____ pictures better than those.
- a. this
- b. that
- c. those
- d. these

9. _____ car at the far end of the lot is mine.
- a. That
- b. This
- c. These
- d. Those

10. I like the feel of _____ fabric.
- a. those
- b. this here
- c. that there
- d. this

11. In _____ early days, space travel was a dream.
- a. That
- b. them
- c. those
- d. this

12. _____ days, we believe humans will go to Mars.
- a. These
- b. This
- c. Those
- d. That

Airbags

In a collision, airbags __inflate__ to cushion passengers from hitting the vehicle's interior or external objects (such as other cars or trees).

Instantaneously upon collision, sensors begin measuring the severity of the hit. If the crash is hard enough, the __sensors__ tell the inflators to fill the bags with gas in a fraction of a second.

In most cases, airbags don't need to be serviced unless deployed during a collision. In this scenario, they must be replaced at a repair shop that utilizes __original__ equipment manufacturer (OEM) replacement parts to verify that the replacement airbag is not counterfeit. During deployment, counterfeit airbags may fail to deploy or __discharge__ metal shrapnel.

Airbags in the front

The federal government has __mandated__ the installation of driver and passenger airbags for frontal collision protection in all vehicles, light trucks, and vans from the 1999 model year.

During moderate to severe frontal collisions, front airbags inflate so that people's heads and torsos do not touch the vehicle's __rigid__ structures.

They provide the maximum protection when riders wear safety belts and sit properly in the seat, but they are designed to protect all occupants.

Newer airbags incorporate a safety belt sensor and a decision-making __algorithm__ to select whether or not to inflate the bag while passengers are wearing their seat belts.

For unbelted occupants, a front airbag will typically deploy when the crash is the equivalent of a 10–12 mph impact with a solid wall. Belted people, on the other hand, usually have a lower __threshold__ for airbag deployment-around 16 mph-because the belts themselves are expected to provide adequate protection up to these modest speeds.

Front airbags can help protect passengers from side collisions if the vehicle moves forward enough during the crash.

The steering wheel contains the driver's airbag. The __dashboard__ houses the passenger airbag.

Knee airbags positioned lower are an option from some manufacturers. Using knee airbags is a good idea if you're concerned about preventing leg injuries due to collisions. It is possible that they may also help lessen the stress on an occupant's chest and __abdomen__ by limiting movement of the lower body.

Airbags on each side

Side airbags are designed to inflate in side accidents to protect people's heads and chests from the vehicle's side structure, a striking car, or a tree or pole. With side airbags, the power of an accident is __dispersed__ evenly across the body, reducing the chance of a direct hit to any one portion.

Due to the possibility of window glass __shattering__ in an accident, a side airbag that protects the occupant's head is very crucial.

Side airbags must deploy within the first 10 to 20 __milliseconds__ of a side impact to protect the people in the car. For narrow object collisions (e.g., trees and poles), deployment thresholds can be as low as 8 mph and 18 mph for the more widely spread side impacts (vehicle-to-vehicle crashes). Some frontal accidents __trigger__ side airbags.

A federal rule about side-impact protection says that all occupants must have a specific head and torso protection level. While it does not technically require side airbags, they are commonly used to provide the necessary protection. A large majority of new passenger cars sold after the 2014 __model__ year are also required to meet this standard. Because of this, side airbags are a standard feature in almost all passenger cars.

Organ Donations

1. You can quickly register to donate organs through the _____ in your state.
    a. Department of Organ Donations
    b. Department of Motor Vehicles

2. Donated organs can be _____ into another _____.
    a. transplanted, person
    b. translational, facility

3. To remove the DONOR label from your driver's license or ID card, visit any _____ office.
    a. DVM
    b. DMV

4. There are many different types of _____ that can be donated, including skin, bone, corneas, heart valves, and _____.
    a. organism, plasma
    b. tissues, veins

5. Those under the age of _____ may be able to donate their organs if they have the _____ of their parents.
    a. 18, approval
    b. 17, agreement

6. If an organ or tissue _____ be transplanted, it may be used for medical research and _____, unless you make other arrangements.
    a. can, placement
    b. cannot, teaching

Lumberjack Paul Bunyan

According to legend, it took five massive storks to deliver the infant (already enormous) Paul Bunyan to his parents in __Bangor__, Maine. As he grew older, a single drag of the mighty lumberjack's massive ax __carved__ out the Grand Canyon, while the giant footprints of his trusty companion, Babe the __Blue__ Ox, filled with water and became Minnesota's 10,000 lakes. There is no way to know for sure, but was Paul Bunyan really a real person? As it turns out, there's more to this iconic figure's past than meets the eye.

Scholars believe that Bunyan was based on a real lumberjack: Fabian Fournier, a French-Canadian who moved south after the Civil War and became the foreman of a logging crew in Michigan after the war. Fournier was __nicknamed__ "Saginaw Joe" because he was six feet tall (at a time when the ordinary person was barely five feet) and had huge __hands__. This man was known to have two full sets of teeth and was known to chew off __chunks__ of rail in his spare time while also indulging in a bit of drinking and a little brawling. Fournier was killed on a November night in 1875 in the notoriously rowdy lumber town of Bay City, Michigan. People told stories about Saginaw Joe's __complicated__ life in logging camps in Michigan, Minnesota, Wisconsin, and other places after his death and the dramatic trial of his alleged killer (who was acquitted).

"Round River," the first Paul Bunyan story, was published in 1906 by __journalist__ James MacGillivray for a local newspaper in Oscoda, Michigan. MacGillivray and a poet collaborated on a Bunyan-themed poem for American Lumberman magazine in 1912, giving Paul Bunyan his first __national__ exposure. Two years later, the first illustrations of the larger-than-life lumberjack appeared in an ad campaign for Minnesota's Red River Lumber Company. His prominent appearance as Red River's mascot and pamphlets rolling tales of his adventures would help turn Paul Bunyan into a __household__ name and an enduring American icon.

Spelling: How Do You Spell It?
Part II

	A	B	C	D
1.	compllain	complian	**complain**	compllian
2.	negattyve	negatyve	**negative**	negattive
3.	**importance**	importence	imporrtance	imporrtence
4.	encourragement	**encouragement**	encourragenment	encouragenment
5.	shallves	**shelves**	shellves	shalves
6.	**mixture**	mixttore	mixtore	mixtture
7.	honorrable	**honorable**	honorible	honorrible
8.	lagall	legall	lagal	**legal**
9.	manar	mannar	**manner**	maner
10.	encycllopedia	**encyclopedia**	encycllopedai	encyclopedai
11.	repllacement	replacenment	repllacenment	**replacement**
12.	medycie	medycine	**medicine**	medicie
13.	experriance	**experience**	experiance	experrience
14.	**hunger**	hunjer	hungerr	hunjerr
15.	sallote	sallute	salote	**salute**
16.	horrizon	hurizon	hurrizon	**horizon**
17.	sestion	**session**	setion	sesion
18.	shorrten	shurten	**shorten**	shurrten
19.	fuacett	faucett	fuacet	**faucet**
20.	haadache	haadace	haedache	**headache**
21.	**further**	furrther	forrther	forther
22.	injurry	injory	**injury**	injorry
23.	disstance	distence	**distance**	disstence
24.	rattio	**ratio**	rattoi	ratoi
25.	independense	**independence**	independance	independanse

Spelling: How Do You Spell It?
Part I

	A	B	C	D
1.	**grade**	grrada	grrade	grada
2.	**elementary**	elenmentary	ellenmentary	ellementary
3.	**marks**	marrcks	marrks	marcks
4.	repurt	reporrt	**report**	repurrt
5.	schedolle	**schedule**	schedole	schedulle
6.	timetible	**timetable**	timettable	timettible
7.	**highlight**	highllight	hyghllight	hyghlight
8.	foell	foel	fuell	**fuel**
9.	instrucsion	insstruction	**instruction**	insstrucsion
10.	senttence	sentance	senttance	**sentence**
11.	**vaccination**	vacination	vaccinasion	vacinasion
12.	**proof**	prwf	prouf	proph
13.	mandatury	mandattury	**mandatory**	mandattory
14.	**final**	fynall	finall	fynal
15.	envellope	**envelope**	envellupe	envelupe
16.	equattor	eqauttor	eqautor	**equator**
17.	bllanks	**blanks**	blancks	bllancks
18.	honorible	honorrable	**honorable**	honorrible
19.	scaince	sceince	**science**	sciance
20.	mussic	mosic	muscic	**music**
21.	**history**	hisstory	hisctory	histury
22.	lissten	liscten	lysten	**listen**
23.	entrence	enttrance	enttrence	**entrance**
24.	especialy	especailly	especaily	**especially**
25.	mariage	maraige	marraige	**marriage**

Spelling: How Do You Spell It?
Part III

Write and circle the correct spelling for each word.

	A	B	C	D
1.	invitation	invittasion	invitasion	invittation
2.	denuminator	denominator	denuminattor	denominattor
3.	personal	perrsonal	perrsunal	persunal
4.	rapkd	rapid	rahid	rapyd
5.	oryginal	original	orryginal	orriginal
6.	liquvd	liqiod	liqoid	liquid
7.	desscendant	descendant	dessendant	desssendant
8.	dissastrous	disastrous	dissastroos	disastroos
9.	cooperasion	cooperation	coperation	coperasion
10.	routine	roottine	routtine	rootine
11.	earleist	earrleist	earrliest	earliest
12.	acidentally	accidentally	acidentalli	accidentalli
13.	rehaerrse	rehearrse	rehaerse	rehearse
14.	quotte	qoote	quote	qootte
15.	capablla	capablle	capable	capible
16.	apointment	appointnment	apointnment	appointment
17.	mussician	mussicain	musicain	musician
18.	nomerrator	numerrator	numerator	nomerator
19.	inquire	inqoire	inquirre	inqoirre
20.	remote	remute	remutte	remotte
21.	pryncipal	prrincipal	prryncipal	principal
22.	sylent	sillent	syllent	silent
23.	locatsion	locasion	location	locattion
24.	edision	edition	editsion	edittion

Grammar: Singular and Plural

1. Which word is NOT a plural noun?

   a. books

   b. [hat]

   c. toys

2. Which word is a singular noun?

   a. bikes

   b. cars

   c. [pencil]

3. Which word can be both singular and plural?

   a. [deer]

   b. bears

   c. mice

4. Tommy _____ badminton at the court.

   a. playing

   b. [plays]

   c. play's

5. They _____ to eat at fast food restaurants once in a while.

   a. likes

   b. [like]

   c. likies

6. Everybody _____ Janet Jackson.

   a. know

   b. known

   c. [knows]

7. He ___ very fast. You have to listen carefully.

   a. spoken

   b. speak

   c. [speaks]

8. Which one is the singular form of women?

   a. womans

   b. [woman]

   c. women

9. The plural form of tooth is

   a. tooths

   b. toothes

   c. [teeth]

10. The singular form of mice is _____.

   a. [mouse]

   b. mices

   c. mouses

11. The plural form of glass is _____.

   a. glassies

   b. [glasses]

   c. glassy

12. The plural form of dress is _____.

   a. dressing

   b. [dresses]

   c. dressy

13. Plural means many.

   a. [True]

   b. False

14. Singular means 1.

   a. [True]

   b. False

15. Is this word singular or plural? monsters

   a. [plural]

   b. singular

16. Find the plural noun in the sentence. They gave her a nice vase full of flowers.

   a. they

   b. [flowers]

   c. vase

17. Find the plural noun in the sentence. Her baby brother grabbed the crayons out of the box and drew on the wall.
    a. crayons
    b. box
    c. brothers

18. Find the plural noun in the sentence. My friend, Lois, picked enough red strawberries for the whole class.
    a. strawberries
    b. friends
    c. classes

19. What is the correct plural form of the noun wish?
    a. wishes
    b. wishs
    c. wishy

20. What is the correct plural form of the noun flurry?
    a. flurrys
    b. flurryies
    c. flurries

21. What is the correct plural form of the noun box?
    a. boxs
    b. boxses
    c. boxes

22. What is the correct plural form of the noun bee?
    a. beess
    b. beeses
    c. bees

23. What is the correct plural form of the noun candy?
    a. candys
    b. candyies
    c. candies

24. Find the singular noun in the sentence. The boys and girls drew pictures on the sidewalk.
    a. boys
    b. drew
    c. sidewalk

Different Types of Dangerous Weather

1. _____ are extremely fast-spinning columns of wind.
   a. Tornadoes
   b. Hurricanes

2. _____ can form when moist warm air rises quickly.
   a. Thunderstorms
   b. Lighting

3. Huge and powerful storms that form over the ocean are known as _____.
   a. hurricanes
   b. tornadoes

4. Lighting will frequently strike the _____ point on the land surface when it comes to landing.
   a. lowest
   b. highest

5. The top of the thunderstorm is _____ charged, but the bottom accumulates a negative charge.
   a. positively
   b. steadily

6. _____ is a powerful electrical blast that can form in thunderstorms and strike the earth with great force.
   a. Lighting
   b. High winds

Science Multiple Choice
Quiz: Tyrannosaurus Rex

Select the best answer for each question.

1. The T-rex usually measures up to _____ and weighs as much as _____.
   a. 43 feet, 2 tons
   b. 43 feet, 7.5 tons
   c. 40 feet, 6 tons

2. The Tyrannosaurus rex was a _____ dinosaur.
   a. quadrupedal
   b. bipedal
   c. tripedal

3. The T-rex is a member of the dinosaur subgroup _____, which includes all the flesh-eating dinosaurs.
   a. Theropoda
   b. Sauropodomorpha
   c. Thyreophora

4. The Tyrannosaurus rex lived in North America between 65 and 98 million years ago, during the late _____ period.
   a. Cretaceous
   b. Triassic
   c. Jurassic

5. Where could we find the only documented track of a Tyrannosaurus Rex?
   a. at the Black Hills Museum of Natural History Exhibit in Hill City, South Dakota
   b. at Philmont Scout Ranch in New Mexico
   c. at the Field Museum of Natural History in Chicago

6. Which of the following is the largest and most complete T-rex specimen that can be found on display at the Field Museum of Natural History in Chicago?
   a. Sue
   b. Stan
   c. Susan

7. The Tyrannosaurus had a life span of around _____.
   a. 30 years
   b. 40 years
   c. 50 years

8. It is one of the most ferocious predators to ever walk the Earth.
   a. Giganotosaurus
   b. Spinosaurus
   c. Tyrannosaurus rex

9. Tyrannosaurus rex was also adept at finding its prey through its keen sense of _____.
   a. hearing
   b. smell
   c. sight

10. The famous Tyrannosaurus Sue fossil was purchased by the Chicago Museum for _____.
   a. $9 million
   b. $10 million
   c. $8 million

11. Given their ability to inflict deep wounds with four-inch claws, the T-rex's arms may have been adapted for _____ at close quarters.
   a. "harmful biting"
   b. "powerful smashing"
   c. "vicious slashing"

12. The word Tyrannosaurus is from the Greek word meaning _____.
   a. "Tyrant Flycatcher"
   b. "Tyrant Lizard"
   c. "Tyrant Dinosaur"

Science Multiple Choice
Quiz: Endangered Animals

Select the best answer for each question.

1. In 1973, an international treaty known as _____ was adopted as a far-reaching wildlife conservation measure.

   a. International Union for Conservation of Nature (IUCN)

   b. Wildlife (Protection) Act

   c. Convention on International Trade in Endangered Species of Wild Fauna and Flora (CITES)

2. _____ programs can help protect endangered species.

   a. Conservation

   b. Restoration

   c. Preservation

3. The Endangered Species Act was signed into law by _____ in 1973.

   a. Richard Pallardy

   b. John Dingell (D-Mich.)

   c. Richard Nixon

4. What percent of threatened species are at risk because of human activities alone?

   a. Roughly 99 %

   b. Below 50 %

   c. Almost 50 %

5. These animals are listed as critically endangered because they are primarily threatened by hunters who kill them for their horns.

   a. Black rhinoceros

   b. Antelope

   c. Oryx

6. Who wrote the Endangered Species Act and argued that "only natural extinction is part of natural order?"

   a. Richard Nixon

   b. John Dingell (D-Mich.)

   c. Julian Huxley

7. Species that only exist in captivity (for example in a zoo), are called _____.

   a. extinct species

   b. extinct in the wild

   c. critically endangered species

8. It is defined as any species that is at risk of extinction because of a sudden, rapid decrease in its population or a loss of its critical habitat.

   a. Distinct Species

   b. Endangered Animals

   c. Exotic Species

9. It is a law that protects endangered animals by taking into account any destruction to a species' habitat, whether it has been over-consumed, any disease or predation that threatens it, and whether any other man-made factors put it in danger.

   a. The United States' Endangered Species Act of 1973

   b. The Republic Act of 1947

   c. The Wildlife (Protection) Act of 1972

10. 10. By the early 21st century, it could be said that _____ are the greatest threat to biodiversity.

   a. human beings (Homo sapiens)

   b. exotic plants

   c. wild animals

11. Choose the correct order of the level of risk, starting with the most threatened animal and working your way down to the least threatened.

   a. Critically endangered, Endangered, Vulnerable

   b. a.Critically endangered, Vulnerable, Endangered

   c. b.Endangered, Critically Endangered, Vulnerable

12. The most pervasive threat to species in the wild is:

   a. Disease

   b. Unsustainable hunting

   c. Habitat loss and habitat degradation

Multiple Choice Quiz: Lebanon

Select the best answer for each question.

1. Lebanon is a country in the _____, on the Mediterranean Sea.

   a. Middle East

   b. Western Europe

   c. Africa

2. Lebanon has _____ rivers all of which are non-navigable.

   a. 17

   b. 18

   c. 16

3. What is the capital city of Lebanon?

   a. Tyre

   b. Sidon

   c. Beirut

4. Lebanon has a moderate _____.

   a. Continental climate

   b. Mediterranean climate

   c. Temperate climate

5. When the Ottoman Empire collapsed after World War I, which country took control of Lebanon?

   a. Russia

   b. France

   c. Britain

6. When did Lebanon become a sovereign under the authority of the Free French government?

   a. November 26, 1943

   b. September 1, 1926

   c. May 25, 1926

7. What is the national symbol in Lebanon?

   a. Cedar tree

   b. Maple tree

   c. Pine tree

8. Lebanon is bordered by _____ to the north and east, _____ to the south, and the Mediterranean Sea to the west.

   a. Syria, Israel

   b. Israel, France

   c. Japan, Korea

9. Lebanon is divided into how many governorates?

   a. 6

   b. 8

   c. 7

10. The Cedar Revolution occurred in 2005, following the assassination of Lebanese Prime Minister _____ in a car bomb explosion.

   a. Jabal Amel

   b. Rafik Hariri

   c. Fakhr al-Din II

11. The city of _____ is one of the oldest continuously inhabited cities in the world.

   a. Beirut

   b. Byblos

   c. Baalbek

12. Lebanon is divided into how many districts?

   a. 24

   b. 22

   c. 25

Biography Multiple Choice Quiz: Calvin Coolidge

Select the best answer for each question.

1. Calvin Coolidge was the _____ of the United States.
   a. 31st President
   b. 30th President
   c. 29th President

2. Calvin Coolidge served as President from _____ to _____.
   a. 1923-1929
   b. 1913-1921
   c. 1929-1933

3. He is also famous for ____ earning him the nickname ____.
   a. bing excellent in academic, schoolmaster
   b. being a man of few words, Silent Cal
   c. breaking up large companies, The Trust Buster

4. Calvin grew up in the small town of _____.
   a. Plymouth, Vermont
   b. Staunton, Virginia
   c. New York, New York

5. Calvin Coolidge signed the _____, which gave full U.S. citizen rights to all Native Americans.
   a. The Dawes Act
   b. Indian Civil Rights Act
   c. Indian Citizenship Act

6. Who was the Vice President under Calvin Coolidge's administration?
   a. Charles Gates Dawes
   b. Charles Curtis
   c. Thomas Riley Sherman

7. Coolidge gained national recognition during the 1919 _____ when he served as governor.
   a. Boston Police Strike
   b. Baltimore Police Strike
   c. NYPD Police Strike

8. Calvin died of a sudden heart attack _____ years after leaving the presidency.
   a. five
   b. four
   c. three

9. Calvin Coolidge became President of the United States after his predecessor, _____ died in office.
   a. William Taft
   b. Warren Harding
   c. Herbert Hoover

10. The _____ is a nickname for the 1920s in the United States as it was a time of hope, prosperity, and cultural change during President Calvin Coolidge's presidential term.
    a. Reconstruction
    b. Roaring Twenties
    c. Gilded Age

11. Which of the following words best describes President Calvin Coolidge's personality?
    a. talkative
    b. adventurous
    c. quiet

12. What was Calvin Coolidge's campaign slogan when he ran for President of the United States?
    a. Keep Cool with Coolidge
    b. Coolidge, For the Future
    c. Peace, Prosperity, and Coolidge

Biography Multiple Choice
Quiz: Charles Lindbergh

Select the best answer for each question.

1. Charles Lindbergh was born on _____ in _____.
- a. February 4, 1902, Detroit, Michigan
- b. January 7, 1900, Lindberg, Germany
- c. January 29, 1905, Minneapolis, Minnesota

2. Charles' mother was _____.
- a. an aviator
- b. a schoolteacher
- c. a doctor

3. On May 20, 1927, Charles took off from New York aboard his plane, the _____.
- a. Spirit of St. Joseph
- b. Spirit of St. Louis
- c. Spirit of St. Luke

4. _____ were pilots that traveled the country performing stunts and giving people rides at air shows.
- a. Recreational pilot
- b. Barnstormers
- c. Sports pilot

5. Charles died in _____ at _____.
- a. August 25, 1975, Detroit, Michigan
- b. August 24, 1976, Minneapolis, Minnesota
- c. August 26, 1974, Maui, Hawaii

6. In 1924, Charles joined the _____ where he received formal training as a pilot.
- a. Army Aviation Branch
- b. Army Signal Corps
- c. Army Air Service

7. Charles Lindbergh was named the first ever _____ by Time Magazine in 1927.
- a. "Man of the Half-Century"
- b. "Man of the Year"
- c. "Man of the Decade"

8. In _____, Charles became a Brigadier General in the U.S. Air Force.
- a. 1928
- b. 1974
- c. 1954

9. When World War II began, Lindbergh flew around _____ during the war and helped to test out new planes.
- a. 50 combat missions
- b. 40 combat missions
- c. 60 combat missions

10. Charles was awarded the _____ by President Calvin Coolidge and a huge parade was held for him in New York City.
- a. Distinguished Flying Cross
- b. Aerial Achievement Medal
- c. Air Force Achievement Medal

11. Charles contributed to the development of _____.
- a. a water pump
- b. an artificial heart pump
- c. an air pump

12. Charles was one of the best-known figures in aeronautical history, remembered for the first nonstop solo flight across the Atlantic Ocean, from New York City to _____, on May 20–21, 1927.
- a. Paris
- b. United Kingdom
- c. Italy

Proofreading
Interpersonal Skills: Peer Pressure

In this activity, you'll see lots of grammatical *errors*. Correct all the grammar mistakes you see.

There are **30** mistakes in this passage. 3 capitals missing. 5 unnecessary capitals. 3 unnecessary apostrophes. 6 punctuation marks missing or incorrect. 13 incorrectly spelled words.

Tony is mingling with a large group of what he considers to be the school's cool kids. Suddenly, someone in the group begins mocking ~~Tony"s~~ Tony's friend Rob, who ~~walk's~~ walks with a limp due to a physical disability.

They ~~began~~ begin to imitate Rob's limping and call him 'lame cripple' and other derogatory ~~terms~~ terms. Although Tony disapproves of their behavior, he does not want to risk being excluded from the group, and thus joins them in mocking Rob.

Peer pressure is the influence exerted on us by members of our social group. It can manifest in a variety of ~~Ways~~ ways and can lead to us engaging in behaviors we would not normally ~~consider~~ consider, such as Tony joining in and mocking his friend Rob.

However, peer pressure is not always detrimental. Positive peer pressure can motivate us to make better ~~choices.~~ choices, such as studying harder, staying in school, or seeking a better ~~jub.~~ job. ~~when~~ When others influence us to make poor choices, such as smoking, using illicit drugs, or bullying, we succumb to negative peer pressure. We all desire to belong to a group and fit in, so developing strategies for ~~resasting~~ resisting peer pressure when necessary can be beneficial.

Tony and his friends are engaging in bullying by mocking Rob. Bullying is defined as persistent, unwanted, aggressive behavior directed toward another person. It is most prevalent in school-aged children but can also affect adults. ~~bullying~~ Bullying can take on a variety of ~~forms~~ forms, including the ~~following~~ following:

· Verbal bullying is when someone is called ~~names~~ names, threatened, or taunted verbally.
· Bullying is physical in nature - hitting, spitting, tripping, or pushing someone.
· Social bullying is ~~intentoinally~~ intentionally excluding someone from activities, spreading rumors, or

embarrassing someone.

· Cyberbullying is the act of verbally or socially bullying someone via the internet, such as through ~~socail~~ social media sites.

Peer pressure ~~exert's~~ exerts a significant influence on an individual's decision to engage in bullying behavior. In Tony's case, even though Rob is a friend and Tony ~~Would~~ would never consider mocking his disability, his desire to ~~belung~~ belong to a group outweighs his willingness to defend ~~His~~ his friend.

Peer pressure is a strong force ~~thit~~ that is exerted on us by our social group ~~mambers.~~ members. Peer pressure is classified into two types: negative peer pressure, which results in poor decision-making, and positive peer pressure, which influences us to make the correct choices. Adolescents are particularly susceptible to peer pressure because of their desire to fit in.

Peer pressure can motivate someone to engage in bullying behaviors such as mocking someone, threatening to harm ~~tham,~~ them, taunting ~~Them~~ them online, or excluding them from an activity. Each year, bullying affects an astounding 3.2 million school-aged ~~chaldren.~~ children. Several strategies for avoiding peer pressure bullying include the following:

- Consider your actions by surrounding yourself with good company.
- ~~acquiring~~ Acquiring the ability to say no to someone you trust.

Speak up - bullying is never acceptable and is taken extremely seriously ~~In~~ in schools and the workplace. If someone is attempting to convince you to bully another person, speaking with a ~~trosted~~ trusted ~~adolt~~ adult such as a teacher, coach, ~~coonselor,~~ counselor, or coworker can frequently help put things into perspective and highlight the issue.

Health Reading
Comprehension: Food & Sports

You have to have equipment if you play sports, right? Would you be willing to play baseball without a _mitt_ ?

Would you play soccer if you didn't have _shin_ guards?

You must eat healthily and fuel up before your _activity_ by eating the right foods at the right times.

You can eat healthy, but if you overeat before exercising, you will feel _sluggish_ and may experience stomach upset or _cramping_ .

On the other hand, if you don't eat anything before working out, you may feel weak, _faint_ , or tired.

It would help if you also ate after exercising to help your _muscles_ recover.

So, what are you going to eat? Carbohydrates are your body's primary source of _energy_ , so eat foods high in carbohydrates but low in fat.

Cereals , breads, vegetables, pasta, rice, and fruit are all good carbohydrate sources.

Meat, _dairy_ products, and nuts are examples of high _protein_ foods.

Water consumption is also essential. Unless you exercise vigorously for more than 60 minutes, water is preferable to _sports_ drinks such as Gatorade.

The American College of Sports Medicine recommends drinking enough fluid to _balance_ your daily fluid losses during exercise to stay healthy and hydrated.

Keep a food _journal_ for a few days to see how much you're eating and if you're getting all of the nutrients you need.

Calcium and iron are two essential _nutrients_ for children. Calcium aids in the formation of strong bones, while iron provides energy.

Dairy products, such as milk, yogurt, and cheese, are high in calcium. Dark, green _leafy_ vegetables and calcium-fortified products, such as orange juice, are also good sources.

Iron can be found in various foods, including meat, dried beans, and _fortified_ cereals.

Remember that if you don't get enough iron, you'll get tired _faster_ .

Avoid any diet _supplements_ or aids as well. These could be harmful to a developing body.

Keeping a cooler in the car with _fresh_ fruit, water, and a sandwich on whole-grain bread is preferable to driving through a fast-food restaurant.

Geography: Himalayas

The Himalayas are an Asian mountain range. The Himalayan region includes Nepal, Tibet, Bhutan, India, Afghanistan, and Pakistan. The Himalayas are home to the majority of the world's ___tallest___ mountains.

I'm almost sure you've heard of ___Mount___ Everest, the world's tallest mountain. Climbers train for years to scale this massive chunk of rock and ice. Because Everest is so high, most climbers require ___oxygen___, which is a pure component of the air we breathe, to reach the summit, and many climbers must abandon their efforts before reaching the summit.

Plate tectonics created the Himalayas, which may sound like a technical term, but it's quite simple. Large swaths of land make up the earth's ___surface___. Plate tectonics is basically what happens when the pieces move slightly and collide with each other. When these plates collide, one piece of land is forced beneath the other, raising the piece on top and eventually forming ___mountains___. Everest grew to a height of 29,000 feet as a result of this process!

The shifting that formed the Himalayas began during the ___Jurassic___ period; I wonder what the dinosaurs thought of the earth moving beneath their feet? But, just like us, they probably couldn't feel anything because plate tectonics is invisible to anyone living on the earth's surface - that is, until an ___earthquake___ occurs, which is an extreme example of how plate tectonics work.

The name Himalayas means "home of snow," but most of the Himalayas are lower than the parts always covered in snow. The Himalayas are home to forests and ___grasslands___ as well as ice. As you descend the mountains, the temperatures rise, and the snow melts. The Himalayas are the source (beginning point) of many important rivers in Asia, including the Ganges and the Yangtze. Many different kinds of animals and plants live in the forests and grasslands.

It's challenging to get past the image of bare mountains, but some areas of the Himalayas have fertile soil. The majority of farmable land in Nepal is in the foothills or lower hilly parts of the mountains. The majority of Nepal's rice is grown there. Apple, cherry, and grape orchards can be found in the Vale of the Kashmir region. ___Sheep___, goats, and yaks are also raised. When the weather is warm, the animals graze higher in the mountains, but they move to lower pastures like snowfalls.

Have you ever heard of a Yeti? The Yeti, also known as the ___Abominable___ Snowman, is a mythical creature that roams the Himalayas and resembles a giant hairy man. It is said to have shaggy, white fur and sharp teeth ready to devour anyone who comes into contact with it! According to monks, there are the remains of a Yeti hand in a Buddhist monastery in Pangboche, Nepal. Scientists believe they have proof that the Yeti is a rare type of polar bear, but others are skeptical. What are your thoughts? Is the Yeti a bear or a previously unknown monster?

Music: History of the Violin

First, read the entire passage. After that, go back and fill in the blanks. You can skip the blanks you're unsure about and finish them later.

| strings | France | soundhole | bowed | ages |
| introduced | Italy | Baroque | existence | existence |

Stringed instruments that use a bow to produce sound, such as the violin, are referred to as __bowed__ stringed instruments. The ancestors of the violin are said to be the Arabian rabab and the rebec, which came from the Orient in the middle __ages__ and were popular in Spain and __France__ in the fifteenth century. A bowed stringed instrument known as a fiddle first appeared in Europe near the end of the Middle Ages.

In terms of completeness, the violin is in a class by itself when compared to its forefathers. Furthermore, it did not evolve gradually over time but instead appeared in its current form abruptly around 1550. However, none of these early violins are still in __existence__ today. The violin's history is inferred from paintings from this era that depicts violins.

The two earliest recorded violin makers are from northern __Italy__: Andre Amati of Cremona and Gasparo di Bertolotti of Salone (Gasparo di Salon). The history of the violin emerges from the fog of legend to hard fact thanks to these two violin makers. These two's violins are still in use today. The oldest violin still in __existence__ today is one built around 1565 by Andre Amati.

Though the violin was __introduced__ to the world in the middle of the sixteenth century, a similar-looking instrument called the viol was made around the fourteenth century.

The viol flourished in the sixteenth and seventeenth centuries, and the violin and viol coexisted during the __Baroque__ period.

The viol family's instruments did not have the f-shaped __soundhole__ of the violin, but rather a C-shaped soundhole or a more decorative shape. The viol differs from the violin in that it has six, seven, or more __strings__ tuned in fourths (as opposed to the violin's four strings tuned in fifths), a fretted fingerboard, and a relatively thick body due to the sloping shoulder shape at the neck-body joint. There are several sizes, but the Viola da Gamba, which has a lower register similar to the cello, is the most well-known.

Art: Visual

First, read the entire passage. After that, go back and fill in the blanks. You can skip the blanks you're unsure about and finish them later.

splattering	Middle	ceramics	pencils	Greece
vases	inking	pharaohs'	oldest	three-dimensional

Visual arts are visible art forms such as drawing, painting, sculpture, printmaking, photography, and filmmaking. Design and textile work are also referred to as visual arts. The visual arts have evolved over time. During the __Middle__ Ages, artists became well-known for their paintings, sculptures, and prints. Today, visual arts encompasses a wide range of disciplines.

Drawing is the process of creating a picture with a variety of tools, most commonly __pencils__, crayons, pens, or markers. Artists draw on a variety of surfaces, such as paper or canvas. The first drawings were discovered in caves around 30,000 years ago.

The ancient Egyptians drew on papyrus, while the Greeks and Romans drew on other objects such as __vases__. Drawings were sketches made on parchment in the Middle Ages. Drawing became an art form when paper became widely available during the Renaissance, and it was perfected by Michelangelo, Leonardo Da Vinci, and others.

Painting is frequently referred to as the most important form of visual art. It's all about __splattering__ paint on a canvas or a wall. Painters use a variety of colors and brush strokes to convey their ideas.

Painting is one of the __oldest__ forms of visual art as well. Prehistoric people painted hunting scenes on the walls of old caves. Paintings became popular in ancient Egypt, where __pharaohs'__ tombs were adorned with scenes from everyday Egyptian life.

Printmaking is a type of art that is created by __inking__ a plate and pressing it against the surface of another object. Prints are now mostly made on paper, but they were originally pressed onto cloth or other objects. Plates are frequently made of wood or metal.

Sculptures are __three-dimensional__ works of art created by shaping various materials. Stone, steel, plastic, __ceramics__, and wood are among the most popular. Sculpture is frequently referred to as the plastic arts.
Sculpture can be traced back to ancient __Greece__. Over many centuries, it has played an essential role in various religions around the world. During the Renaissance, Michelangelo was regarded as one of the masters of the art. David, a marble statue of a naked man, was his most famous work.

Art: Mary Cassatt

First, read the entire passage. After that, go back and fill in the blanks. You can skip the blanks you're unsure about and finish them later.

influenced	private	Fine	museums	techniques
pastels	Pittsburgh	Japanese	childhood	enrolled

Mary Cassatt was born on May 22, 1844, into a prosperous family near __Pittsburgh__, Pennsylvania. She spent a significant portion of her __childhood__ in France and Germany, where she learned French and German. She developed an interest in art while in Europe and decided that she wanted to be a professional artist early on.

Despite her parents' reservations about Mary pursuing a career as an artist, she __enrolled__ in the Pennsylvania Academy of __Fine__ Arts in 1860. Mary studied art at the academy for several years but became dissatisfied with the instruction and limitations on female students. Mary moved to Paris in 1866 and began taking __private__ lessons from art instructor Jean-Leon Gerome. She also studied paintings in museums such as the Louvre on her own. One of her paintings (A Mandolin Player) was accepted for exhibition at the prestigious Paris Salon in 1868. Cassatt continued to paint with some success over the next few years.

By 1877, Mary Cassatt had grown dissatisfied with Paris's traditional art scene. Fortunately, Mary became close friends with Impressionist painter Edgar Degas around this time. She began to experiment with new painting __techniques__ and discovered a whole new world of art in Impressionism. She began to exhibit her paintings alongside the Impressionists and gained further acclaim in the art world.

Early on, Cassatt's artistic style was __influenced__ by European masters, and later, by the Impressionist art movement (especially Edgar Degas). Mary also studied __Japanese__ art, which is evident in many of her paintings. Mary wanted to use her art to express light and color. She frequently used __pastels__. The majority of her paintings depict people. She primarily painted her family for many years. Later, scenes depicting a mother and child together became a major theme in her paintings.

Mary Cassatt is widely regarded as one of America's greatest artists. She rose to prominence in the art world at a time when it was extremely difficult for women to do so. Many of her paintings are currently on display at __museums__ such as the National Gallery of Art, The Metropolitan Museum of Art, and the National Portrait Gallery.

English: Apostrophe

An apostrophe is a punctuation mark used to indicate where something has been removed. It can be used in contractions, to show possession, to replace a phrase, for the plural form of family names, for irregular plural possessives, and, on rare occasions, to provide clarity for a non-possessive plural. Avoid common apostrophe mistakes, such as using 'it's' for the possessive 'its,' which should be 'its.' Omitting the apostrophe, putting it in the wrong place for a possessive plural, and using 'of' when you mean to contract a word with 'have' are other common errors.

Apostrophes, like any other aspect of language, are prone to errors. The omission of the apostrophe is one of the most common.

Here are some examples:

'Let's go to McDonalds.' Correct: 'McDonald's'
'Whos responsible for the bill?' Correct: 'Who's'
'Its about five o'clock.' Correct: 'It's.' We are saying 'it is' here, so we need the apostrophe.

1. Where should the apostrophe go in didnt?
   a. didn't
   b. didn't

2. How do you make the contraction for was not?
   a. was'nt
   b. wasn't

3. How do you make Jimmy possessive?
   a. Jimmy's
   b. Jimmys'

4. Where should the apostrophe go in shouldnt?
   a. should'nt
   b. shouldn't

5. How do you make the contraction for she would?
   a. she'd
   b. she'd

6. What is the correct use of the apostrophe?
   a. brother's toys
   b. brother's toys

7. Which of the following is the correct way to show possession with a plural noun ending in 's'?
   a. Add an apostrophe at the end.
   b. No apostrophe is required

8. How would you express the plural possessive of the word 'child'?
   a. Child's
   b. Children's

9. What is the proper way to contract the possessive form of 'it'?
   a. Its
   b. It's

10. The _____ awfully good today.
    a. weather
    b. weather's

11. Adam believes _____ going to snow later.
    a. it's
    b. its

12. The dog was wagging _____ tail excitedly.
    a. its
    b. it's

13. Where did you leave _____ book?
    a. your
    b. you're

14. _____ going to Ms. Katy's room.
    a. Were
    b. We're

15. Bobby always kicks _____ dolls around.
    a. Kim and Sandy's
    b. Jennifer and Kate's

16. _____ not allowed to listen to music while they read.
    a. They're
    b. Their're

ELA: Informational Text

An informational text is a nonfiction piece of writing that aims to educate or inform the reader about a specific topic. An informational text, unlike fiction or some other types of nonfiction texts, does not contain any characters. It presents information in a way that allows the reader to learn more about something of interest to them.

Informational text is a type of nonfiction that is intended to convey factual information about a specific topic. The purpose of informational text is to deliver information about a topic, and it is distinguished by its formatting, which includes organization, written cues (visual variations in text), and visuals/graphics.

Literary nonfiction, expository writing, persuasive/argumentative writing, and procedural writing are the four basic types of informational text. Examples of informational text can be found in a variety of formats both online and in print.

Select the best answer for each question.

1. Identify the main idea: "You wouldn't use a nail file to peel carrots. You can't tune an engine with a cheese grater, either. So why would you buy a wrench to do the job of a screwdriver?"
   a. Always use the right tool.
   b. Wrench and screwdrivers are basically the same.
   c. Use nail file for your fingernails.

2. Autobiographies are written in which point of view?
   a. second
   b. third
   c. first

3. Differentiate between a plot and a theme.
   a. A plot is the ending in a story, a theme conveys the message in first person
   b. A theme is a collection of the main idea, while a plot conveys the point of the ending
   c. A plot is more of what happens in a story, whereas a theme conveys the message of the story

4. Which is not an article in a reference book?
   a. thesaurus entry for the word army
   b. encyclopedia article on World War II
   c. a review of a novel

5. When creating summaries, it's important to _____.
   a. tell the ending of the story
   b. Write down the main points in your own words
   c. Use the first person exact words

6. Which type of literary nonfiction is not meant to be published or shared?
   a. biography
   b. diary
   c. memoir

7. Which of the following should you do as you read an informational text?
   a. Take notes
   b. find clue words and text
   c. read as quickly as possible

8. What makes a speech different from an article?
   a. speeches are meant to be spoken aloud to an audience
   b. speeches do not inform about a topic
   c. articles can persuade a reader

9. Which type of literary nonfiction is a short piece on a single topic?
   a. essay
   b. letter
   c. memoir

10. Procedural writing example:
    a. letter to the editor, blog entry
    b. textbook, travel brochure
    c. cookbooks, how-to articles, instruction manuals

Science: Temperate Forest

Rainforests are found near the equator in the tropics.

Taiga forests are found in the far north.

Temperate rainforests are found in the middle.

The temperature ranges between -20 and 90 degrees _Fahrenheit_ .

Four distinct seasons - Winter, _spring_ , summer, and fall are the four distinct seasons.

Fertile soil - Rotted leaves and other decaying matter create a rich, deep soil that allows trees to grow

strong roots.

The forest floor, which is made up of _wildflowers_ , herbs, ferns, mushrooms, and mosses, is the

lowest layer.

There are a few _evergreen_ trees that keep their leaves throughout the winter.

Sap - sap is used by many trees to help them _survive_ the winter. It keeps their roots from freezing

and is then used as energy to start growing again in the spring.

Animals that live here include black bears, _mountain_ lions, deer, fox, squirrels, skunks, rabbits,

porcupines, timber wolves, and a variety of birds.

Science: Coral Reefs

One of the most important marine __biomes__ is the coral reef.

Coral reefs are home to approximately __25%__ of all known marine species, despite being a relatively small biome.

Coral reefs may appear to be made of __rocks__ at first glance, but they are actually __living__ organisms.

When polyps die, they __harden__ and new polyps grow on top of them, causing the reef to expand.

Because polyps must eat to __survive__, you can think of the coral reef as eating as well.

They eat plankton and __algae__, which are small animals.

__Photosynthesis__ is how algae get their food from the sun.

To form, coral reefs require warm, __shallow__ water.

Southeast Asia and the region around __Australia__ are home to a sizable portion of the world's coral reefs.

The __Great__ Barrier Reef is 2,600 miles long.

__Fringe__ reefs are reefs that grow close to the shore.

__Barrier__ reef - Barrier reefs grow away from the shoreline, sometimes for several miles.

An __atoll__ is a coral ring that surrounds a lagoon of water. It begins as a fringe reef surrounding a volcanic island.

Some atolls are large enough to support human __habitation__.

ADDITIONAL ASSIGNMENTS PLANNER

○ MONDAY

GOALS THIS WEEK

○ TUESDAY

○ WEDNESDAY

WHAT TO STUDY

○ THURSDAY

○ FRIDAY

EXTRA CREDIT WEEKEND WORK
○ SATURDAY / SUNDAY

ADDITIONAL ASSIGNMENTS PLANNER

○ MONDAY

GOALS THIS WEEK

○ TUESDAY

○ WEDNESDAY

WHAT TO STUDY

○ THURSDAY

○ FRIDAY

EXTRA CREDIT WEEKEND WORK
○ SATURDAY / SUNDAY

ADDITIONAL ASSIGNMENTS PLANNER

○ MONDAY

○ TUESDAY

○ WEDNESDAY

○ THURSDAY

○ FRIDAY

EXTRA CREDIT WEEKEND WORK
○ SATURDAY / SUNDAY

GOALS THIS WEEK

WHAT TO STUDY

ADDITIONAL ASSIGNMENTS PLANNER

○ MONDAY

GOALS THIS WEEK

○ TUESDAY

○ WEDNESDAY

WHAT TO STUDY

○ THURSDAY

○ FRIDAY

EXTRA CREDIT WEEKEND WORK
○ SATURDAY / SUNDAY

GRADES TRACKER

Week	Monday	Tuesday	Wednesday	Thursday	Friday
1					
2					
3					
4					
5					
6					
7					
8					
9					
10					
11					
12					
13					
14					
15					
16					
17					
18					

Notes

GRADES TRACKER

Week	Monday	Tuesday	Wednesday	Thursday	Friday
1					
2					
3					
4					
5					
6					
7					
8					
9					
10					
11					
12					
13					
14					
15					
16					
17					
18					

Notes

GRADES TRACKER

Week	Monday	Tuesday	Wednesday	Thursday	Friday
1					
2					
3					
4					
5					
6					
7					
8					
9					
10					
11					
12					
13					
14					
15					
16					
17					
18					

Notes

End of the Year Evaluation

Name: _____

Grade/Level: _____ Date: _____

Subjects Studied: _____
_____
_____
_____

Goals Accomplished: _____
_____
_____
_____
_____

Most Improved Areas: _____
_____
_____
_____

Areas of Improvement: _____
_____
_____
_____

Cut out book

Main Curriculum Evaluation	Satisfied		A= Above Standards S= Meets Standards N= Needs Improvement	Final Grades
_____	Yes	No	98-100 A+ 93-97 A	_____
_____	Yes	No	90-92 A 88-89 B+	_____
_____	Yes	No	83-87 B 80-82 B	_____
_____	Yes	No	78-79 C+ 73-77 C	_____
_____	Yes	No	70-72 C 68-69 D+ 62-67 D	_____
_____	Yes	No	60-62 D 59 & Below F	_____

Most Enjoyed: _____
_____

Least Enjoyed: _____
_____

Made in the USA
Middletown, DE
02 September 2024